Essays on "The Soul's Logical Life" in the Work of Wolfgang Giegerich

Essays on "The Soul's Logical Life" in the Work of Wolfgang Giegerich: Psychology as the Discipline of Interiority is the second collection of essays dedicated to the study and application of psychology as the discipline of interiority–a new 'wave' within analytical psychology which pushes off from the work of C. G. Jung and James Hillman.

Reflecting upon the notion of psychology developed by German psychoanalyst Wolfgang Giegerich, whose Hegelian turn sheds light on the notion of soul, or the objective psyche, and its inner logic and 'thought', forms a radical new basis from which to ground a modern psychology with soul. The book explores the theme of "the soul's logical life" as it displays itself in various modern phenomena, from overwhelming anxiety, cryptocurrency, the dreams of Japanese college students, and contemporary psychoanalysis, to myth, music, social movements, and the question and relevance of truth in psychology and consciousness. The authors, comprising clinical psychologists, teachers, Jungian analysts, and international scholars, aim to reveal and convey the dialectical inner workings and speculative logic of the modern soul.

Essays on "The Soul's Logical Life" in the Work of Wolfgang Giegerich: Psychology as the Discipline of Interiority will be essential reading for depth and clinical psychologists, Jungian psychoanalysts, and academics and students of post-Jungian studies, and for all those interested in what it means to *think* in the highly sophisticated and technological world of the twenty-first century.

Jennifer M. Sandoval is a clinical psychologist residing in Southern California and the author of *A Psychological Inquiry into the Meaning and Concept of Forgiveness* (2017) and co-editor of *Psychology as the Discipline of Interiority: The "Psychological Difference" in the Work of Wolfgang Giegerich* (2017).

Colleen EL-Bejjani is an English teacher and poet living in Rochester, New York. She has served on the Executive Committee for the International Society for Psychology as the Discipline of Interiority since 2012, and presented her work on PDI in Canada, Ireland, California, and Germany.

Pamela J. Power is a clinical psychologist and Jungian psychoanalyst living in Santa Monica, CA. She is the past clinic director and past training director of the C. G. Jung Institute of Los Angeles. She has lectured nationally and internationally on a variety of topics and has published numerous articles and chapters in books. She is a member of the C. G Jung Institute of Los Angeles, the Interregional Society of Jungian Analysts, the IAAP, and ISPDI, where she currently serves on the executive committee.

Essays on "The Soul's Logical Life" in the Work of Wolfgang Giegerich

Psychology as the Discipline of Interiority

Edited by Jennifer M. Sandoval,
Colleen EL-Bejjani and
Pamela J. Power

Routledge
Taylor & Francis Group

LONDON AND NEW YORK

Designed cover image: Getty Images

First published 2024
by Routledge
4 Park Square, Milton Park, Abingdon, Oxon OX14 4RN

and by Routledge
605 Third Avenue, New York, NY 10158

*Routledge is an imprint of the Taylor & Francis Group, an informa
business*

British Library Cataloguing-in-Publication Data
A catalogue record for this book is available from the British
Library

ISBN: 978-1-032-46325-4 (hbk)
ISBN: 978-1-032-46324-7 (pbk)
ISBN: 978-1-003-38115-0 (ebk)

DOI: 10.4324/9781003381150

Typeset in Times New Roman
by SPi Technologies India Pvt Ltd (Straive)

Contents

Acknowledgements

The editors wish to express their heartfelt gratitude to their families, the ISPDI Executive Committee, and all members of the International Society for Psychology as the Discipline of Interiority, past and present, for their continued and steadfast fellowship in this work.

Sources and Abbreviations

For frequently cited sources, the following abbreviations have been used:

CEP   Wolfgang Giegerich, *Collected English Papers*, 6 vols (New Orleans, LA: Spring Journal Books, 2005 ff; now London and New York: Routledge, 2020).

CW   C. G. Jung, *Collected Works*, 20 vols. (Ed. Herbert Read, Michael Fordham, Gerhard Adler, and William McGuire. Trans. R. F. C. Hull. Princeton: Princeton University Press, 1957–1979). Cited by volume and, unless otherwise note, by paragraph number.

Letters   C. G. Jung, *Letters*. 2 vols. (Ed Gerhard Adler. Bollingen Series XCV: 2. Princeton University Press, 1975).

MDR   C. G. Jung, *Memories, Dreams, Reflections* (Edited by Aniela Jaffe. Translated by Clara Winston and Richard Winston. Reissue edition. New York: Vintage, 1989). Cited by page number.

CON   Wolfgang Giegerich, *Coniunctio: Reflections on a Key Concept of C.G. Jung's Psychology*, (London, Ontario, Canada: Dusk Owl Books, 2021).

DAP   Wolfgang Giegerich, David L. Miller, Greg Mogenson, *Dialectics and Analytical Psychology: The El Capitan Canyon Seminar*, (New Orleans: Spring Journal Books, 2005).

HEI   Wolfgang Giegerich, *The Historical Emergence of the I: Essays about One Chapter in the History of the Soul* (London, Ontario, Canada: Dusk Owl Books, 2020).

NLMI   Wolfgang Giegerich, *Neurosis: The Logic of a Metaphysical Illness* (New Orleans: Spring Journal Books, 2013).

PIT   Wolfgang Giegerich, *Pitfalls in Comparing Buddhist and Western Psychology* (Create Space Independent Publishing Platform, 2018).

Contributors

Daniel Anderson is a clinical psychologist in private practice in Santa Monica, California, where he works with adults, children, and their parents. Daniel trained in Jungian psychology at the Jung-von Franz Center in Zürich, Switzerland, received his doctoral degree from Pacifica Graduate Institute, and did his pre-doctoral internship at the Los Angeles Jung Institute and his post-doctoral Fellowship at the Reiss-Davis Child Study Center. Daniel's doctoral dissertation, "Giegerich's Psychology of Soul: Psychotherapeutic Implications" addressed the implications for therapy of psychology as a discipline of interiority, and he formed a case consultation group of ISPDI members to continue this exploration. His published works include "Reflections on a Case Study of Neurosis" (2018) and "The Soul's Logical Life and Jungian Schisms" (2021). He is a member of the International Society for Psychology as the Discipline of Interiority, where he served on the Executive Committee for many years.

Marco Heleno Barreto (Brazil) received a PhD in philosophy and teaches philosophy at FAJE – Faculdade Jesuíta de Filosofia e Teologia, in Belo Horizonte, Brazil. He is a Jungian psychotherapist, working in private practice. He is the author of *Símbolo e Sabedoria Prática. C. G. Jung e o Mal-estar da Modernidade* (Loyola, 2008), *Imaginação Simbólica. Reflexões Introdutórias* (Loyola, 2008), *Pensar Jung* (Loyola, 2012), *Homo Imaginans. A Imaginação Criadora na Estética de Gaston Bachelard* (Loyola, 2016), *Estudos (Pós)Junguianos* (Loyola, 2018), *Psychology and the Irrelevantification of Man. From Jung's Project to the Post-Human Times* (Dusk Owl Books, 2020), and *Psychology and Metaphysics. On the logical Status of Psychology as the Discipline of Interiority* (Dusk Owl Books, 2021), having also contributed articles to *Spring Journal, International Journal of Jungian Studies, Journal of Analytical Psychology* and *Jung Journal*. He served on the Executive Committee of the International Society for Psychology as the Discipline of Interiority from 2012 to 2023.

Michael R. Caplan has engaged with Hillman and Giegerich's work for over 30 years and presented at gatherings of the International Society for Psychology as the Discipline of Interiority since 2012. Recent writings on contemporary antisemitism for *White Rose Magazine* connect to his broader project, "One Full Revolution (Meaning Now)," relating language, the Axial Revolution, and the monotheisms as trinity. With extensive editing and design experience (including Spring Journal Books), decades in theatre and special events, a BFA in Contemporary Dance, and singing down-home country classics for countless crossover audiences, he is founder and "Renaissance Man" of the House of ShAkE –a publishing and production company launched in 2017 with *A Handbook for Ecstatic Survival* by choreographer David Earle, Current House ventures include Gilles Goyette's *Random Generated Text Project*, dancer Bill Coleman's *Prepare for the Truth*, on boxing, and Michael's live/online *Back to Bacchae*, inspired by Euripides, and ongoing "Porch Songs." www.houseofshake.ca

Robert Dommett is a systems analyst, researcher, and developer of social profiling systems and web applications for use in the corporate sector and has an MBA. He is President of the CG Jung Society of Sydney and is an avid reader in the areas of depth psychology, ancient religions, consciousness and artificial intelligence, and has a particular interest in the work of Wolfgang Giegerich and Henry Corbin. Robert has presented at ISPDI conferences in Berlin (2012), Dublin (2018), at the ISPDI Summer Gathering in 2020, The Soul's Logical Life Online Conference in 2021, and on various occasions to Jung Societies in Australia.

Colleen EL-Bejjani holds an MA in Liberal Arts and an MAT in English. She is a long-time member of the ISPDI and serves as the communication director. She has presented essays on PDI at conferences in Berlin, Malibu, Toronto, and Dublin. After a 30-year career in the performing arts, she now writes poetry and teaches English at an urban high school in Rochester, New York.

John Hoedl received his diploma from the C. G. Jung Institute Zurich in 2006. He received a bachelor's degree in physical education from the University of Alberta, Canada and a masters in counseling from Gonzaga University, Spokane. He is a past president of the Western Canadian Association of Jungian Analysts as well as the current president and founding member of the International Society for Psychology as the Discipline of Interiority.

He has published in the *Journal of Analytical Psychology*, including the article, "The alchemical 'not' and Marlan's stone that remains a stone." He has a private practice in Edmonton, Canada.

George B. Hogenson is a senior training analyst in the Chicago Society of Jungian Analysts. He earned his Ph.D. in philosophy from Yale University, and his MA in clinical social work from the University of Chicago. He is a former vice president of the International Association for Analytical Psychology and a member of the Editorial Board of *The Journal of Analytical Psychology*. His book, *Jung's Struggle with Freud*, marked a turning point in scholarship surrounding the relationship between the two founders of depth psychology. With Thomas Kirsch he edited *The Red Book: Reflections on*

C. G. Jung's Liber Novus, a collection of essays from the first conference on Jung's *Red Book*. Dr. Hogenson has published extensively on the theory of archetypes and synchronicity, focusing on the application of complex dynamic systems theory to these central elements of Jung's system of psychology. He is in private practice in Chicago and Oak Park, Illinois.

Philip Kime is an analyst in private practice in Zürich, Switzerland. He is a past vice president, curatorium member and lecturer at the C.G. Jung Institut, Küsnacht with a background in philosophy and artificial intelligence.

Greg Mogenson is a registered psychotherapist and Jungian psychoanalyst practicing in London, Ontario, Canada. He is a founding member and past Vice-President of The International Society for Psychology as the Discipline of Interiority and the publisher of the imprint, Dusk Owl Books. The author of numerous articles in the field of analytical psychology, his books include *Psychology's Dream of the Courtroom*; *A Most Accursed Religion: When a Trauma becomes God; Greeting the Angels: An Imaginal View of the Mourning Process*; *The Dove in the Consulting Room: Hysteria and the Anima in Bollas and Jung*; *Northern Gnosis: Thor, Baldr, and the Volsungs in the Thought of Freud and Jung*, and (with W. Giegerich and D. L. Miller) *Dialectics & Analytical Psychology: The El Capitan Canyon Seminar*. He is also the author of the monographs: *Dereliction of Duty and the Rise of Psychology, as Reflected in the "Case" of Conrad's Lord Jim*; *That Glimpse of Truth for which you had Forgotten to Ask; Inwardizing Rilke's Dog of Divine Inseeing into Itself*; and *Jungian Analysis Post Mortem Dei*.

Josep M. Moreno is a psychologist who graduated from the University of Barcelona and the International Center for Psychology and Psychotherapy, Miami, Florida. His clinical and research experiences and interests include assisting adults, children, and adolescents in the fields of psychotherapy, consultation, and counseling, in Spain, the United States, and Mexico. He was a professor of child psychopathology at ISEP, a center specializing in postgraduate programs and courses in psychology, attached to the University of Barcelona. He is the author of *Symbolism of the Houses* published by Arbor Scientae, Barcelona (1987). His most recent works are several papers presented at ISPDI Conferences (2012, 2016).

Andrés Ocazionez is a Jungian analyst with a private practice in Berlin. He is a graduate from the C.G. Jung Institute Zürich and has received a *cum laude* recognition for his doctoral work, *The Psychology of Analytical Training*, presented in the Faculty of Philosophy of Universidad Complutense de Madrid. In addition to his clinical work, Dr. Ocazionez is a regular lecturer at the C.G. Jung Institute, supervisor and training analyst.

Pamela J. Power is a longtime member of the ISPDI. She attended and presented "The Negation of the Negation" at the inaugural international conference of the ISPDI in Berlin in 2012 and in 2014 a paper titled "The

Psychological Difference in Jung's *Mysterium Coniunctionis*." In 2016 she presented "How Does Music Think?" at the conference in Malibu. She currently serves as member-at-large on the executive committee of the ISPDI. She is a Jungian analyst and clinical psychologist practicing in Santa Monica, CA. She is a member of the Los Angeles Jung Institute and the Interregional Society of Jungian Analysts where a few years ago she presented a paper titled, "Does Giegerich Make a Difference?"

Jennifer M. Sandoval is a clinical psychologist, author, and teacher. She received her doctoral degree in clinical psychology from Pacifica Graduate Institute, her MA in counseling psychology from the University of Santa Monica, and her BA in theoretical mathematics from the University of California, Santa Cruz. Her current interests include the study and practice of psychology as the discipline of interiority (PDI) and from within the framework of *A Course in Miracles* (ACIM). Dr. Sandoval is the author of *A Psychological Inquiry into the Meaning and Concept of Forgiveness* (2017) and co-editor of a book of collected essays, *Psychology as the Discipline of Interiority: The 'Psychological Difference' in the Work of Wolfgang Giegerich* (2017). Jennifer resides in southern California with her two dogs, three birds, nine chickens, and many fish.

Nanae Takenaka is an associate professor at the Kyoto University of the Arts, where she is also a clinical psychotherapist, where she is also a clinical psychotherapist. Her published articles are "The Realization of Absolute Beauty: An Interpretation of the Fairytale Snow White" (*Journal of Analytical Psychology*, 2016), "Voices from Nature and Withdrawal (*Hikikomori*) in Japanese Culture" (In: *Cultural Complexes in China, Japan, Korea, and Taiwan*. Ed. Thomas Singer, Routledge, 2020).

Michael Whan is a senior Jungian analyst with the Independent Group of Analytical Psychologists, the International Association for Analytical Psychology, the College of Psychoanalysts – UK, and a member of the International Society for Psychology as a Discipline of Interiority. He is also a senior associate of the Royal Society of Medicine and a patron of the Department of Germanic Studies of the Institute of Modern Languages, University of London. He has published extensively in various psychology journals and chapters in several books; the latest is "Nihilism and Truth: Tarrying with the Negative," in *Shame, Temporality and Social Change*: *Ominous Transitions*. Eds., Ladson Hinton and Hessel Willemsen.

Peter White is a retired secondary school teacher of music, recording, native studies, and philosophy. He has delivered papers and presentations at several ISPDI conferences and workshops. His paper, "Thinking 'Murder,' Following the Trail of Psychology's Uroboric Knowing of Itself in No Country for Old Men," was published in *Jung Journal: Culture and Psyche* in 2011.

Peter is also a songwriter whose many recordings can be enjoyed at www.thepeterwhitewebsite.com. His deep appreciation for Giegerich's work led him to compose a piece of music in Giegerich's honor. Written in 2004, the instrumental "Alchemy (for Wolfgang Giegerich)" was performed at the closing of the inaugural ISPDI conference in Berlin, 2012.

Introduction

Jennifer M. Sandoval, Colleen EL-Bejjani and Pamela J. Power

We begin our introduction to this volume of collected essays on "the soul's logical life" with an observation from eminent Jungian psychoanalyst, Dr. Wolfgang Giegerich:

> Mozart reported that he was able to hear a symphony or opera instantaneously, synchronistically, as *we* might grasp the plan of a house all at once, without having to imaginally go through each room and story one after the other. Mozart did not have to go discursively through a piece of music as a sequence of movements and notes. His hearing was sublated hearing – or: thought. He could *think*, or conceptually apprehend, a piece of music. Unlike us ordinary humans, he did not have to *listen* to it (be it in his imagination or literally). This thinking is *logical* (not sensual) hearing; and it is not emotional, but soulful (sublated emotion: sober frenzy). When I said that Mozart could hear a whole symphony instantaneously, this does not mean that it was merged into an undifferentiated one, and when I said that he could conceptually apprehend a piece of music this does not mean that he subsumed it under an abstract concept. The inner complexity and all its tension (the identity of the identity and difference of the opposites) were, of course, preserved. It was the vibrating of the rich, fluid life of the soul, not in the medium of empirical time, but in the soul's native medium of thought.[1]

The astonishing notion that the "soul's native medium" happens to be *thought* – and as such the mode of our comprehending soul[2] – is at the heart of psychology as the discipline of interiority. Mozart's ability to *think* music provides a clear example of discerning the invisible movement of *the soul's logical life* and recognizing that movement in the world (here in the form of a symphony).[3] The psychological exploration of the logical life of the soul is the primary aim of psychology as the discipline of interiority and the theme of this book.

This volume is the second of collected essays that emerged from conferences given by the *International Society for Psychology as the Discipline of Interiority* (ISPDI).[4] The current volume originated from a summer online conference in 2021 celebrating the publication of the landmark book, *The Soul's Logical*

DOI: 10.4324/9781003381150-1

Life, first published in 1998 by Giegerich. This groundbreaking work questioned and critiqued the fundamental identity and structure of analytical psychology and archetypal psychology, arguing for a psychology based in 'thought.' In the many years since, Giegerich produced a total of six volumes of collected essays, nearly a dozen books, and many articles further expounding upon the initial thesis set forth in *The Soul's Logical Life*. In all, Giegerich has opened up a new dimension of psychology that re-establishes its roots with its philosophical history and the soul from which it comes; it 'completes' the psychology originating in Jung and further developed by Hillman, resulting in a modern psychology that has truly come home to itself in thought.

What Is Psychology as the Discipline of Interiority?

Like analytical and archetypal psychology before it, psychology as the discipline of interiority (PDI) is decidedly not an "ego" psychology; in fact, the *psychological difference* between the subjective ego and the objective psyche, or soul, is foundational to PDI. The traditional notion of psychology as a mode of studying the behaviors, thoughts, feelings, and experiences of individuals, families, or groups of people is expressly *not* that of psychology as the discipline of interiority and is deemed to be un-psychological, relegated to the disciplines of sociology, anthropology, phenomenology, and the like. The primary object of study for psychology is the soul and not the person; the essential question regarding any subject matter of study is, "What is the soul saying about *itself* with this phenomenon?" In making the crucial differentiation between speaking of soul in a subjective way (e.g., as referring to a personal soul) and soul as consciousness or mindedness per se, we speak of the ego dimension and the soul dimension, the *opus parvum*, the work of the individual, and the *Opus Magnum*, the work of the objective soul. It is psychology as a discipline because the effort required to do psychology with soul requires each time, each moment that we do psychology to leave the given world of ego and positivity and enter the invisible realm of negativity, or thought – the dimension of soul. When described this way, there is of course no leaving or entering in any literal way, but doing rigorous work to negate ordinary or ego ways of seeing, thinking, feeling, and hearing.

What Is Soul?

The subject of this collection of essays is "the logical life of the soul." But what do we mean by "soul" to begin with? The ineffable nature of soul denies us an easy answer to this question. Giegerich's important book, *What Is Soul?* is devoted to such inquiry and is considered to be required reading for students of psychology as the discipline of interiority. While we cannot hope to answer the question here, arguably the most important quality of soul in modernity is its very *absence*, that is, the soul exists only as absolute negativity.

The Soul as Absolutely Negative

In the soul, the dance as logical negativity … has truly come home to itself. It is really just a *dance* with no dancers, nothing but a dance. It is and stays logically negative, exclusively negative, not even metastable.[5]

The soul is not imagined to exist as an abiding, ever-present entity but is generated ever anew: "Where the soul does not stir, where it does not produce (feelings, ideas, symptoms, dreams, works of art or culture…), there simply is no soul."[6] Thus, the soul must not be positivized in our thinking and "does not exist. But this does not at all mean that it is simply nothing."[7] Indeed, Giegerich offers some illuminating examples of the use of the term "soul" below:

- soul in a very general sense as a whole dimension or status of existence, the "world" of the mind, in contrast to natural, positive-factual being, and
- soul in the sense of the soul of and in the Real, i.e., the mercurial logical life stirring within the real developments,
- The soul as subjectivity and self-relation,
- soul manifesting as particular phenomena, i.e., certain motifs, symbols, narratives, symptoms, and teleological interests in contrast to other ones that are "not soul,"
- soul as a particular ("soulful") style of approach, a way of seeing.[8]

Giegerich also distinguishes speaking of the soul in the context of the modern person's life, such as it may be revealed in personal analysis, on the one hand, contrasting it with "the wholly other context of the soul's *opus magnum*, its historical process, on the other."[9]

The Need to Approach Soul Thought-Fully

As we have seen, the notion of soul can be elusive due to its incorporeal, intangible nature:

The life of the soul, rather than being metastable and having a natural existence, is totally ephemeral. Even its very form of realization and actualization is incorporeal, unnatural, fundamentally sublated, distilled, vaporized, momentary act. It is only in the doing: in the act or process of awareness, feeling appreciation, thinking comprehension.[10]

Here Giegerich emphasizes again the soul, and psychology, are not given. Rather, psychology and soul must be created over and over again, each time anew, through the work of interiorizing *thought*, described by Giegerich as the "*quinta essentia* of, and beyond, all four functions."[11]

Thought is privileged in psychology because it serves as

the breakthrough ... to the entirely different level of logic or the Notion. ...
Basically, thought is the soul's (or "the whole man's") openness to what is, the
capacity to express and respond to the truth of the age. It is what allows the
human being to enter Actaeon's wilderness, to extend into the realm of origins and pre-existence. What is meant by thought in this context is, therefore,
not abstract, but living thought, or better: logical movement, logical life.[12]

What Is Meant by the "Logical Life" of the Soul?

The term "logic" can be a source of confusion or even dissension to some as
used to characterize the soul's life. Giegerich relates such protests:

Would we not, with [psychology's] emphasis on thought and on "logical
life," betray the soul? Would we not leave the "vale of soul-making" and
instead ascend into the heights of abstractions and to "the peaks of spirit"?
... [W]hen we try to go beyond "image"
to thought, do we not necessarily turn our back on the soul?[13]

The problem with this objection is that at the outset, it sets up its own "logic"
wherein vales and peaks are associated with soul and thought in a Cartesian
topography, setting them apart from one another in space, precluding a dialectical relation. Such imagistic thinking

is a thinking in terms of otherness and externality: the one has the other
outside of itself. What I offer instead is a psychology of interiority. There
are not two, but only one, and this "one" contains its own "other" within
itself. Thought is not an external other to the image, but it is the very "soul"[14]
of the image itself; the image is, as it were, the
external garment of the thought...

For Giegerich, "the pleading for 'thought' is not a call to turn our backs on
'image' and on what archetypal theorizing had accomplished, 'but rather to
continue it radically in an attempt to complete it...'"[15]

Distinct from formal logic,[16] psychology's version of logic refers to the
inherent character of a thing, or *the way it works*, so to speak. Peter Moore, the
Nike engineer who designed the famous Air Jordan basketball shoe, achieved
something new with his masterpiece: the shoe, he declared, "is the logic of
water." Here we might understand its form to reflect fluidity, motion, flow,
power, speed, even stillness – qualities consistent with the extraordinary performance and character of the shoe's namesake, Michael Jordan. What inherent operational principles are revealed in view of the soul's logic? How does
soul work?

Dialectics or the Negation of the Negation

The logic of soul unfolds dialectically. To comprehend the movement of soul, dialectical thinking is needed. Such thinking

> begins with one single idea, notion, phenomenon and then shows its internal contradiction. It makes one conscious of the fact that what from outside looks like a unitary and self-consistent unit is not unitary, but within itself contradicts itself. It is within itself different (distinguishing itself from itself). In this sense, dialectical thinking is *recursive*. ... [It is] a stepping backwards so as to widen the horizon before oneself.[17]

The "stepping backwards" is accomplished through the *absolute negation* of one's current position. Absolute negations afford ever-deepening understanding, ever-widening horizons and perspectives, enabling the only *true* escape from within the existing logic. As related to problem-solving, one must (dialectically) push off from the logic that gave rise to the problem in order to solve it. In this way, consciousness can further itself, in effect "pushing off" from its position into ever-deepening knowledge of itself.

How is a simple negation distinct from the absolute negation required in dialectial thinking?

> In his writings, Giegerich frequently distinguishes between the "semantic" or content level of consciousness and the "syntactic" level of its overall structure or form. Change at the semantic level merely involves a shifting around of the contents of consciousness in the light of their having been contradicted in some way. This shifting around, however, as extensive as it may be in many cases, poses no challenge to the *form* of consciousness. None of its contents, that is to say, has yet become the straw that breaks the camel's back. In the negation of the negation, by contrast, the camel's back is broken, the structure of consciousness torn asunder.[18]

With a true negation, that which is negated is not fully lost but rather sublated, having "fulfilled" its function as an integral moment of the logical life of which it is a part, such as the blossom gives way to the fruit. As Hegel explains:

> The bud disappears when the blossom breaks through, and we might say that the former is refuted by the latter; in the same way when the fruit comes, the blossom may be explained to be a false form of the plant's existence, for the fruit appears as its true nature in place of the blossom. These stages are not merely differentiated: they supplant one another as being incompatible with one another. But the ceaseless activity of their own inherent nature makes these stages moments of an organic unity, where they not merely do

not contradict one another, but where one is as necessary as the other; and this equal necessity of all moments constitutes alone and thereby the life of the whole...[19]

Eachness and Interiorization

Drown in it
and grow gills.

– Greg Mogenson

A favorite expression of Jung's is said to be, "*Hic Rhodus, hic salta*" (literal translation: Here is Rhodes, jump here!). From one of Aesop's Fables, we read:

A man who had traveled in foreign lands, boasted very much, on returning to his own country, of the many wonderful and heroic things he had done in the different places he had visited. Among other things, he said that when he was at Rhodes he had leaped to such a distance that no man of his day could leap anywhere near him—and as to that, there were in Rhodes many persons who saw him do it, and whom he could call as witnesses. One of the bystand-ers interrupting him, said, "Now, my good man, if this be all true there is no need of witnesses. **Suppose this to be Rhodes; and now for your leap.**"[20]

The power of the phrase *Hic Rhodus, hic salta* as we contemplate our approach to soul lies in its remarkably psychological nature; we are invited to relinquish the personal ego (the boast), abandon the tale, and face reality here and now ("Suppose *this* to be Rhodes"), and then "leap," that is, dive in, give it our full effort! In *Memories, Dreams, and Reflections*, Jung writes:

For me, ... irreality was the quintessence of horror, for I aimed, after all, at *this* world and *this* life. No matter how deeply absorbed or blown about I was, I always knew that everything I was experiencing was ultimately directed at this real life of mine. I meant to meet its obligations and fulfill its meaning. My watchword was: *Hic Rhodus, hic salta!*[21]

In this spirit, Jung offers a clear description of the deeply *psychological attitude* that begins to approach the notion of absolute interiorization of the subject matter at hand:

Take the unconscious in one of the handiest forms, say a spontaneous fan-tasy, a dream, an irrational mood, an affect, or something of the kind, and operate with it. Give it your special attention, concentrate on it, and observe its alterations objectively. Spare no effort to devote yourself to this task, follow the subsequent transformations of the spontaneous fantasy atten-tively and carefully.[22]

Similarly, for Giegerich, each real situation, each dream, each image invites us to say to it,

> "This is it!" "*hic rhodus, hic salta*"! "This is it!" implies a double presence: 1. "I am here," reporting for duty, as it were, and unconditionally staking myself. 2. *This* situation that I am in has, regardless of what it is like, everything it needs (and thus also the potential of its fulfillment) *within* itself. Here and now, in this life of mine, in this world, must be the place of ultimate fulfillment.[23]

A requirement for recognizing the soul's logic is the mind's thinking capacity to apperceive the fullness of what is right in front of it. An example of this mindful relation to life is described by the Vietnamese Buddhist monk Thich Nhat Hanh:

> When you contemplate the big, full sunrise, the more mindful and concentrated you are, the more the beauty of the sunrise is revealed to you. Suppose you are offered a cup of tea, very fragrant, very good tea. If your mind is distracted, you cannot really enjoy the tea. You have to be mindful of the tea, you have to be concentrated on it so the tea can reveal its fragrance and wonder to you. That is why mindfulness and concentration are such sources of happiness. That's why a good practitioner knows how to create a moment of joy, a feeling of happiness, at any time of the day.[24]

Hanh's description approaches Giegerich's notion of interiority, as distinct from interiority in a traditional sense. Interiority as defined in PDI refers to the interior life of the soul *as such* –wherein the soul "is not the (literal, in itself external) inwardness in man, not traditional psychology's 'the unconscious,' but [the soul' s] inwardness in itself, absolute interiority."[25] The infinite interiority of the soul is reached through a logical act, that of the dialectical negation of externality as such, or the dialectical interiorization into absolute negativity. In our example of the tea, the negation of exterior distracted impulses allows for concentrated mindfulness upon the subject. As the ego personality is left behind, the mind finds itself drowning in the subject matter and dropping into its inner infinity, invited to witness the delightful "revelation of fragrance and wonder" in a simple cup of tea.

The Two Opposing Purposes [Movements] of the Soul (Manifesting/Absolving)

A complicating wrinkle in understanding the soul's logic is the existence of two completely opposing directions of the soul's logical life. These two movements are discussed in detail the final chapter of *What Is Soul?* The following describes the soul's longing for initiation into the world:

The whole point or intentionality of the soul's logical life is that "the soul" wants to become real in empirical life; it wants to have an affirmative presence in consciousness; more than only in subjective consciousness: it wants to be objectively *born* into the world. Through this self-representation it wants to become real and explicit to itself. ... The soul also wants to unfold and display its full reality in the empirical world and real life. It wants to represent itself in its whole circumference, in all its possible forms and stages of refinement. This aiming for the completion of its self-representation, for its self-display in its fullness, is what gives to the soul its fundamental process and *opus* character (opus in the alchemical sense, but applied to the history of the soul). It is and happens as the ongoing *opus magnum*.[26]

It is important to note that the soul's birth into the world and becoming "real" in empirical life consists not of substantive reality but exists strictly as "absolutely negative presences"[27] in the invisible form of myths, rituals, symbols, ideas, and so on.

The soul's opposing movement heads in the direction away from initiation and toward emancipation:

The soul of the archaic ancestor cults, of religion, and of metaphysics has in the course of the long history of the soul's logical life – please note the intentional equivocation of the first and the second term "soul"! – transmuted into *psychology*, which is nothing but a methodological approach or style of seeing (and perhaps of being). The formerly objectified notion *of* subjectivity and personal identity has come home to itself, been reflected into itself, so that it now reveals itself truly as subject (the subject that one *is*), rather than object ("the soul" that one *has*). It thereby has attained the form of form and left the form of substance behind.[28]

Ultimately, the soul longs for an unmediated encounter with itself, as form absolved of content: it "wants to be born *out* of itself as anima and into the world *as itself*: as subjectivity, as subjective mind, subjective consciousness as such... [T]he soul wants to come home to *itself* and to human consciousness."[29]

The Soul's Logic as Revealed by Historical and Cultural Shifts Over Time

On the way to its ever fuller self-unfolding, the soul pushes off from a given historical situation of itself, and it does so predominantly by means of a determinate negation or sublation of the status quo, in order to adapt to the changes encountered. The fact that it is a determinate negation of the prevailing situation gives to the soul's response to this situation, or to its move beyond it, its logical consistency, ... [which is] always unforeseeable.[30]

Giegerich offers a personal reflection about the soul's pushing off from its former self: "I am very comfortable with Goethe or Bach, more than, e.g., with very modern compositions. But I know that they do not connect me with our world today. They keep me in the world of the good old days and my consciousness in the logical status that had been reached then."[31] The task of the psychologist is to discern and attend to the logic of the current age. In this collection, several essays track psychologically relevant phenomena, documenting the modern soul's cultural and technological manifestations.[32]

The Soul's Logic vs. the Ego's Logic (or the Psychological Difference)

> True psychology depends on the awareness of what I call the "psychological difference" (a kind of analogy to Heidegger's "ontological difference"). It is the difference that runs through the meaning of the word psychology itself and divides "psychology" as the account of the psychologies that people have (personalistic psychology) from "psychology" as description of the life of the soul.[33]

The logic of the ego and the logic of soul bear no similarities. The logic of the ego is, in its most fundamental form, the logic of its own survival. In service to protecting its self-definition (whether physical or existential), the ego tends to insist on the literal, practical, predictable, and measurable, suspicious of the invisible, abstract, spontaneous or unknown. Where the ego is defined by a past narrative and invested in a projected future, the objective psyche is atemporal, only ever existent *now* (history documents soul, not the other way around), unconcerned with defending itself because it knows no threat by anything other than itself, as there is nothing else. As such, soul and ego are unrecognizable to one another, in the same way that, for example, a third dimension is unknowable from within a two-dimensional framework.

However, the logic of ego and soul can form a relation, albeit a nonlinear one; one might imagine the relation between the mechanical logic of a record player as related to the ethereal logic of music. In themselves, they are utterly unrelated. Yet one is wholly dependent on the other for its meaning. Still, the soul's internal atemporal, dialectical logic is completely foreign to the ego's, evident in Giegerich's description of Actaeon's transformation into the stag:

> There is only the (atemporal) Now of one single, atomic moment or archetypal truth, together, however, with the unfolding of its internal logical complexity, its inner logical, not temporal, life. No development, no transition, no literal initiation, no transformation as a process in time. Under the particular perspective of this particular moment in the soul's logical life, the

moment of "cognition," our myth shows the identity of the different and the difference of the identical. It shows the soul as the identity of identity and difference and thus as logical *life*.[34]

It is important to understand that what is impossible is a *personal* (egoic) relationship to soul. An objective relation *is* possible (and necessary from the soul's perspective) to the extent that the ego-personality gives way. "The human subject is, as it were, merely the antenna or the receiver which, however, makes [the soul's] self-relation not only audible but also possible in the first place... The human subject is merely a moment in the soul's self-relation and yet also its precondition."[35] Soul utilizes the individual as an instrument for its self-expression, for example in the creation of art or literature. Giegerich writes, "What makes a poet a true poet is precisely his capacity to allow himself to become sublated as a being in his own right and to become instead an integral moment of the self-production of his poem."[36] Indeed, "Psychology is possible only out of *Ergriffenheit*, one's being deeply affected and moved by the soul...."[37]

As psychologists, our ability to comprehend and attune to the logical life of the soul is of vital importance if we are to succeed in doing psychology and being of service to the modern soul. Giegerich maintains:

> We need logic for the benefit of a real aesthetic response to our world, for the benefit of the things in the world as it is today, so that they can be seen with soul. We need logic to educate and differentiate our senses to the degree of sophistication that would match the state of logical sophistication already real in the things of our world out there, which is a world of steel-and-glass architecture, asphalt streets, airplanes and spacecraft, electronics, computer tomography, shopping malls, etc. Tremendous changes have occurred since the days of mythological man: they are the assignment, we have to do our homework.[38]

Explorations of the Soul's Logical Life

The variety of subject matter that appears in this collection of essays speaks to the many ways in which the authors have grasped and been grasped by the soul's logical life. Giegerich writes that "Jung had been reached and touched, indeed 'gripped,' by the Notion of the soul. And because he had been touched and gripped by it, he had a grasp, a Begriff, a Notion, of it and he could grasp it."[39] Like the poet who writes of the essence of his subject by collapsing his subject into the thing it is-and-is-not, soul itself can only be grasped by the is-and-is-not character of itself, which must also exist in the mind of the thinker. In each thinker's work presented in the following pages, we are introduced to the soul coming home to itself as consciousness.

Jungian analyst **Andrés Ocazionez** takes the first step of an attempt to assess Wolfgang Giegerich's impact on depth psychology in his chapter, "Soul-Making

IS Psychology-Making: Wolfgang Giegerich's Essential Insight." Its main objective is to present Wolfgang Giegerich's essential psychological insight. This initial presentation, however, inevitably leads to a discussion of the difference between psychological insights and traditional theoretical insights and of how the observance of this difference is crucial for genuine psychological work and understanding. Consequently, an understanding of Wolfgang Giegerich's impact on the discipline requires consideration of both the content of his essential insight and the specific nature of psychological insights.

In his chapter, "The Uroboric Logic of Anxiety: 'Not Out, But Through'," Jungian analyst **Michael Whan** explores the psychological 'disorder' of anxiety, which in modernity has reached epidemic proportions. Whan approaches anxiety from the standpoint of the psychology of interiority, deriving initial inspiration from Kierkegaard, who discerned within anxiety a dialectical movement, associating it in his writings with an existential notion of a *"yawning abyss."* Whan connects this fundamental image with the notion of the modern soul's bottomlessness, its *groundlessness*, drawing on Giegerich's concept of neurosis and the "neurotic soul." Anxiety is then shown to exhibit a uroboric logic, a self-othering in relation to the psychological difference, analogously understood like the alchemical axiom, "the stone that is not a stone." Anxiety can then in this way be comprehended as "the fear that is not a fear," – *sublated fear*, fear raised up to a higher, more complex logical level. Whan then turns to a particular phobia described by the psychoanalyst Wilfred Bion, in which a symptomatic anxiety reveals more deeply a terror of the *lacunary* nature of existence.

In "Discerning the Dialectic between Form and Content," psychologist **Jennifer M. Sandoval** explores the conditions of consciousness for distinguishing between mere contents of consciousness and their underlying form or soul logic. She illustrates this through various examples, including a young woman's experience in a strip club, the prodigal son parable, and Ibram X. Kendi's perspective on racism. The chapter highlights the importance of preparing and conditioning the mind to be attuned to the dialectic, using the example of psychoanalytic companioning to demonstrate the need to stay attuned to form above content to grasp the truth of an encounter. Sandoval draws parallels between the capacity to listen beyond apparent meaning to true meaning and the *melos* in music, understanding its "true spirit." The chapter concludes by noting the relation between relinquishing hope and transformation, particularly in Beethoven's case, where his deafness allowed him to "hear" the inner sounds so powerfully and beautifully conveyed in his music.

Jungian analyst **George B. Hogenson's** chapter, "Returning to the Wilderness: Jung, Giegerich and the infinite task of interiority," examines Giegerich's use of the myth of Thor and the giant Utgard Loki to approach the question of whether and how Giegerich's Hegelian interpretation of Jung's system runs the risk of settling into stasis. The chapter raises this question by disputing Giegerich's contention that Thor experiences the universal in the particularity of Utgard Loki's cat in the myth. This argument is framed in contrast to

Giegerich's dynamic reading of the Artemis and Actaion myth, which concludes *The Soul's Logical Life*. The two myths, while intended to frame the book's argument, may point to a fundamental tension in Giegerich's work that Jung might have resisted.

"Mandamin 'Food of Wonder'" is **Peter White's** engaging examination of the Anishnaabe story from the standpoint of psychology as the discipline of interiority, the unique interpretive style that begins with the position that myths are to be read in terms of their internal relations, seen from within. In this story, a boy must prove his worth by killing Mandamin, a spirit figure who has searched far and wide for a good Anishnaabe. Each section of the story unfolds in the light of the one thought that all of its images are ultimately the simultaneous and mutually mediating expression of soul's desire to become real in this world. In an approach that sees every image in the story as being allegorical of a psychological reality, conventional everyday thinking slowly gives way to understanding the myth as the expression of this one archetypal idea. In White's exploration of the psychological difference between "the soul" and Man, characters and events in this story that seem to be opposites are revealed to also share an identity, the logical process of which culminates in the death of Mandamin. In this way, the killing of the corn god is simultaneously the influx of soul into the consciousness of his challenger Zhowmin.

Through a fascinating psychological interpretation of dreams, Jungian analyst **Nanae Takenaka** explores the phenoenon of non-attendance in Japanese university students in her chapter, "The Difficulty of Encountering One's Own Other." The author introduces a clinical case of a student who stayed in university for eight years without attending classes as an example of how this type of student is prone to psychology's logical movement. Through dreamwork, Takenaka emphasizes the importance of exploring the psyche's self-relation and interplay of archetypes to gain insight into the underlying logic of this modern phenomenon.

In "You Are Here (Now): Psyche's Logic or Sense of Soul in Jung, Hillman, and Giegerich," **Michael R. Caplan** explores the mutual contributions of James Hillman and Wolfgang Giegerich toward the advancement of what both considered foundational to C.G. Jung's project: his insight into the necessarily uroboric structure of psychology itself, its lack of an external "Archimedean" point from which to interpret ourselves and our world. Using their own words to bring the dialectic of syzygy into relief, Caplan articulates the logos of a truly psychological psychology, one that Giegerich would say deserves its name. Through an examination of their shared idea of "soul," of the duplicitous phenomenology of the dream, and of the discipline of image as entry to uroboric interiority, the chapter addresses the "divergence" sparked by Giegerich's critique of Hillman, concluding with the question of psychology's response to modernity. Psychological thinking is presented as a contra-natural realism bringing us home to our very nature and our actual lives, but not without first subverting our every natural habit of thought and alienating us from the day-world perspective by means of what Hillman called the "underworld," as illustrated by the author's youthful experience of clinical depersonalization. Giegerich goes further than Hillman, as Hillman went further than Jung, in drawing out the implications of Jung's insight into psyche and psychology as uroboric; to go "further" than Giegerich is only to go, ever and anew, into the real phenomena addressing us.

Occasions in which the analytic psychotherapist gives interpretative utterance to the soul situation of the patient by saying "I ..." on his or her behalf are highlighted in Jungian analyst **Greg Mogenson's** chapter, "Vicarius I-Statement: From Substance to Subject." Such "vicarius I-statements," as these may be called, are not concocted by the therapist as a matter of technique. When authentic, they rather have *phenomenon* character and are the spontaneous expression in "the form of subject" of what Jung variously referred to as "the coming to consciousness of the psychic process," "the soul's speaking about itself," and "interpretation from above. ..." Topics include Giegerich's concepts of "the psychological difference" and "the psychological I," these in relation to Hegel's insistence that the truth must be known not only as substance, but also as subject.

The rise of evolutionary psychology is an important development in evolutionary theory. In "Consciousness, Reflexivity and Evolution," Jungian analyst **Philip Kime** maintains the necessity of demarcating the properly psychological in the face of the undeniable success of such recent theory so as not to lose it to important and essentially accurate empirical science. Kime argues that attempts to accommodate depth psychology to the framework of empirical theory are conceptually confused and doomed to failure, as they give up the fundamentally psychological, right out of the gate. Therefore, we must agree on a definition of the psychological that stands apart in a motivated sense from the framework of evolutionary theory and which does not pander, as Giegerich has so famously urged, to the irrelevant and logically limited framework of standard empiricism. The reflexive nature of human consciousness is the root of the properly psychological and embodies a structure that does indeed have an evolutionary genesis but which, once extant, the author contends, can no longer in principle be addressed by evolutionary theory.

In "A Temporal Dance with the Psychological Difference: Lessons from *Lesson of the Mask*," **Colleen EL-Bejjani** shares a personal experience of participating in a cleansing ritual in Kibola, Guinea, led by a village elder, which sets the stage for a discussion of the lessons of the mask and their relevance to both traditional drum and dance and traditional Jungian psychology. The author, who has spent decades studying and teaching Guinean drum and dance alongside her interest in Jungian psychology, reflects on how the two began to crumble as her interest in psychology as the "Discipline of Interiority" expanded. EL-Bejjani discusses Giegerich's essay, "Lesson of the Mask," which shows how the mask dance sets the performance of the psychological difference into motion. The author suggests that every topic and subject matter for psychology has a mask character, and that implicit in the lesson of the mask is the need for psychologists to put on the mask of whatever phenomena lay claim to their attention. By doing so, psychologists set themselves up as, enact, and become the psychological difference, the difference between themselves as individuals and themselves as soul, spirit, or divinity. The author concludes by suggesting that the lessons of the mask are relevant not only to traditional drum and dance, but also to the discipline of psychology, and that a disciplined approach is necessary for any learning endeavor.

In "Deconstruction and the Modern Self," psychologist **Daniel Anderson** contends that the history of psychoanalysis is simultaneously the history of culture, the objective psyche, the "I" and the unconscious. The author's examination of the original symptoms that served to generate the field of psychoanalysis demonstrates great differences between the times of Freud and Jung and the symptoms therapists see today as a result of the dramatic changes the ego has undergone. Anderson shows how the ego significantly impacts the nature of experience that must be made unconscious and the symptoms that result, tracing the changes in the nature of the ego over the last century, from the "atomic self" to the current "smeared self." The smeared self results from multiple cultural changes, especially the prevalence of ambient societal deconstruction. Deconstruction operates on narrative and discourse, which powerfully impacts identity and ego, reconfiguring them. Anderson argues that this new configuration of the ego, driven by deconstruction, yields a new configuration of the unconscious and new challenges that our patients present for treatment.

Late in his life, Jung voiced concern that after his death his psychology, which he viewed as a modern form of soul, would lose the vitality that burst forth at its inception. Without this living presence keeping it alive, rooted, and "objective." Jung feared his psychology would become interred in dry concepts and fundamentally misunderstood. Jungian analyst **John Hoedl's** chapter, "'It's Not Art!': Interiorizing Jung's 'Confrontation with the Unconscious,'" examines Jungian psychology's founding story, that is, Jung's "confrontation with the unconscious" from the perspective of "interiority", in other words, as the *soul's confrontation with itself*. The author demonstrates that through the negation/sublation of its old forms (religion and myth) and also the subjective, egoic activities and concerns of Jung the person, the soul came into its new form, that of psychology. Hoedl explores how logical negation, present as the "Not" in "It's Not Art!" is constitutive to psychology's requisite *sublated* perspective and is the living spirit that keeps it from becoming entombed in applications foreign to its nature.

In "Bitcoin, Utopia & Soul," psychologist **Josep M. Moreno** develops a psychological analysis of a specific soul movement that is present in one of the major topics of our times, where the real action is carried out: the economy, its fundamental token, money, and the cultural institutions that are in the center of gravity of our way of life which today lie in the intersection of economy and technology. This analysis stems from the perspective of one of the major teleologies of soul, emancipation: a dialectical soul movement that historically accounts for major transformations in the general logical form of consciousness. This examination considers a recent paper published in the sphere of technology.

In the chapter, "How Does Music Think?," Jungian analyst **Pamela J. Power** describes how the "soul's logical life" manifested in the history of Western music. Beginning with plainchant and moving through the development of a complex harmonic system, Power addresses changes in the syntax of music, that is, the underlying structures and forms. The author examines how in modern times, soul has both abandoned music and absconded *with* music into the media and digitization but has left a residue in the wake of its departure.

Robert Dommett's chapter, "Churchill's Shroud" offers a speculative investigation of the archetypal forces underlying the Western Great White Male's (GWM) ascension to the role of divine intelligence, based on the Enlightenment and industrial revolution. It then follows their recent loss of power, as evidenced by their lost monopoly on financial and technical power and the more recent emergence of a successor in the form of a powerful multifaceted, multiracial, democratized technological hive mind in social media, and technology more generally. The author considers the now-deprecated state of GWM leadership and uses the Persian myth of Jamšid to identify a fatal lie that is the mythological source of their fall. Keeping with the Zoroastrian theme, GWM's are described as being greeted by an abomination derived from their lie at the bridge of judgment and by a demon called the Loosener of Bones (in the guise of Black Lives Matter protests) who is rendering judgment on the bronze symbols of their lost power. The chapter encourages us to adopt the perspective of Nietzsche's Noble (Hu)man whose mastery of the underlying dialectic would enable us to move on from this phase of consciousness to face the greater challenges of an uncertain, technology-lead future.

In "The Great Hunt: Psychology and the Question of Truth," Jungian psychotherapist **Marco Heleno Barreto** contends that psychology as the discipline of interiority is essentially related to the question of truth. This relation, as well as the specific notion of truth proper to psychology, is exposed in the last chapter of *The Soul's Logical Life*, through an interpretation of the myth of Actaion, the hunter, and his meeting with the goddess Artemis, who allegorically means the truth that implicitly governs Actaion's hunt. Psychology is thus seen as the great hunt for truth. Now, Nietzsche uses the same metaphor-image of the great hunt (and of truth as a woman) to present his notion of psychology. However, in *The Soul's Logical Life*, Nietzsche is seen as one of the destroyers of the notion of truth, and thus his stance should be in full opposition to the one that is embodied in psychology as the discipline of interiority. In this chapter, the author explores both stances in order to highlight their opposition, on the one hand, and to point to a problem that arises in psychology's claim for being "the discipline of truth."

The essays in this volume vary considerably, and each is stamped by the individual author. This collection is not meant to be a textbook of accuracy about the ideas or methodology of PDI. For that, we refer the reader to the growing volumes of work being published by Wolfgang Giegerich himself and by others who follow from his inspiration.

The editors of this volume share a deep interest in facilitating the creative output of those who have been affected by the works of Wolfgang Giegerich because we ourselves have been irrevocably changed by encounters with his work, his thinking, his feeling, and his person. That this book is dedicated to him goes without question.

Notes

1 Wolfgang Giegerich, *The Soul's Logical Life: Towards a Rigorous Notion of Psychology* (4th ed. Frankfurt am Main; New York: Peter Lang GmbH, 2007), 267–8.
2 Not the ordinary definition of thinking, but rather: "Thinking is the art to allow the matter that we are dealing with to speak for itself. Psychology is not concerned with what we, what people think, but with what 'the soul' of/in the real thinks." Wolfgang Giegerich, *The Soul Always Thinks (Collected English Papers, Vol. IV)* (Woodstock, Conn.; Lancaster: Spring Journal, Inc., 2010), 16.
3 See Pamela J. Power's essay, "How Does Music Think?" in this volume wherein she describes how the soul's logical life manifested in the history of Western music, beginning with plainchant through the development of a complex harmonic system, addressing changes in the syntax of music, i.e., the underlying structures and forms.
4 The first collection featured papers presented at the International Conference of the ISPDI held in Berlin in 2014. See: Jennifer M. Sandoval and John C. Knapp, eds. *Psychology as the Discipline of Interiority*. 1 edition (London; New York, NY: Routledge, 2017).
5 Giegerich, *What Is Soul?*, 50.
6 Giegerich, *What Is Soul?*, 41.
7 Giegerich, *What Is Soul?*, 22.
8 Giegerich, *What Is Soul?*, 26.
9 Giegerich, *What Is Soul?*, 26.
10 Giegerich, *What Is Soul?*, 50.
11 Giegerich is here referring to Jung's typology and intending to make clear that thinking in this sense is not reducible to Jung's thinking function.
12 Giegerich, *The Soul's Logical Life*, 125.
13 Wolfgang Giegerich, David L. Miller, David L., and Greg Mogenson, *Dialectics & Analytical Psychology: The El Capitan Canyon Seminar* (New Orleans, La.: Spring Journal, Inc., 2005), 108.
14 *Dialectics*, 109.
15 *Dialectics*, 108.
16 E.g., if a→b and b→c, then a→c
17 *Dialectics*, 3.
18 *Dialectics*, 93.
19 Georg W. Friedrich Hegel, *The Phenomenology of Mind: Volume 1* (New York, NY: Cosimo Inc., 2005), 62.
20 https://en.wikisource.org/wiki/Three_Hundred_%C3%86sop%27s_Fables/The_Boasting_Traveller
21 C. G. Jung, *Memories, Dreams, Reflections*, ed. Aniela Jaffe, trans. Clara Winston and Richard Winston, Reissue edition (New York: Vintage, 1989), 189.
22 C. G. Jung, *CW* 14 § 749.

23 Giegerich, *The Soul's Logical Life*, 223.
24 https://uhs.berkeley.edu/sites/default/files/article_-_five_steps_to_mindfulness.pdf
25 Giegerich, *What Is Soul?*, 333.
26 Giegerich, *What Is Soul?*, 43.
27 Giegerich, *What Is Soul?*, 319.
28 Giegerich, *What Is Soul?*, 294. He goes on to note, "Although what I have just described is the truth of our time, *it is not its reality*. The actual general reality is that the subjectivity of the subject has itself precisely been again construed in the same old substantial form and not in the form of form."
29 Giegerich, *What Is Soul?*, 320.
30 Giegerich, *What Is Soul?*, 43.
31 Giegerich, *The Soul Always Thinks*, 70.
32 For examples, see "Deconstruction and the Modern Self" (Daniel Anderson), "The Difficulty of Encountering One's Own Other" (Nanae Takenaka), "Bitcoin, Utopia & Soul" (Josep M. Moreno Alavedra), and "How Does Music Think?" (Pamela J. Power) in this volume.
33 Giegerich, *The Soul's Logical Life*, 124.
34 Giegerich, *The Soul's Logical Life*, 250.
35 Giegerich, *What Is Soul?*, 94.
36 Giegerich, *What Is Soul?*, 95.
37 Wolfgang Giegerich, *The Neurosis of Psychology (Collected English Papers, Vol. I)* (New Orleans, LA: Spring Journal, Inc., 2005), 136.
38 Giegerich, *The Soul Always Thinks*, 70.
39 Giegerich, *The Soul's Logical Life*, 41.

Chapter 1

Soul-Making IS Psychology-Making

Wolfgang Giegerich's Essential Insight

Andrés Ocazionez

Introduction

The first and main purpose of this chapter is to present what I believe to be Wolfgang Giegerich's essential insight, namely that in our times and within Western culture psychology-making is the only genuine way of soul-making. Now, this discussion produces for itself a seemingly problematic side effect. As will become evident in the course of its development, the identity of soul-making with psychology-making implies that a genuine psychological insight is not free-floating but bound to, or better said, in itself *identical* with each concrete individual psychological work. This, of course, challenges my initial proposition of there being an *essential* insight from Wolfgang Giegerich. So, how can I justify my speaking about a psychologist's essential insight? And how can we assess the impact of a psychologist's work on the discipline if that work is not only based on but also leads to a radical redefinition of psychology and of the nature of psychological insights themselves? The second purpose of my chapter is to at least begin to address these questions.

Giegerich's use of the term psychology-making is certainly not new and the insight that in our times and within Western culture soul-making can only happen as psychology-making runs consistently throughout his work. I would even venture to say that this insight IS his work. With this, I don't mean to say that the purpose of Giegerich's work is to arrive at this formulation. That would be a mistake. Clearly, the purpose of Giegerich's work is to make psychology and not to come up with a formula. However, the result of each one of his individual works, as long as he has successfully made psychology (*as a psychology with soul*), is a reenactment or "celebration" of this insight.

To say it in vulgar terms, Giegerich's work does not "talk the talk, but walks the talk" or, more precisely, it simply *walks*, simply makes psychology. Consequently, the insight that soul-making is psychology-making is not always written explicitly in his published works. This happens only sporadically, depending on the specific needs of each individual one of his tasks. Nonetheless, we can identify, here and there, this explicit formulation. In *What Is Soul?*, for example, we find the following statement, "The whole purpose of psychology (OF the psychological *opus*) is to

DOI: 10.4324/9781003381150-2

produce psychology. Soul-making is psychology-making, and psychology-making is soul-making."[1] And in a similar vein, we read,

> *The soul* of the archaic ancestor cults, of religion, and of metaphysics has in the course of the long history of the soul's logical life (…) *transmuted* into *psychology*, which is nothing but a methodological approach or style of seeing.[2]

Or, "Having become psychology, the soul has come down to earth."[3]

But it seems to me that in his latest English publication, *Working With Dreams*, this insight becomes, so to speak, aware of itself as an essential psychological insight. I am referring to the section "Psychotherapy – the making of psychology"[4] from the third chapter of the book. Here Giegerich summarizes Jung's, Hillman's, and perhaps unwittingly, his own essential insight.[5] In this specific discussion, Giegerich's insight is put forward as the solution to the fundamental dilemma of a psychology with soul within the context of psychotherapy. For the most part, my discussion will be orbiting around Giegerich's argumentation, which reads as follows:

The dilemma:

Our task as psychologists is to *make* soul; this means that it has to become in some way *real* in empirical reality.

The soul or logical movement must be fundamentally kept apart from empirical reality and understood as "background" or "underworldly" or "absolute-negative" process, and yet it must be made real in empirical reality (which also means that it cannot be located behind or above the world in a metaphysical realm).

How can soul and its logical movements become real without losing their "underworldly," that is, "ghostly" background quality?

The solution:

The answer is: soul-making is psychology-making and it happens in consciousness, not in empirical states or the conditions of people. (…) the way it is made in the world, in the real, and thus also in dreams, is not physically, but noetically: When soul has successfully been *made*, then the result is psychology, as a psychology of soul, as truly psychological thinking and understanding. Psychology *is* the form of the SOUL *as real*, as realized.[6]

This dilemma builds on and is irrigated by Jung's and Hillman's essential psychological insights, achievements, and shortcomings. What follows is a brief review of Giegerich's presentation of these insights with some additional comments. This will allow us to return to what I argue is Giegerich's own essential insight from a somewhat informed position.

C. G. Jung's Essential Insight

Giegerich presents Jung's essential insight as follows:

> The *psyche* is certainly personal, each individual has his or her own psyche, just like each person possesses his or her own body (...). In contrast to the subjective psyche, the soul is objective and cultural. This was Jung's decisive discovery. The Jungian understanding of psychology is that it is in the first place the study of the objective soul.[7]

Jung was well aware that the precondition for the making of psychology was the departedness of the soul as substance or as an external objective reality. As he writes in CW 10:

> [T]he soul is not always and everywhere on the inside. There are peoples and epochs where it is outside, peoples and epochs that are unpsychological, as, for example, all ancient cultures. ... Whenever there exists externally a conceptual or ritual form in which all the yearnings and hopes of the soul are absorbed and expressed, that is, for example, a living religion, then the soul is outside and there is no soul problem, just as there is the no unconscious in our sense. It was therefore logical that the discovery of psychology took place exclusively during the last decades, although former centuries possessed enough introspection and intelligence to gain knowledge about psychological facts. ... the reason for this is that there existed no compelling predicament. ... It needed the spiritual predicament of our time to force us to discover psychology.[8]

Nonetheless, Jung did not always conclude from this that the soul as the object of psychology had to be replaced with the human organism or with what goes on inside people. He persuades us to, "summon up courage to consider the possibility of a 'psychology with soul'—that is, a theory of the psyche ultimately based on the postulate of an autonomous, spiritual principle"[9] and maintained that psychology is, "neither biology nor physiology nor any other science than just the knowledge of the soul."[10]

Jung's recommended courage is not to be underestimated, especially if one considers the important theoretical problem that confronts psychology as the science or knowledge of the soul. If, "everything I have observed lies in the soul; everything, so to speak, on the side of the inner"[11] then, "everything we can possibly know consists in psychic stuff,"[12] including psychology. In other words, if there is no "outside" for the soul, then every attempt to approach the soul is already, from the outset, inner and subjective. Therefore, objectivity, knowledge, and neutral observation in the traditional empirical-scientific sense is not possible for psychology. Jung was aware of this:

> The soul is the beginning and end of all cognition. It is not only the object of its science, but the subject also. This gives psychology a unique place

among all the other sciences: on the one hand there is a constant doubt as to the possibility of its being a science at all, while on the other hand psychology acquires the right to state a theoretical problem the solution of which will be one of the most difficult tasks for a future philosophy.[13]

Jung therefore faced an important dilemma: *is psychology as the study of the objective soul possible in a world without soul?* That is, in a world without soul as an external or substantial form. This question runs throughout Jung's whole body of work. According to Sonu Shamdasani in *Jung and the Making of Modern Psychology*:

> In reading Jung's work and correspondence, one encounters two distinct modes of thinking and presentation. In the first, specific theories are advanced, established, and considered to be proven. This mode, heavily accentuated in the first generation of Jungian analysts and in numerous introductory and expository works, is the most well known. Thus, as "everybody knows," he put forward theories of complexes, psychological types, and most notoriously, of the archetypes of the collective unconscious. *The second mode of his thinking consists in an ongoing questioning concerning the conditions of possibility of psychology.*[14]

The author adds:

> When considering Jung's strictures on the possibility of psychology and his statements about the premature status of general theories in psychology, it is important to realize that he is including his own work in this assessment. *It is precisely this mode of his thinking that tends to be filtered out. These two modes thread themselves throughout his work.*[15]

Shamdasani presents the way in which Jung grappled with this dilemma throughout his work. He also points out that, at least in some instances, Jung found the solution to his own dilemma by precisely going deeper into it. An excellent example of this can be found from Jung in CW 8. This paragraph is outstanding because it includes both Jung's central dilemma and solution:

> As I have said, the psychology of complex phenomena finds itself in an uncomfortable situation compared with the other natural sciences because it lacks a base outside its object. It can only translate itself back into its own language, or fashion itself in its own image. The more it extends its field of research and the more complicated its objects become, the more it feels the lack of a point which is distinct from those objects. And once the complexity has reached that of the empirical man, his psychology inevitably merges with the psychic process itself. It can no longer be distinguished from the latter, and so turns into it. *But the effect of this is that the process*

attains consciousness. In this way, psychology actualizes the unconscious urge to consciousness. It is, in fact, the coming to consciousness of the psychic process, but it is not, in the deeper sense, an explanation of this process, for no explanation of the psychic can be anything other than the living process of the psyche itself. *Psychology is doomed to cancel itself out as a science and therein precisely it reaches its scientific goal. Every other science has so to speak an outside; not so psychology, whose object is the inside subject of all science.*[16]

Jung, at least in his "second mode of thinking," was little impressed by psychology's production of theories, gathering of evidence, or therapeutic efficacy. For Jung, psychology's own reflectedness and sophistication, whereby the psychic process can become conscious of itself, is what really counts, not its conceptual, social or therapeutic products. This is the real interest that inspires *Psychological Types,* where, as Shamdasani correctly remarks, "The first "subject" of psychology was psychology itself, and psychology had to study the psychology-making process."[17] We see another example of Jung's interest in psychological sophistication over and above psychological propositions in the preface to the planned English edition of one of Tina Keller's books:

A ceaseless and limitless talk about psychology has inundated the world in the last twenty years, but it has not as yet produced a noticeable improvement of the psychological outlook and attitude. Laymen, as well as scientists, are bewildered by the luxuriant growth of theoretical standpoints, and by a maze of unbalanced propositions.[18]

Again, what counts is the "psychological outlook and attitude," what happens within psychology itself, not the production of theoretical standpoints and propositions.

Now, from all the Jungians that came after Jung, James Hillman stands out as one who dedicated his life's work to refining the outlook and attitude of psychology as well as to reorient the object of psychology toward the study and care of the soul.

James Hillman's Essential Insight

Giegerich presents James Hillman's insight as follows:

James Hillman's essential insight was that the aim of psychology is "soul-making". The term "making" in "soul-making" implies that, to begin with, the soul does not exist. (...) Therefore it has to be MADE, produced, in order to come into existence. From this it follows that if our task as psychologists is to *make* soul, this means that it has to become in some way *real* in empirical reality.[19]

As mentioned previously, a fundamental aim of James Hillman's work is pre-cisely to offer a deepening of "the psychological outlook and attitude" of the discipline. He opens *Re-visioning Psychology* by saying:

> This book is about soul-making. It is an attempt at a psychology of soul, an essay in re-visioning psychology from the point of view of soul. ... The job of psychology is to offer a way and find a place for soul *within its own field.* [20]

Hillman's whole psychological enterprise starts off from the soul's change, noted by Jung, from substance to subject:

> *By soul I mean, first of all, a perspective rather than a substance, a viewpoint toward things rather than a thing itself. This perspective is reflective*; it medi-ates events and makes differences between ourselves and everything that happens.[21]

Hillman was well aware of Jung's statement that "the psyche creates reality every day"[22] and furthermore, that the psychological discipline inevitably cre-ates the psychic realities that it sets out to study. This is nicely put in *The Myth of Analysis* where he observes that "Freud's fantasy *of* the little girl's mind becomes a Freudian fantasy *in* the little girl's mind."[23] But soul-making for Hillman was something else and something more than the type of, so to speak, "innocent" or "un-reflected" psyche-making[24] that we see in this example. Soul-making is essentially reflective, and part of its task is to identify the archetypal perspectives that "influence our consciousness, particularly the ideas and attitudes of psychology."[25] An important part of Hillman's thinking is dedicated to reflect these perspectives *within the field of psychology.* There-fore, according to Hillman, *"essential to soul-making is psychology-making."*[26] From this point of view, making psychology is essentially a deepening and reflecting of psychology's own perspectives. What Hillman achieves in this regard is truly impressive. He gives a partial summary of this in *The Dream and the Underworld*:

> I have looked at the psychology of ego development and growth in terms of the child archetype (1971), at the psychology of age versus youth in terms of the puer-senex pair (1967), at the diagnosis of hysteria and inferior fem-ininity by means of the archetypal configuration of Dionysos (1969), and at the therapeutic concern with changing abnormality into normality through the figures of Ananke and Athene (1974). Each of these has been an attempt to see through accepted psychological positions by placing them against a relevant mythic background. *The hope has been that arche-typal perspectives can rectify our vision of the psyche and give a more psycho-logical (i.e., self-reflective, imaginal, and deeper) of what psychology is saying and doing.*[27]

We could say about these contributions what Shamdasani said about Jung's work with *Psychological Types*, that here the first "subject" of psychology is psychology itself. However, their object would not be merely to "study the psychology-making process" but rather to *make psychology* as a self-reflected and self-deepening discipline.[28] As Hillman writes in *Re-Visioning Psychology*: "Here psychology is conceived as a necessary activity of the psyche, which *constructs vessels and breaks them* in order to deepen and intensify experience."[29] If I may be allowed an oxymoron: *archetypal psychology stands on this deepening and reflectedness.*

Therefore, as Giegerich rightly notes, Hillman's psychology is "a major step forward, a real advance of psychological theory beyond conventional Jungianism,"[30] and supersedes all other psychological schools, including Jungianism (Jung's "first mode of thinking"), by reaching and establishing itself at a new level of reflection.

Wolfgang Giegerich's Essential Insight

We can now return to Giegerich's dilemma and solution and approach it again with some additional comments.

The dilemma:

Our task as psychologists is to *make* soul; this means that it has to become in some way *real* in empirical reality.

The soul or logical movement must be fundamentally kept apart from empirical reality and understood as "background" or "underworldly" or "absolute-negative" process, and yet it must be made real in empirical reality (which also means that it cannot be located behind or above the world in a metaphysical realm).

How can soul and its logical movements become real without losing its "underworldly", that is, "ghostly" background quality?[31]

Our task as psychologists, as Hillman remarked, is to *make* soul.[32] To, in some way, make it *real* in empirical reality. The soul, however, has always come into being in its absence.[33] As Hillman would put it, the soul's possibility to endow events with depth and significance "derives from its special *relation with death*."[34] The soul is, and has always been, negation, its own departedness. In other words, the *soul is not*, and therefore, has to be *made*.

"There were times and epochs," Jung remarks, where soul-making could take place in empirical reality as, for example, in a living religion, where "all the yearnings and hopes of the soul are absorbed and expressed."[35] This possibility, however, has been lost to us as the soul has migrated to "the side of the inner," from substance to subject. And this loss is precisely the precondition for psychology.

This "subject," however, is not the patient and not the analyst; it's not the world as Hillman suggested. And this "inner" is not the personal or collective unconscious, not the imaginal. People, the world, and psychological topologies have the form of substance and the soul, as mentioned previously, has transmuted into subjectivity and interiority as such. In fact, the soul, as *psychological subject*, only comes about through psychology.[36] Therefore, soul-making cannot genuinely happen as the "individuation process" (in Jung's sense) or as "the rescue of the world" (in Hillman's sense). Soul-making can only take place in its own "ghostly" or "underworldly" form as thought (*Geist*) and *under*standing: as psycho*logy*.

The solution:

The answer is: soul-making is psychology-making and it happens in consciousness, not in empirical states or the conditions of people. (...) [T]he way it is made in the world, in the real, and thus also in dreams, is not physically, but noetically: When soul has successfully been *made*, then the result is psychology, as a psychology of soul, as truly psychological thinking and understanding. Psychology *is* the form of the SOUL *as real*, as realized.[37]

With this solution, Giegerich's psychology reaches a still deeper level of reflection than that of Hillman's. It is not, as Hillman puts it, *that psychology-making is essential for soul-making* or that *psychology is a necessary activity for the psyche*, but that *psychology-making IS soul-making* and "psychology *is* the sublation of the soul."[38] For Giegerich, psychology-making is not only an essential form of soul-making among other possible forms, for example, individuating, becoming Self, or restoring the anima to the world. Psychology-making is the *one and only* genuine way in which soul can be made.

This exclusivity is not capricious but corresponds to the sublatedness of the soul (which is at the same time the fundamental precondition for psychology). To recapitulate: the soul throughout its long history of transformations has mutated, as Jung would put it, from being outside to being on the side of the inner, from substance to subject. The soul has *gone **under*** and fully come home to itself as "absolutely-negative," "ghostly," "underworldly." The soul is *not*. Therefore, soul has to be made as perspective, reflection, way of ***under***standing (Hillman). Psychology (the logos of the soul) is therefore the one genuine place where *the soul as knowing or understanding subject* can reflect itself, know itself, or, more precisely, become *realized*. It is *only* as a psychological event in consciousness that soul is made in the here and now.

Soul (or soul-making) IS psychology-making and nothing else.

The Summit (or Nadir) of Psychology

Giegerich's essential insight has important implications for psychology. I would like to discuss this by turning back to Jung's passage in CW 8. Here Jung momentarily brings psychology home to itself when he mentions that in psychological work the psychic process cannot be distinguished from psychology, but that,

> the effect of this is that the process attains consciousness. In this way, psychology actualizes the unconscious urge to consciousness. It is, in fact, the coming to consciousness of the psychic process.[39]

Giegerich's comment on this passage is spot on. "With this view," he writes,

> **Jung's theoretical standpoint has arrived at its summit (or better said; its nadir)**: at the standpoint of subjectivity, of subject come home to itself, and at the uroboric logic of interiority. The psyche observes *itself – this*, according to Jung, is what *psychology* is. "Psychology inevitably merges with the psychic process itself" – this presupposes that **the soul itself as substance has gone under into what formerly might have been the abstract** *theory* or *knowledge* or science **ABOUT the soul. The soul now has** *itself* **attained the form of psychology.**[40]

Indeed, a theoretical summit, and one with tremendous implications for psychology. Jung might have been aware of this when he comments further down that,

> Psychology is doomed to cancel itself out as a science and therein precisely it reaches its scientific goal. *Every other science has so to speak an outside; not so psychology, whose object is the inside subject of all science.*[41]

By attaining the form of subject, of "I," of psychology, the soul finds a medium in which it can know itself. In the context of another discussion, Jung writes that psychology may very well be "the Schopenhauerian mirror in which the unconscious [or better, the soul] becomes aware of its own face."[42] The Austrian scholar and psychologist Ernst Falzeder points out that, being well versed in philosophy, it is possible that with these comments Jung had in mind the fundamental problem in Schopenhauer's philosophy as well as Nietzsche's demand, namely, "that psychology again be recognized as queen of the sciences, and that the rest of the sciences exist to serve and prepare for it."[43] As is noted by Falzeder, Jung explicitly asked himself, "Will Nietzsche be proved right in the end with his '*scientia ancilla psychologiae*' [science (is) the handmaiden of psychology]?"[44] It seems evident that, at least in paragraph 429, Jung managed to show how psychology is at a logically higher level than all the sciences and does not fall short of its highest aspiration: to own up to its own name as the knowing or understanding of the soul.

Regrettably, right after this, Jung comes to see this phenomenon exclusively in terms of personalistic psychology, that is, in terms of the "remarkable effects" that this phenomenon can have "on ego-consciousness" and in terms of the "indispensable business of coming to terms with the unconscious components of the personality."[45] It seems to me that with this step Jung falls short of his own theoretical summit.

Giegerich's work, however, *stays* within the summit of Jung's theoretical standpoint and is therefore able to intensify, sophisticate, and clarify it throughout his multiple works.[46] From this perspective, Giegerich's achievement is tremendous. As far as I can tell, in each and every one of his published works, he confronts the fundamental dilemma of modern psychology and finds the solution, which is nothing less than *the making and refinement of a psychology with soul*. In a myriad of ways, Giegerich's work shows us that *in a world that is characterized by the departedness of soul, a psychology with soul is possible, and therefore soul can be made, but only in, as, and during the making of psychology*.[47] It is no accident that in the preface of *The Soul's Logical Life*, before the very first thrust of the spear, the author hints to the reader that through a rigorous notion of psychology the discipline "can at long last redeem the promise of *alchemical* psychology and do justice to the *Dionysian* as a psychological concept."[48] This is reminiscent of Nietzsche's demand and of Jung and Hillman's essential insights, and directly answers to the discipline's deepest longing.

So, it might not be hyperbolic to say that in each psychological work (of Giegerich, or Jung, or Hillman or of any of us), as long as it is a work with soul, psychology reaches its highest aspiration and claims its place as a Dionysian, Alchemical (or one could add Ecstatic) psychology, indeed as the Queen of all science. This is on the one hand. On the other hand, we shouldn't let this go up to our heads. A psychological work cannot last beyond its time and is therefore not expansive, accumulative, or progressive. Psychology's crowning achievement is but an instant and turns back to dust in its fulfillment. Nothing remains.

The Nature of Psychological Insights and of Progress in Psychology

This brings me back to a specific aspect of psychological insights in Giegerich's work. For Giegerich, soul-making and psychology-making are synonymous with gaining psychological insights. In *Working With Dreams* he writes,

> *Soul can only be made in or as truly psychological insights.* ... Gaining psychological insights means something like one's being momentarily "initiated" into a general self-contained soul truth as a truth of the objective soul.[49]

And here we can bear in mind his own distinction between strictly psychological insights and conventional theoretical insights. "Theoretical insights," writes Giegerich, last beyond the time and exist outside of the experiments or studies through which they were achieved, and they retain their significance beyond the time of their production (at least until future experiments will disprove or supersede them. ...). Theoretical insights are logically "positive" items; you can transmit them to others in scientific journals or books.

However, a psychological insight,

> comes into being, and exists only, in that mind that actually performs the *opus* of absolute-negative inwardization and exists only for the duration of this inwardization ... It IS its own time.[50]

Therefore, "If psychology comes up with insights that correspond to scientific knowledge, these are not truly psychological, but at best byproducts, as important and valid that they may be in other (for example, technical) regards."[51] Psychology-making is essentially different from *applied psychology* which can count on ready-made insights, methods and approaches. Psychology-making, on the other hand, starts out from scratch and has to slowly work its way *into* and *down to* the *interiority* and *depth*, the *in*sight and *under*standing, of each specific phenomenon. And this is it. Once that insight as a momentary event in consciousness has passed we are left "empty handed" and back to an external and un-psychological standpoint.

The gain of a psychological insight is out of reach for practical reality or for us as ego personalities, as ordinary civilian men and women. It does not make us wiser, richer, or more individuated. In all practical regards a psychological insight is useless and unprofitable. Psychology, as Giegerich reminds us, has "no external purpose."[52] Here we can remember the alchemical difference between *aurum vulgi* and *aurum nostrum*:

> Whereas *aurum vulgi* can be given as a present to others or can be turned into coins with which you can buy things, *aurum nostrum* cannot be bartered.[53]

Looking back at Jung's example mentioned earlier, we could say that he bartered his impressive theoretical insight for the *aurum vulgi* of a personalistic ego-psychological project and, conversely, that Giegerich stays on Jung's theoretical summit precisely by refusing to barter its underlying insight for practical purposes. Yet another way to say this is: *Giegerich's theoretical summit is Jung's and Hillman's unbartered psychological insights*. Giegerich maintains that the only purpose or gain of a psychological insight is the momentary making of psychology:

> The whole purpose of psychology is to *produce* psychology. Soul-making is psychology-making and psychology-making is soul-making, i.e., the establishing and further development, further deepening, of the psychological level

in everything one studies. Psychology does not aim for theoretical knowledge about the soul, for a kind of scientific doctrine, new information. *The psychological standpoint or perspective is itself that lapis that it tries to reach.*[54]

As far as I can tell, Giegerich's work is tenacious in this regard. I see this as a kind of methodological sobriety. Borrowing Freud's abstinence principle for psychoanalytic treatment we could say that Giegerich's psychology-making has been "carried through, as far as possible, under privation – in a state of abstinence."[55] He never sets out to create his own school of psychology or even to "rectify our vision of the psyche"[56] as Hillman hopes to do with *The Dream and the Underworld*, much less to heal or improve the world. Again, no external purpose. Not even rectifying or advancing the field of psychology as a whole.

It might then come as a surprise to read his evaluation of Hillman's work as "a major step forward, a real advance of psychological theory beyond conventional Jungianism"[57] or that in paragraph 429 "Jung's theoretical standpoint reaches its summit."[58] Clearly, both comments imply a form of progression. However, psychology, as we have seen, has no external purpose apart from producing itself. And this production does not outlast the momentary attainment of a psychological insight in each specific work. So, how can I justify my talking about the author's essential insight and how can we evaluate the impact of his work on the field of psychology? I will not be able to answer these questions in this discussion, but here are some preliminary remarks.

In *The Soul Always Thinks*, Giegerich offers a distinction between the factual progress that takes place in science and psychological progress by taking Jung's, Hillman's, and his own psychology as an example:

> Jung further developed Freud's views only within *his own* psychology and *for* his own thinking. As one can show, there is really a move beyond Freud in Jung's theory. By the same token Hillman re-visioned psychology only within his own psychology and for it, just as I pushed off from imaginal psychology only within my own psychological position and for it. What is overcome in each case is only overcome within and for the new scheme, but does in neither case overcome its predecessor *outside* this scheme. So there can indeed be *logical* progress *in* a psychology, but not *factual* progress *of* psychology as such.[59]

This is reminiscent of a very moving passage by Hillman. In *Re-Visioning Psychology* he writes:

> Since my soul, my psychological constitution, differs from Freud's and from Jung's, so my psychology will be different from theirs. Each psychology is a confession, and the worth of a psychology for another person lies not in the places where he can identify with it because it satisfies his psychic needs, but where it provokes him to work out his own psychology in response. Freud

and Jung are psychological masters, not that we may follow them in becoming Freudian and Jungian, but that we may follow them in becoming psychological.[60]

Giegerich not only lives up to this phrase but refines it. Phrases like "my own psychology" or "becoming psychological" acquire a more methodological, immediate, and defined tone with Giegerich, as in: *my task of becoming psychological or acquiring my psychological position within the HERE and NOW of THIS specific psychological work*. This, I think, is the main purpose of *The Soul's Logical Life*: an attempt to describe in detail the inner complexity of psychology-making.

So, here I might have to amend my previous comment, when I said that "psychology's crowning achievement is but an instant and turns back to dust in its fulfillment." It is clear that, at least for some of us, Giegerich's psychology-making does leave a trace. It stands as a clear example of what a psychological work looks like and sets the standard for true psychology. His fierce consistency allows us to learn about psychology-making from multiple perspectives while his sobriety invites us to focus on what Jung called "a noticeable improvement of the psychological outlook and attitude" instead of on ego-psychological or salvationist projects. In *The Neurosis of Psychology*, Giegerich reminds us that the place where our psychological efforts should be directed is

> the objective, impersonal, and yet almost subjective, third person: psychology. Integrating, developing, compensating, healing, "recollecting" (erinnern, interiorizing), imagining, introspection, initiation, analysis, expanding one's consciousness and what else psychotherapy aims for are the tasks to be accomplished not by the person, but by psychology. Only on this level, on the "higher plane of psychological and philosophical dialectic" (*CW* 10 § 333), can psychology become psychological (...) Instead of needing psychological methods for obtaining more intensive personal experiences, we might find out that that psychology itself can be our richest and more personal experience: the experience of soul-making.[61]

So, something definitely remains, but the real beneficiary of this is psychology itself. Yet, not necessarily the psychological discipline as a whole but YOUR PSYCHOLOGY or MY PSYCHOLOGY. I still maintain, however, that MY or YOUR psychology-making (when we have successfully made psychology with soul) does answer to the (whole) discipline's deepest aspiration. I would have to come back to clarify what I mean with "the discipline's deepest aspiration" and I won't be able to do this here. For now, I will just mention that this aspiration could also be described in William James' words as "the hope of a science"[62] and what Isabelle Stengers called "la volonté de faire science."[63] Giegerich consistently chooses to do psychology (a psychology that could be also described as sublated or cancelled science). Now, this consistency answers I think to the discipline's aspiration, but not so much in the form of a hope, or wish, or longing, but in the form of the fully committed WILL to do psychology. Borrowing Stengers' diction, one could say that with Giegerich, but also with Jung and with Hillman, "la volonté de faire science" is transformed into "la volonté de faire de la psychologie" and it is only in such conditions, with fierce commitment, that one "can at long last redeem the promise of *alchemical* psychology and do justice to the *Dionysian* as a psychological concept."[64] Again, I can't develop this in detail here. But I do suggest that an assessment of the impact of Giegerich's essential insight on the discipline could be approached in this light.

Notes

1 Wolfgang Giegerich, *What Is Soul?* (New Orleans, LA, Spring Journal, Inc., 2012), 302.
2 Giegerich, *What Is Soul?* 294.
3 Giegerich, *What Is Soul?* 292.
4 Wolfgang Giegerich, *Working With Dreams: Initiation into the Soul's Speaking about Itself* (New York, Routledge, 2021), 57–66.
5 Giegerich, *Working Dreams*, 60–61.
6 Giegerich, *Working With with Dreams*, 61.
7 Giegerich, *Working With with Dreams*, 60.
8 C. G. Jung, *CW 10*, §§ 158–159, trans. modified.
9 Jung, *CW 8*, § 661, trans. modified.
10 Jung, *CW 9i*, § 63, trans. modified.
11 Jung, *CW 10*, § 158, trans. modified.
12 Jung, *CW 8*, § 680, trans. modified.
13 Jung, *CW 8*, § 261, trans. modified.
14 Sonu Shamdasani, *Jung and the Making of Modern Psychology: The Dream of a Science* (Cambridge: Cambridge University Press, 2003), 16, my emphasis.
15 Shamdasani, *Jung and the Making of Modern Psychology*, 17, my emphasis.
16 Jung, *CW 8*, § 429, my emphasis.
17 Shamdasani, *Jung and the Making of Modern Psychology*, 73.
18 C.G. Jung, Preface to Proposed English Edition of *L'Ame et les Nerfi* by Tina Keller ca. 1938, quoted by Shamdasani, *Jung and the Making of Modern Psychology*, 3, my emphasis.
19 Giegerich, *Working WithDreams*, 61.
20 James Hillman, *Re-visioning Psychology* (New York: Harper Perennial, 1975 [1992]), ix, my emphasis.
21 Hillman, *Re-visioning Psychology*, x, my emphasis.
22 Jung, *CW 6*, § 78.
23 James Hillman, *The Myth of Analysis. Three Essays in Archetypal Psychology* (Michigan: Northwestern University Press, 1972), 172.
24 I offer a discussion on the confluence between the (a) psyche-making process, (b) psychology-making process, and the (c) psychologist-making process in the fourth chapter of my doctoral work:
    Andrés Ocazionez, *La Psicología de la Formación Analítica* (PhD diss., Universidad Complutense de Madrid, 2014), 130–181. Available online: https://eprints. ucm.es/id/eprint/28570/1/T35807.pdf
25 Hillman, *The Dream and the Underworld* (New York: Harper Row, 1979), 3.
26 Hillman, *Re-visioning Psychology*, xii, my emphasis.

27 Hillman, *The Dream and the Underworld*, 3, my emphasis.
28 Shamdasani offers a compelling argument. For him, *the study of the psychology-making process* is, in itself, a form of psychology-making:

> "When confronted with psychology today, there are several options available. One could simply attempt to ignore it, though this becomes increasingly hard to do. Alternatively, one can take up an active interest in it, install oneself into one of the already existing schools of psychology, take up an eclectic position or form a school of one's own. The majority of responses to psychology fall into one of these options. *However, there is another possibility, which would be to study the psychology-making process itself.*"

> At first sight I don't entirely agree with this (in short: the "study of" creates a gap between the psychologist and the process itself). I still believe, however, that this is an idea that is worth considering in depth.
> See Shamdasani, *Jung and the Making of Modern Psychology*, 10.

29 Hillman, *Re-visioning Psychology*, xii, my emphasis.
30 Wolfgang Giegerich, *The Soul's Logical Life: Towards a Rigorous Notion of Psychology* (Frankfurt am Main; New York: Peter Lang, 1998), 104.
31 Giegerich, *Working With with Dreams*, 61.
32 Hillman, *Re-visioning Psychology*, ix.
33 I have attempted to clarify and expand on this (rather bold) statement in:

> "Death and the Soul" (lecture, Winter Semester 2021–2022, Zurich: C.G. Jung Institute Zürich, Küsnacht, November 01 & 03, 2021).

34 Hillman, *Re-visioning Psychology*, x, Hillman's emphasis.
35 Jung, *CW 10*, §§ 158–159. trans. modified.
36 This is another statement that will be expanded in a proposed upcoming seminar entitled *The Subject of Psychology* in which I try to illustrate the crucial distinction between the psychological discipline's production of identities or subjectivities (a byproduct of what I call the "psyche-making process") and the production of the "psychological subject" or "the soul as subject" as an essential aspect of the psychology-making process.
37 Giegerich, *Working With with Dreams*, 61.
38 Giegerich, *What Is Soul?* 287.
39 Jung, *CW 8*, § 429.
40 Giegerich, *What Is Soul?* 290, my emphasis in bold.
41 Jung, *CW 8*, § 429, my emphasis.
42 Jung, *CW 14*, § 129.
43 Ernst Falzeder, "Types of Truth. Jung's Philosophical Roots" (lecture, *Psychological Types, Then and Now: The Relevance and Application of Jung's Theory*. New York: The Philemon Foundation & the Jungian Psychoanalytic Association, April 11, 2015).
44 Jung, quoted by Falzeder, "Types of Truth. Jung's Philosophical Roots."

> "Queen of the sciences" and "*scientia ancilla psychologiae*" may give the wrong impression as if psychology were still a science, although only a superior one, and that it wanted to rule supreme. But psychology is not in competition with the sciences. It may only be able to reflectingly "see through" and psychologically understand them.

45 Jung, *CW 8*, § 430.
46 As will be discussed below, one major difference between Giegerich and both Jung and Hillman is that he does not attempt to *apply* his psychology-making. Psychology for Giegerich is an end in itself and not the means to an end (to individuate

people, or to restore the anima to the world, etc.). I have attempted to elaborate on the main difference between *psychology-making* and *applied psychology* in: Andrés Ocazionez, "Psychology-Making vs. Applied Psychology. A Respectful Critique of Jungian Activism" (lecture, IAAP International Congress, Buenos Aires, August 2022).

47 It seems to me that Giegerich's arguments and work literally *bring to life* the insight made by Michel Henry in *The Genealogy of Psychoanalysis*:

"When objectivity ceaselessly extends its reign of death over the devastated universe... then we must say that psychoanalysis is the soul of a world without soul, the spirit of a world without spirit."

Henry's statement, however, stems from an entirely different standpoint. An important difference to note is that, unlike Giegerich. Henry's position comes out as rather critical of the Western philosophical tradition:

"Psychoanalysis is not a beginning, but an ending, an ending of a long history that is no less than the history of Western thought, of its incapacity to take possession of the only thing that matters and, thus, of its inevitable decomposition. Freud is an heir, and a late heir."

See Michel Henry, *Genealogía del psicoanálisis* (Madrid: Editorial Síntesis, 1985), 27, 22, respectively.

48 Giegerich, *The Soul's Logical Life*, 9.
49 Giegerich, *Working With with Dreams*, 63, my emphasis.
50 Giegerich, *What Is Soul?* 303.
51 Giegerich, *What Is Soul?* 303.
52 Giegerich, *What Is Soul?* 302.
53 Giegerich, *What Is Soul?* 303.
54 Giegerich, *What Is Soul?* 302.
55 Sigmund Freud, *SE17*, 162.
56 Hillman, *The Dream and the Underworld*, 4.
57 Giegerich, *The Soul's Logical Life*, 104.
58 Giegerich, *What Is Soul?* 290.
59 Wolfgang Giegerich, *The Soul Always Thinks* (Collected English Papers, vol. IV) (New Orleans, LA, Spring Journal, Inc., 2010), 576.
60 Hillman, *Re-visioning Psychology*, xii.
61 Wolfgang Giegerich, *The Neurosis of Psychology. Primary Papers towards a Critical Psychology* (Collected English Papers, vol. I) (New Orleans, LA, Spring Journal, Inc., 2005), 67.
62 William James, *Text-Book of Psychology* (London: Macmillan, 1892).
63 Isabelle Stengers, *La volonté de faire science. À propos de la psychanalyse* (Paris: Les Empêcheurs de Penser en Rond, Synthélabo, 1992).
64 Giegerich, *The Soul's Logical Life*, 9.

Chapter 2

The Uroboric Logic of Anxiety
'Not Out, But Through'*

Michael Whan

By Way of a Conclusion

In his *The Concept of Anxiety*, Søren Kierkegaard, in his intricately insightful
way describes the dialectical nature of anxiety. In this, considered his most
difficult book, he writes:

> When we consider the dialectical properties of anxiety, it appears that these
> possess precisely the ambiguity of the psychological. ... What then is the
> human being's relation to this ambiguous power; how does spirit relate to
> itself and to that which conditions it? It relates as anxiety. ... Flee from anx-
> iety he cannot, for he loves it; really love it he cannot for he flees from it.[1]

As Kierkegaard notes, anxiety is intimately a "psychological" matter. What
does he mean, that *it belongs to the essence of what we call psychology*? Following this insight, I want to explore the dialectical notion of anxiety from the
standpoint of what Jung called a *psychology with soul*; for Jung this was the
essence of a true psychology, the *logos* of the *soul*. Logos indicates a *methodological* principle, a way of thinking or accounting ("*methodos*," "a following
after," a "way"), that enables a thinking of the soul or psyche: "Psychology,
however, is neither biology nor physiology nor any other science than just the
knowledge of the psyche."[2] In the original German text, the expression "soul"
(*Seele*) replaces the term "psyche." The logos of the soul, thinking about and
from the soul, enables us to approach the intelligibility of such as an anxiety
symptom. That is, the inner dialectic of anxiety as understood from the position of *psychology as a discipline of interiority*. Recognizing anxiety's internal
dialectic, its uroboric logic, helps us to understand anxiety as containing its
"cause" as wholly *within itself*. The mythological expression "soul" here is *not*
meant in a mythic, religious, metaphysical, occult, or humanistic sense, but
rather as the logic of being-in-the-world at this time and age.

Fundamental to this approach is the notion of *the psychological difference*, the
difference between the psychic "inner life" of the individual, human personality,

---

* *The dream figure of 'Jung' speaking in one of his patient's dreams.*

DOI: 10.4324/9781003381150-3

and the psychology of the soul itself. What then does the psychological difference look like? The difference goes as follows:

> The soul as subject is I. However, the I or subject is within itself the dialectical unity and difference between itself as that function primarily oriented towards "survival" in the general sense ... the pragmatic, technical I (in the sense of the one side of the subject-object opposition), on the one hand, *and* the internal not-I as the subject of true knowing, the organ of truth and of syntactical or logical form, on the other. The latter is "not-I" because it is the *objective* subject, experienced by the ego-personality as an internal other with an intentionality (and often impelling necessity) of its own. We could also say an autonomous other, however one that despite its otherness is nevertheless also I (me). ... We must much rather comprehend the I and the not-I as different styles of knowing and understanding: egoic knowing versus soul knowing.[3]

The soul as this dialectical unity of opposites means the soul appears within it as but "one *moment* of itself." It is the: "whole relation (the entire psychological difference, *homo totus*) and at the same time the one *relatum* of this relation ... the one moment ... the not-I, the organ of truth and true knowing, in contradistinction to the other moment, the pragmatic I, the egoic type of knowing and understanding."[4] We see then that in the psychological difference the soul's dialectical movement pushes off from the psychic, the ego-personality, not outwardly but further *inwardly*. This entails a self-negation of the I, the pragmatic I, as the soul's movement self-sublates into the not-I. It negates the ego-personality, negates its positivistic style of knowing, releasing psychology into itself, freeing its logos into itself, as "the spirit of logical negativity."[5] From an egoic knowing, it transforms itself, *auto-poetically*, into that of the *psychological I*.

Anxiety is the neurotic soul's realisation of the *truth* of its condition today, and simultaneously its resistance to that truth – hence, we can speak of the "neurotic soul." Anxiety is the neurotic soul's reaction, its "fight/flight" from the truth of its groundlessness, its *unhomely* condition. Kierkegaard among others has linked the experience of anxiety to the notion of *abyss*, of the *abysmal*. As Hinton observes: "The 'black hole' is a floating signifier. ... It involves a cluster of experiences involving acute anxiety and terror ... such experiences are enigmatic, uncanny, they are the gaps and holes in experience."[6] Oscar Wilde wrote on this: "I never knew what terror was before; I know it now. It is as if a hand of ice were laid upon one's heart. It is as if one's heart were beating itself to death in some *empty hollow*."[7] Wilde appears to be describing what today we would describe as a "panic attack": "terror" and an "empty hollow." This loss of mythic, religious, or metaphysical "ground," of meaning with a big M, of "grand narratives," of when these once "ful-filled" us, now have become an "empty hollow," that is, the soul's condition within the historical, cultural situation of modernity. Indeed, neurosis and depth psychology have evolved in a co-determinant manner in modern times. This co-evolving, from the standpoint of psychology, arises by way of the soul's self-negation, its self-emptying (*kenôsis*). Its self-emptying consists of the self-negation of its former modes of being, expression *as* myth, religion, and metaphysics.

Consciousness has historically, culturally, psychologically, reached the realisation of the soul's *logical negativity*, namely, as empty, cold, alien, uncanny; even if our individual consciousness has not yet caught up with this realisation or defends against knowing it. Soul has realised its truth as groundlessness, the abysm of existence. Anxiety is the neurotic resistance to this truth, as well as its realisation. From the position of psychology's understanding of neurosis as an "organic form," containing its own internal nature, it is a "Work," a *poiêis*, an *opus*, "personally" experienced, but transpersonal or impersonal in kind. As a "Work," neurosis, hence, anxiety, needs to be thought alchemically, as a "work against nature," as an *opus contra naturam*. *Contra naturam*, in this context, means against a *naturalistic consciousness*, a naiveté, or logical innocence. For instance, it works against an empirical-positivist or literal mode of consciousness. Thus did Kierkegaard speak of anxiety as reaching the "peak" of "innocence."[8]

Lacan, the French psychoanalyst, in his seminar on anxiety[9] remarked that Freud's essay *The Uncanny*[10] was Freud's fundamental statement on anxiety. In his essay, Freud discusses the German word "*Die Unheimlichkeit*," which translates in English as "the Uncanny." Literally translated, it signifies the "the Unhomely," namely the disturbing, dis-placing, estranging feelings that belong with states of anxiety. Heidegger, too, draws much on this term in his discussions of anxiety in his *magnum opus*, *Being and Time*.[11] For Heidegger, these expressions, the uncanny or unhomely, depict intimately the mood of anxiety, the feeling of not-being-at-home-in-the-world. That is, they belong intimately with the logic or logos of our being-in-the-world, feelings we have being with others and ourselves. Put otherwise, it belongs to the present-day condition of the soul, having thrown, projected (liberated), itself out of its previous states of "in-ness," of containment in its former logical modes as myth, religion, and metaphysics.

An understanding of anxiety can be furthered in terms of the dialectical, alchemical depiction of the *Philosophers' Stone*, "The Stone that is not a stone." It follows, then, that anxiety can be seen dialectically as "The fear that is not a fear." Initially there is fear in its (mediated) immediacy, then a negation of fear, and finally the sublation (or negation of negation) of fear, cancelling it out, yet preserving and raising it to a higher level of complexity. Put another way, it is the immediacy of the psychobiology of fear complexified to a higher historical, cultural, logical, existential level of what we term as anxiety; the soul pushing off from "instinctual," our human, animal being. Of course, these sequential steps are not experienced as so, but occur as a singular, dialectical, simultaneous, autonomous movement in the soul. Fear is but a *moment* in the movement of a uroboric logic, anxiety's dialectic. The initial negation cancels out the immediacy of fear, the following negation cancels out the first nega-tion, transforming or sublating fear into anxiety. *Anxiety is sublated fear, fear dialectically negated.* Anxiety arises from the neurotic soul's resistance and realisation of its *uncanny* state, its state of no longer being, feeling, and think-ing its "at-homeness" in the world. It is, as it were, a sublation from the ontic to the onto-logical. Namely, it is the loss of "in-ness," of worldly and "other-worldly" containment (states of derealization and depersonalization as extreme instances). Anxiety negates our everyday, familiar modes of being-in-the-world, our familiar experience, *de-realised*. Further, there is a crucial difference between fear and anxiety. Fear always has an "object," it is always intentional, a fear *of*, whether known or not known. Anxiety is otherwise, for instead of an "object," there is an uncanny *indefiniteness* or as Heidegger describes it: a "peculiar indefiniteness."[12] Sufferers of anxiety, what psychiatry labels as "Generalised Anxiety Disorder," sometimes try to find some or other "object" to eradicate the "peculiar indefiniteness," so, a defensive *phobia* forms with its specific focus, say, a fear *of* dogs or *of* open spaces. In phobic anxiety, anxiety employs "intentionality," "consciousness of," as a defence against anxiety's "peculiar indefiniteness." This is an attempt to transform anxiety back into fear, to reverse anxiety's dialectic, to reverse the sublation. Anxiety as Kier-kegaard and Heidegger have argued, has a world-disclosive function. It is an existential, (onto-)logical *mood* of worldly disclosure.

The neurotic soul's resistance attempts to maintain the onetime *Absolute* of its former mythic, religious, or metaphysical states. It attempts to reverse history, to reverse consciousness' logic of being-in-the-world, as now in modernity, emp-tied out of any overarching, totalizing meaning. Giegerich portrays it thus:

> Neurotic symptoms are characterized by what I call *the inflation of empiri-cal-reality aspects with metaphysical significance* ... the excessive significance is characterized by the quality of *unconditionality*: something is experienced as *absolutely* intolerable, *absolutely* unthinkable, *totally* menacing, *at all cost* to be avoided, *by all means* controlled. ... For the *soul*, it's much rather a question of all or nothing, life and death. ... Something absolute is at stake.[13]

Anxiety displays just such a compelling, all-embracing ("The Absolute") impact on its sufferers. Neurosis is the revenant of the metaphysical, mythic, or religious "Absolute," of "things that once were."

It is surely worth noting that as a recent translator of Freud's essay, "Inhibi-tion, Symptom, Fear," puts it regarding his preferred substitution of "fear" instead of the usual shibboleth by Freud translators of "anxiety":

> But the fact remains that in the great majority of cases Freud uses the word *Angst* in its normal sense – which corresponds very closely to the English "fear," and which does *not* cover "anxiety" in the ordinary sense of the word (indeed, when Freud means "anxiety" he uses the standard word *Ängstlichkeit*).[14]

It would seem then that Freud in his seminal writings differentiated "fear" from "anxiety." *Ängstlichkeit* has more the sense of "apprehension," "worry," "timorousness," "timidity," whereas *Angst*, though overlapping the former has more the sense of "fear," "dread," "to be afraid," "trepidation." From the standpoint of psychology, however, what matters here is the difference in the logical status, the logical levels between fear and anxiety.

*

A Stocking Phobia, Anxiety, and the Psychological Difference

By maintaining the psychological difference, that which is between the psychology of soul (Jung's "objective psyche") and the psychology of the human, individual personality, the ego-personality including its unconscious, we can further understand the distinction between fear and anxiety. For, as I suggested earlier, fear revolves around some real or imagined, conscious or unconscious "object." It belongs to the psychobiology of the human being. Anxiety arises from a wholly different level of (existential) complexity, its logic is more intricate, it is sublated fear, "The fear that is not a fear." Once we conflate the psychological difference, we reduce and lose the difference to one or other side of itself. Even though many psychologies, including analytical psychology, *rhetorically evoke* the notion of soul, usually the soul difference gets reduced to the individual's personality and its psyche. Thus even "archetypes" become *subjectivised*, understood as underpinning our personal psychology. For instance, *my* "Mother," the mother of my personal experience and psychic development, my *inner* "Maternal Imago" is conflated with the archetype of "The Great Mother." Or another "soul" trope invoked often is that of depression likened to the alchemical *nigredo*. However, as Jung points out, the *melancholy* the alchemist suffered in his alchemical practice was *not* always his own: "The *nigredo* not only brought decay, suffering, death … visibly before the eyes of the alchemist, it also cast the shadow of melancholy over his own solitary soul. In the blackness of a despair which was not his own, and of which he was merely the witness."[15] It belonged to the alchemical process. This insight of Jung into the alchemical *nigredo* distinguishes between the alchemist's personality and the spirit (or soul) of alchemy. Fashionable in contemporary psychologies, including analytical psychology, is the notion of one's "personal myth," a complete contradiction in terms, an *abstraction*. For myth belongs overarchingly to the whole culture, it is communal, always transpersonal. One might rightly speak here of a *mis*appropriation, taking ownership as belonging to "*my* deeper self" what in fact *belongs in and to* a certain historical, cultural context, to a *people*, to the logic of the *objective psyche*, at that time and place.

Anxiety, I suggest, embodies the psychological difference in its very structure. It opens onto the soul level, the deeper logic of being-in-the-world. Hence, its disturbing "peculiar indefiniteness," its uncanniness, betrays its nature of *self-othering*. Amid my everyday familiar worldly experience, suddenly or chronically, I suffer a sense of estrangement, of unfamiliarity and alienation. Something indefinitely *Other* perturbingly enters my experience. Anxiety has an absolute, compelling, and intrusive nature (*Ananke*, Necessity).

The psychoanalyst Wilfred Bion describes a highly relevant instance of such a disturbing feeling in the seeming context of the familiarity and common-sense reality of everydayness. A patient told Bion that he could not buy any new clothes and that his socks were full of holes, adding that "though they are full of holes they constrict" his foot. Bion interpreted this as a castration fantasy with an underlying existential anxiety. He declared that the patient: "has eaten the penis and that therefore there was no interesting food left, only a hole. But this hole was now so persecutory that he had to split it up. As a result of the splitting the hole became a mass of holes that came together in a persecutory way to constrict his foot."[16] Bion also refers to a patient of Freud: "who was working out his castration complex on his skin and that he began to think there was a deep cavity wherever he had got rid of a blackhead."[17] Whilst these patients may have been susceptible to sexual anxiety, fantasies, complications, in these instances the anxiety took the imaginal form of "a hole" and a "deep cavity." The protective, "continuous," layer of skin (representing a fragile, ontic, "outer continuity of being"), when the "blackhead" was removed, was left with a persecutory hollow. As if, the "surface" opened, by way of its "hole," onto a dimension of a disturbingly deep, existential feeling and logic. Clearly, in its persecutory intensity such anxiety demonstrates the "super-charge," the "surplus values" of the Absolute of the neurotic soul, its compelling, compulsive necessity and intrusiveness.

In both these instances, the persecutory images pertaining to anxiety connect to the notion of an "abyss" that Kierkegaard dramatized and identified in his existential, theological-psychological writing on anxiety. For him, anxiety was associated with abysmal groundlessness, bottomlessness, nothingness, absence (the Danish, "*Afgrunden*"): "Although there is no unified concept of 'the abyss' in Kierkegaard's writings, its image is one that Kierkegaard and his pseudonyms persistently evoke with stylish flourish and existential pathos." One he further relates to "dizziness."[18] As Kierkegaard himself writes, making this comparison of anxiety and abyss: "Anxiety can be compared with dizziness. He whose eye happens to look down into the yawning abyss becomes dizzy. ... In anxiety there is the selfish infinity of possibility, which does not tempt like a choice but disquietens seductively with its sweet apprehensiveness."[19] With this statement, Kierkegaard reveals the dialectic of anxiety, the desire and fear, the seductive disquiet, the "sweet" apprehension. In both the cases of Freud and Bion, with their "stocking phobia," there is an echo of Kierkegaard's "yawning abyss" ("hole," "deep cavity").[20]

McCarthy, commenting on this sense of a "yawning abyss," says:

> the experience of possibility is fascinating in the sense that it excites and rouses one's entire being and compels attention to oneself. On the other hand, as an un-actualized possibility [it] is undecided and sensed as a potentially perilous course, because unknowable in advance ... and thus alarm equally permeates the person. Fascination and alarm correspond to the sympathy and antipathy ... which are essential characteristics of the anxiety experience.[21]

In this sense, the "holes" open onto a disturbingly existent, dimension of *depth*, that, as already suggested, is personally suffered, but is *not* personal. The "hole" is the persecutory suffering of *negation* in imaginal form. It is felt as an existential predicament, not so much at the level of *what* one is, but *that* one is, and, indeed, *that* or *if* the world is? For us, the question raised by this symptomatic experience of anxiety with its accompanying "ontic/ontological" fantasy concerns the psychological difference and its impact and interpretation.

In his *Brazilian Lectures*, Bion goes some way towards recognizing a fundamental difference that runs decisively through the stocking phobic symptom of Freud's patient. For Freud, it is an undoubted sexual fantasy, an infantile-sexual complex. Bion, however, detects a deeper sense in that the holes of the stocking trigger a panic attack. The patient is experiencing not only the empirically real (the ontical-concrete): "lacunary nature of the stocking fabric but that with it he is having the ontological experience of a lacunary quality that is general and fundamental because it concerns the being of all things"[22] (concrete universal). Holzhey-Kunz concludes: "The stocking's hole-ridden fabric becomes so deeply threatening for the patient because the *truth* dawns on him through this ontical perception that on closer inspection the supposed compactness and constancy of all things and so all the entire world turns out to be an illusion."[23] (My italics) The solidity of the world dissolves, negates, in lacunae. Karl Marx once asserted that "All That Is Solid Melts into Air." The patient is suffering the soul truth of modernity – "the lacunary quality that is general and fundamental" (concrete universal) – the logical negativity (dialectical fluidity) of the soul, its groundlessness.

A similar (borderline, quasi-psychotic) intimation of the "lacunary quality" of things afflicted a patient, who in adolescence suffered a quasi-psychotic "breakdown." Part of this experience was the idea of "having no self"; beset by the terror of fragmentation, annihilation (an-*nihil*-ation) – the patient's words some forty years later. The aftermath of this episode was a chronic fear of breaking down again and being "sucked into a mad idea." One fear included losing the sense of "self" again, instead of the fragile sense of "self" and reality, there would be "nothing." A further persecutory anxiety was the world's loss of solidity. And thus, the concretization and atomization (fragmentation) that everything was ultimately composed of atoms left them with a profound sense of meaninglessness, isolation, and nihilistic suicidal depression. This atomization also included their defensive necessity to conceive of the solidity, the concretization, of the "self." Like Freud's and Bion's patients, this individual suffers the abyss of anxiety, the groundlessness, "empty hollow," of a lacunary world. These profound anxieties concern the lacunary logic of being, as indicated by Kierkegaard's statement on anxiety: "But what effect does nothing have? It begets anxiety."[24] "Nothing" is *pregnant* with anxiety. This individual had to defend their self against the fluid dynamics of the age, against "fluid identity," "fluid personality" ("BPD"), and so speaks of the "natural," of "being natural," of oneself rooted *naturalistically*, thus in constancy, to "solidify" their self by way of a *naturalistic* thinking and language. This represents a *substantializing* way of comprehending, against the *opus contra naturam* of anxiety. They characterise the "self" – as does much positivistic psychological theorising – as "substance" rather than "subject." In their anxiety, they tormentingly reduce the "lacunary quality" of existence to their self personally, wherein it becomes the threat of madness.

In speaking of the lacunary logic of existence in imaginal terms such as "holes," "deep cavity," "abyss," one falls into a category error. For it might appear that one is speaking of the psychological difference between personal psychology and the soul. Yet, such talk is the opposite of what it seems. For this speaking is from the ego-personality. The psychological difference spoken imaginally is to speak semantically. The syntax of consciousness is left untouched. In speaking imaginally, the personalistic, positivistic, immediate (semantic) position is maintained, whilst seemingly spoken against. Wrongly, the psychology of the soul becomes caught in positivistic, personalised terms, seemingly speaking in soul terms, whilst actually reinforcing the ego's position, trapping psychology into the anthropological, personalistic fallacy:

> "the unconscious" and "the imaginal" have the logical form of "ego," although they of course pretend to be "non-ego" (and, semantically viewed, are indeed non-ego). They speak immediately to the ego, presenting it with easily accessible positive contents and evoking emotions of mystery, bewilderment, thrill, fear, guilt, shame, exaltation, higher meaning, deeper significance. They appeal to the ego's desire for what can be sensibly imagined. This is even true in those cases where imaginal psychology penetrates precisely to the very opposite of visibility, to alchemy's "Black Sun," to the ideas of the Unassimilable and Unspeakable, the Void. They are all merely *semantic* and in itself *imaginal* negation of the visible and celebrate the semantic orientation even while seemingly transcending or destroying it. They are well suited to satisfy the ego's mystical longings.[25]

To imagine anxiety as a "hole," a "deep cavity," imaginally, points in the direction of the soul's logical negativity, yet remains a form of external reflection and egoic standpoint. When we diagnose it in terms of a "generalised anxiety disorder," hence in positivistic terms, the predicate refers to the subject as an external referent. It is a neurotic interpretation of the neurotic soul. Anxiety is that *as which* the neurotic soul manifests empirically. Anxiety is its exteriorized symptomatic form, its self-display.

What does it mean, therefore, to approach anxiety from within its internal logic? Jung's alchemical principle of interpretation was: "Above all, don't let anything from outside, that does not belong, get into it, for the fantasy-image has 'Everything it needs.'"[26] This means that in approaching anxiety, if approached from within, the dichotomy of "inner" and "outer" are overcome dialectically. That is why Kierkegaard is so useful. He offers a methodological, dialectical approach from *within* anxiety. Its "cause" lies within itself, revealing a uroboric logic. Mogenson offers a valuable insight as to what Jung meant by his alchemical hermeneutic: "This conception, this attitude, is itself the retort or alchemical *vas*. Unlike an actual glass vessel, which has a delimited positive inside that contains only those contents that we literally place inside of it, the *notional* vessel which is indicative of psychology is constituted by our think-ing."[27] Interiority in Jung's alchemical "*notional* vessel" is absolute, it has its "outside" within itself.

As a practising psychologist sitting in person with a patient, one neverthe-less may refer to the semantics, the contents, the emotional content of anxiety, "desire" and "fear," that belong to the pragmatics of the work. But what mat-ters as *different* in the psychology of soul is its sublated moments, the syntax. From this standpoint, we listen to the soul speaking of itself, contemplating itself, of the soul *seeing through* the content, image, emotion, fantasy, *to itself*. We listen for the impersonal or transpersonal *sounding through* the negated personal.

Already as a symptom, anxiety unfolds in its first immediacy as negation. As Freud perceived it, the symptom is that which is more alien to the ego than anything else in the mind.[28] Jung offers a further elaboration on this: "as Freud rightly says, we turn the ego into a 'seat of anxiety,' ... As soon as the ego becomes a 'seat of anxiety,' we all run away from ourselves and refuse to admit our fear. That dreaded 'other self.'"[29] Jung, here, identifies the dialectic of anx-iety's self-othering, an alienation from within.

Further, Jung's attitude to anxiety was, as Giegerich has pointed out: "against the interpretation of anxiety ... as a result of repression and thereby dismiss it as inauthentic." Indeed, Jung saw anxiety in a more complex way, that it "is in itself legitimate and an authentic psychological way that one may have to follow. 'To be freed of anxiety' therefore cannot be a truly psychologi-cal goal."[30] To which, Giegerich adds: "The soul even *hungers* for anxiety and produces it from within itself where there is nothing real to be feared ... as Jung states, we have a downright panic fear of the soul and seek to protect ourselves in psychology from it, e.g., by taking a medical or scientific stance."[31]

With anxiety, therefore, a naïve unity of one's sense of self, of identity as being self-identical, is broken up. As Kierkegaard remarks, anxiety is the peak of "innocence."[32] In this sense of self-division, of self-contradiction, fear arises in the hyphenated space between self- and contradiction, as the ego seeks to flee that "dreaded 'other self,'" its sense of self-contradiction. The feeling of anxiety, its *self-contradiction felt as conflictual*, is a surface feeling, for it is an unconscious *acting out* of anxiety's dialectic. The notion of "pathologizing" introduced by James Hillman: "makes the most of the dialectical unfolding, or 'falling apart' ... of the one into the many via symptom formation."[33] What Hillman calls pathologizing, the soul's autonomous capacity to create illness, disorder, suffering, is understood here as the "Work," the *opus contra*, of the neurotic soul: "Like the stage of the alchemical opus known as *putrefactio* or *mortificatio*, pathologizing is a transforming corruption or going under of the naïve A=A self-identical starting point."[34] Kierkegaard regarded anxiety as an alien force that seizes one. The taken-for-granted "unity," the "innocence" of naïve subjectivity, undergoes an inner rupture. "I'm falling apart," is a phrase patients commonly employ to describe how they feel as they suffer: "the negativizing action of self-contradiction."[35] "Falling apart" is falling *into* apart-ness. Nietzsche's Noon-tide experience in which 'One becomes Two' is the first immediacy of the dialectic of anxiety. The alien nature of the symptom's effect is to *corrupt* the naïve interiority of the "inner life" of one's personal psychology, which otherwise, and to the degree that thinking comprehends it as an unfolding dialectic via the negativizing symptom, enables a different notion of unity to be thought. That is, "a unity of identity and difference, and inclusive thinking-it-all-at-once mode of thought, dialectics overcomes the distinction between the external and internal. For reflecting everything external into itself ... the dialectic inaugurates an absolute form of interiority or soulful intensity."[36] Understood in this way, the symptom reflects *unconsciously* the psychological difference in its initial negation of corrupting the naïve subjective unity, as it impinges on the individual personality, who thereby suffers the "otherness" of the symptom as a positive-factual reality.

Suffering anxiety as described by Kierkegaard is to be seized by an alien force, akin to Freud's notion of the symptom as "foreign." Anxiety's dialectic reverses the "externality" of the symptom into itself. For the qualities of alien force, foreignness, and the "dreaded 'other self'" are the "outwardness" interiorized into itself, inherent in the "self-othering" of anxiety. The empirical facticity of the symptom exhibits itself as self-identical, whilst also being the rupture of that "unified" self-identicality. The *alterity* of the symptom confounds its empirical self-identicality, being felt also as *something else*, indefinite, or not identical with itself, as when we say, self-contradictorily, "I am/was not myself." Or "I" feel *de*personalised.

Returning to Bion and the difference between thinking from anxiety's implicit dialectic and our ordinary "clinical" conception of it, Bion's writing on this resonates with Jung. In Jung's *Alchemical Studies*, he states: "One does not become enlightened by imagining figures of light, but by making the darkness conscious."[37] Here, then, is Bion's insightful echo:

Instead of trying to bring a brilliant, intelligent, knowledgeable light to bear on obscure problems, I suggest we bring to bear a diminution of the 'light' – a penetrating beam of darkness. ... The darkness would be so absolute that it would achieve a luminous, absolute vacuum. So that, if any object existed, however faint, it would show up very clearly. Thus, a very faint light would become visible in maximum conditions of darkness. ... Suppose we are watching a game of tennis, looking at it in increasing darkness. We dim the intellectual illumination and light, forgetting imagination or phantasy or any once-conscious activities; first we lose sight of the players, and then we gradually increase the darkness until only the net is visible. If we can do this, it is possible to see that the only important thing visible to us is a lot of holes which are collected together in a net. Similarly, we might look at a pair of socks and be able to see a mass of holes which have been knitted together. Freud described something of this kind but said that the patient had a phobia which made it impossible for him to wear socks. I suggest that the patient did not have a phobia of socks but could see that what Freud thought were socks were a lot of holes knitted together. If this is correct, terms like 'phobia' in classical analysis do not do justice to the facts, and in particular do not do justice to the extreme capacity for observation which is natural to some patients. Just as it is natural for me in my gross, macroscopic way classically to see a pair of socks, this kind of patient has a visual capacity which is different, making him able to see what I cannot see. What I think, with the light of my intelligence, brains, knowledge, experience, is a pair of socks, *he* can see is not. We should reconsider this domain of thought, because as psychoanalysts we must be able to see that it is a pair of socks ... and at the same time to be able to turn down the light, turn off the brilliant intuition, and see these holes, including the fact that they are knitted, or netted together.[38]

Bion's striking metaphorical phrase, "a penetrating beam of darkness," represents a reference to implicit dialectic negation. His talk of dimming "intellectual intuition" unfortunately is a mistaken conception of *thinking*. Clearly, he understands it from the position of positivism, as indicated with his reference to clinical and psychoanalytic notions of "phobia" (also his attempt at a "algebraic grid"). The assumption links together "intellectual intuition," clinical and psychoanalytic thought, as closely akin. Nevertheless, this misrepresents thinking solely as "analytic," which is but a *moment* within any dialectic. His brilliant metaphor is, of course, *thinking*, imaginally stated. I believe the difficulty Bion is up against is a misunderstanding of an initial negation, a *contradiction* in the clinical notion of a "sock phobia," namely, the lacunary logic. Not able to make room in his positivistic, analytic thinking, Bion misrepresents dialectical negation. Negation in his positivistic thinking treats negation as a simple "not," rather than dialectically. Hence, Bion with his metaphor of a "penetrating beam of darkness," talks of cancelling out "intellectual intuition" as thinking.

The logically innocent claim, which Bion questions, is that of psychopathology's "phobic anxiety," the "sock phobia." Against this, Bion proposes the lacunary logic of the "sock" as, in essence, "holes knitted together." He questions the limitations (logical level) of the clinical notion of "phobia." Bion's errant listening comprehends the logic of emptiness, gaps, voids, in the patient's anxiety. He perceives the dialectic of the "pair of socks" as *not* a "pair of socks." Clinical knowledge falters. The "is not" comprises the immediacy of negation, the self-othering of anxiety. Bion is in his own way seeking to make, as Jung proposed, "the darkness conscious." But one does not need (by egoic effort) to make the "darkness conscious," for the "darkness" is an imaginal expression of an unfolding dialectical negation. It *makes itself* conscious. Alchemically, this could be described as the "dividing sword" of Mercurius,[39] a thinking that penetrates and divides. If left to unfold, the work of negation brings consciousness to itself. The soul speaks of itself and from itself, comprehending itself: namely as psychology.

As a practising analyst, Bion stresses seeing both the "pair of socks" (the positive-factual) and the "holes" (the lacunary logic, logical negativity). After stating this, he further says: "we have to tolerate infinity."[40] Here, Bion is groping unconsciously to the notion of "inner infinity," the inner dialectic of the anxiety-ridden "pair of socks." As Bion recognizes: One becomes Two. In Bion's position both cannot be (analytically, formally logically) true. For psychoanalysis, different accounts, as Mogenson observes in another context: "when measured against themselves in the other, both accounts cannot be true at the same time ... consciousness may accept negation, if only in a manner that is still indicative of the immediate-mindedness of the former mode of knowing."[41] Thus, Bion cannot accredit such a way of thinking *as thinking*. He then continues by describing a reversal in which the immediate certainty of psychoanalytic knowledge is undermined by negation, referring to a: "flexibility of mind of all of us who concern ourselves with the human mind." Bion states: "This can be difficult; Descartes, while suggesting philosophical doubt, failed completely to doubt philosophical doubt. 'Cogito, ergo sum' is a failure to doubt doubt."[42] Whereas before, for Bion, an immediate analytic (sense) certainty underpinned psychoanalysis, its logic of self-identicality, he appears caught in a self-identical *uncertainty*, trying to hold both together.[43] Put otherwise, the patient's lacunary notion is treated semantically, set alongside a "pair of socks" and "phobia." The syntactical level of psychoanalytic consciousness remains, however, untouched. The patient's transformed syntax of consciousness gets incorporated into the psychoanalytic syntax as semantics, content, without letting psychoanalysis itself undergo the necessary *putrefaction* of a dialectical negation.

Of course, psychoanalysis, to be fair, *does not recognize anything like the psychological difference in its theory*. So, I am only borrowing Bion's account as an instance to illustrate the conflation of the psychological difference in relation to anxiety, namely, the psychological difference being reduced to one side of itself, to the "inner life" of the patient's psyche. For Bion, the insight, "the penetrating beam of darkness," into the lacunary logic, that the "pair of socks" is *also* "not a pair of socks," itself derives from the patient's "extreme capacity for observation," that is, to his subjective "visual" sensibility. The neurotic soul thus draws on the psychic vulnerabilities of individual patients to manifest itself in the empirical-factual world of the symptom, here clinically named as "anxiety phobia." Anxiety as far as psychoanalysis is concerned is always thought in relation to the patient's subjectivity, the human all-too-human. Alchemically, it is treated wholly as the *opus parvum*, the "little work," treated as a subjective matter, personalistically, developmentally, losing any sense as a "logical universal."[44] The nature of the psychological difference as a "sublated moment *within*" psychology itself, which *pushes off* from within the subjective psyche, its immediate psychology of the matter-at-hand, remains unconscious. The possibility of the psychological difference from ever emerging is itself occluded by psychoanalysis' positivistic analytic. Similarly, in much contemporary Jungian thinking, the same holds true. Rather, it is externalised into the positivistic binary and differential of the "conscious" and the "unconscious."

This *reduction* of the psychology of the soul to the human all-too-human leaves the soul in: "self-immurement ... the whole difference, semanticizing and diminutizing it" in the subjective "inner."[45] Anxiety points to the logical negativity of the soul, but which Jung described basically in a "negative" idiom, though only, obliquely, and unsaid, by referencing the soul: as "symbol-lessness," the yawning "void," "the cold light of consciousness," and "blank barrenness of the world."[46] Anxiety points to the soul in its alien, cold, bottomless, and not positivistically perceivable condition. Or as Kierkegaard pointed out, again in his theological-psychological way, the *abyss* of anxiety, indicating its existential, abyssal, groundlessness. Bion's striking metaphorical insight yet immured itself in the frame of the personalistic and clinical concept of the "inner," comparing the "pair of socks" as positivistic "substance" and the knitted or netted "holes," the logically negative, as if these were on the same logical level.

To end then as we began, with a praiseworthy quotation from Kierkegaard. For anxiety *per se* is not the difficulty only in itself, belonging as it does to the "spirit of the times," but the difficulty is being able *to be anxious in the right way*. Anxiety opens us onto both the neurotic and existential condition of the soul today: "learning to be anxious so as not to be ruined either by never having been in anxiety or by sinking into it. Whoever has learned to be anxious in the right way has learned the ultimate. ... But anxiety makes short work of it, instantly playing the trump card of infinity ... the anxiety within ... has already fashioned fate and has taken away ... absolutely all that any fate could take away."

And further, acknowledging the dialectic of finitude and infinity *within* anxiety: "From finitude one can learn much, but not how to be anxious, except in a very mediocre and corrupting sense. Anyone who has truly learned how to be anxious, on the other hand, will tread as if in a dance when the anxieties of finitude strike up."[47]

In anxiety, we encounter a self-othering, the dialectic between finitude, the empirical-factuality, the human all-too-human, of the symptom *and* the fathomlessness of the *logos* of the soul, its inner infinity, its uroboric logic. So, anxiety needs to be thought not in the "mediocre and corrupting sense" solely of finitude, but in the dialectic between finitude and infinity.

Notes

1 Søren Kierkegaard, *The Concept of Anxiety. A Simple Psychologically Orientated Deliberation in View of the Dogmatic Problem of Hereditary Sin.* A New Translation with an Introduction by Alastair Hannay (London: Liverlight Publishing Corporation, 2015), 51–53.
2 C. G. Jung, *CW* 9i, § 63.
3 Wolfgang Giegerich, *What is Soul?* (New Orleans: Spring Journal Books, 2012), 146, 298–301. (Now alsopublished by London, New York, Routledge, 2020).
4 Giegerich, *What is Soul?* 299–300.
5 Giegerich, *What is Soul?* 301.
6 Ladson Hinton, "Black Holes, Uncanny Spaces and Radical Shifts in Awareness." *Journal of Analytical Psychology*, 2007, 433–447.
7 Oscar Wilde, *An Ideal Husband* (London: Methuen & Co. Ltd., 1893) Act 2.
8 Kierkegaard, *The Concept of Anxiety*, 53.
9 Jacques Lacan, *Anxiety. The Seminar of Jacques Lacan*, Book X. Edited by J-A Miller, trans. by A. R. Price (Cambridge: Polity Press, 2014), 41.
10 Sigmund Freud, *The Uncanny* (London: Modern Classics, 2003).
11 Martin Heidegger, *Being and Time.* Translated by J. Strambaugh. Revised and with a Foreword by D. J. Schmidt (Albany: State University of New York Press, 2010), 182–184.
12 Heidegger, *Being and Time*, 182.
13 Wolfgang Giegerich, *Neurosis. The Logic of a Metaphysical Illness* (New Orleans: Spring Journal Books, 2013), 31–34. (Now also published by London, New York: Routledge, 2020).
14 Freud, *Beyond the Pleasure Principle and Other Writings.* Translated by J. Reddick with an Introduction by M. Edmundson (London: Penguin Classics, 2003), 264–265.
15 C. G. Jung, *CW* 14, § 493.
16 Wilfred R. Bion, *Second Thoughts, Selected Papers on Psycho-Analysis* (London Maresfield Library, 1987), 28–29.
17 Bion, *Second Thoughts*, 29.
18 Simon D. Podmore, *Kierkegaard and the Self Before God. The Anatomy of the Abyss.* (Bloomington: Indiana University Press, 2011), 2–3.
19 Kierkegaard, *The Concept of Anxiety*, 2–3.
20 Podmore, *Kierkegaard and the Self Before God*, 75.
21 V. C. McCarthy, *The Phenomenology of Moods in Kierkegaard* (The Hague: Marinus Nijhoff, 1978), 42.
22 W. R. Bion, *Brazilian Lectures, 1973 São Paulo, 1974 Rio de Janeiro* (London: Routledge). Cited by A. Holzhey-Kunz, *Daseinanalysis.* Translated by S. Leighton (Free Association Books, 2014), 219–221.
23 Holzhey-Kunz, *Daseinanalysis*, 221.
24 Kierkegaard, *The Concept of Anxiety*, 50.
25 Giegerich, *What Is Soul?* 150. Also see G. Mogenson, "Marlin's Bardo Thödol." *San Francisco Jung Library Journal*, 2005, 6–16.

26 Jung, *CW* 14, § 794.
27 Greg Mogenson, "Different Moments in Dialectical Movement," in Wolfgang Giegerich, David L. Miller, Greg Mogenson, *Dialectics and Analytical Psychology, The El Capitan Canyon Seminar* (New Orleans: Spring Journal Books, 2005.) 80–81. (Now also London and New York, Routledge, 2020.)
28 Sigmund Freud, *Beyond the Pleasure Principle and Other Writings*. Translated by J. Reddick with an Introduction by M. Edmundson (London: Penguin Classics).
29 C. G. Jung, *CW* 10, § 360.
30 Wolfgang Giegerich, "The Present as Dimension of The Soul," in *The Neurosis of Psychology. Primary Papers towards a Critical Psychology* (*Collected English Papers, Vol. I*) (New Orleans: Spring Journal Publications, 2005. Now also in London and New York, Routledge, 2020), 109.
31 Giegerich, *The Neurosis of Psychology*, 109.
32 Kierkegaard, *The Concept of Anxiety*, 53.
33 James Hillman, "On the Necessity of Abnormal Psychology, Ananke and Athene," in *Facing the Gods*, ed., J. Hillman (Irving: Spring Publications, 1980), 1.
34 Mogenson, "Different Moments in Dialectical Movement," 89.
35 Mogenson, "Different Moments in Dialectical Movement," 89.
36 Mogenson, "Different Moments in Dialectical Movement," 86–87.
37 C. G. Jung, *CW* 11, § 265–266. Quoted in Mogenson, "Interiorizing Psychology into Itself: Following the movement from Kant to Hegel in the Background of Giegerich's Psychology Project," *Dialectics and Analytical Psychology*, 73.
38 Bion, *Brazilian Lectures*, 21–22.
39 C. G. Jung, *CW* 13, § 110.
40 Bion, *Brazilian Lectures*, 22.
41 Mogenson, "Different Moments in Dialectical Movement", 90.
42 Bion, *Brazilian Lectures*, 22.
43 Mogenson, "Different Moments in Dialectical Movement."
44 Giegerich, *What Is Soul?* 146.
45 Giegerich, *What Is Soul?* 147.
46 C. G. Jung, *CW* 9i, § 28.
47 Kierkegaard, *The Concept of Anxiety*, 195.

Chapter 3

Discerning the Dialectic between Form and Content

Jennifer M. Sandoval

A friend related a story in which a priest visits a hospital room to offer holy communion to a very ill patient. When the priest opens the door, he sees the dying woman on a bed surrounded by family and friends who are tenderly holding hands and singing to her. Upon reflection, the priest realizes that though he initially thought he was there to give communion, he was in fact *receiving* it by entering their midst. The priest's recognition traverses semantic content to logical form, radically elevating awareness to the vertical or psychological dimension; he comprehended the *inner truth of the meaning* of holy communion. In this vastly expanded horizon, the notion of the Eucharist is absolved from its literal definitional constraints, that is, the breaking of bread and drinking of wine, and released into its infinite truth as a living expression of logical love: communion as a living embodied act of remembrance and recognition of the soul returning home to itself, as Love. How does the priest see this? *What manner of perceiving allows the priest to recognize the dialectic?* This essay attempts to explore the conditions of consciousness for discerning the dialectic or distinguishing between mere contents of consciousness and their underlying form or soul logic (i.e., the psychological difference).[1]

The Relation between Form and Content

From a psychoanalytic perspective, Slavoj Zizek describes an inverse relation between content and form via a brief dream interpretation made by Freud wherein his patient initially refuses to describe their dream "because it was so indistinct and muddled." Freud noted that the patient was pregnant but in doubt regarding the identity of the baby's father (i.e., the lineage was "indistinct and muddled"). Freud here recognizes the relation between the dream's underlying form and presenting content:

> [T]he lack of clarity shown by the dream was a part of the material which instigated the dream: part of this material, that is, was represented in the *form* of the dream. *The form of a dream or the form in which it is dreamt is used with quite surprising frequency for representing its concealed subject-matter.*[2]

DOI: 10.4324/9781003381150-4

Freud also notes the significance of linguistics when, in his *Interpretation of Dreams* (1900/1976), he insists that, "the wording chosen [of a remembered dream] is itself part… of the dream."[3]

Zizek affirms that a dialectical relation between form and content does not correlate linearly. He describes the tension between content and form wherein "the very gap between content and form is to be reflected back into the content itself, as an indication that the content is not all, that something was repressed/ excluded from it."[4] Take, for example, a young woman, who happens to be a budding and talented film director, describing a recent night out with friends:

> We decided to go to a strip club. We sat down near the stage where women were dancing as one might expect. Then the stage got quiet and I noticed that everything was red – the stage, the curtains, the lights. The next performer came onto the stage and began to dance to Nina Simone's *I Put A Spell On You* and she was *signing* the lyrics. Sign language! It was completely amazing. I looked to my right and noticed the other dancers were sitting at the end of the bar counting money. My friends were talking and laughing and didn't seem to notice what was happening. I want to make a film of that experience, of that woman!

We could say here that the young director recognized or saw through to the invisible form via the reflection back into the content itself, the "very gap between content and form," the excess, which manifested itself in the transcendent impact of the dancer's expression through sign language, dance, and music. We might say the director successfully detected the excess because she is compelled to make a film (and bear witness to this new seed of consciousness).

The biblical story of the prodigal son is another example in which semantic logic is dimensionally transgressed. The son of a loving father left his home and thought he squandered the treasure his father gave him for nothing of any value, though he did not know its worthlessness at the time. He was ashamed to return to his father because he thought he had hurt him. But when he came home the father welcomed him with joy, because the son *himself* was his father's treasure (his father wanted nothing else). Here we note the dimensional upgrade from semantics to syntax, from content to form, from *having* literal treasure to *being* (treasure in its true sense as Love or Being), achieved through the negation (squandering) of not only the literal treasure but of the son's value of himself.

Ibram X. Kendi offers another example of the dialectic in the context of racism. He begins by describing the initial position (Position A)[5] of the racist as one who harbors racist ideas. "A racist idea is any idea that suggests one racial group is inferior or superior to another racial group in any way. Racist ideas argue that the inferiorities and superiorities of racial groups explain racial inequities in society."[6] Upon further reflection and awareness, the negated position would be achieved, namely, the relinquishment of the idea of such discrimination based on race. One might then declare themselves to be a "non-racist" or "race-neutral." However, according to Kendi,

> The most threatening racist movement is not the alt right's unlikely drive for a White ethnostate but the regular American's drive for a "race-neutral" one. The construct of race neutrality actually feeds White nationalist victimhood by positing the notion that any policy protecting or advancing non-White Americans toward equity is "reverse discrimination."[7]

So here we see the negated position does not logically hold up. To merely deny that one is racist is to stay on the same logical level or reality of the racist. What is needed is an absolute negation, which results in the notion of *antiracism*:

> An antiracist idea is any idea that suggests the racial groups are equals in all their apparent differences – that there is nothing right or wrong with any racial group. Antiracist ideas argue that racist policies are the cause of racial inequities.[8]

The dialectic involves the *absolute negation* of the logical form of the content from within itself which arrives back at the starting point, albeit a transformed starting point. In Kendi's example, antiracism allows for the original idea of discrimination in an *objective* sense, wherein: If discrimination is creating equity, then it is antiracist. If discrimination is creating inequity, then it is racist.[9] Furthermore,

> The only remedy to racist discrimination is antiracist discrimination. The only remedy to past discrimination is present discrimination. The only remedy to present discrimination is future discrimination.... And in order to treat some persons equally, we must treat them differently.[10]

Kendi's discussion on the phenomenology of antiracism is quite remarkable, wherein notions such as beauty, culture, class and power are explored from the new landscape made possible by the dialectic.

Preparing the Mind

So how does one prepare or condition the mind to be attuned to the dialectic? For Giegerich, to think psychologically is truly an *opus contra naturam* and must be consciously entered into, learned, and practiced. As he wrote of training to be a psychoanalyst,

> Apart from a comprehensive knowledge about the phenomenology of the soul's life as manifested in the history of mankind, the training of candidates should be a differentiation of their mind: mind processing! The mind needs to

learn to easily make the complex logical, dialectical movements that are required if an understanding is to be truly psychological and if the logical level of soul is to be reached at all. It needs to acquire truly psychological categories and forms of thought, and thorough practice in working with them.[11]

When a student asked Lacan how to do psychoanalysis, Lacan responded, "Do crossword puzzles."[12] David Miller writes[13]:

So, why did Lacan tell the student that if he wanted to learn psychoanalysis he should do crossword puzzles? Let me give two real examples from recent *New York Times* crossword puzzles. Clue: Santa Fe or Tucson. The answer is an abbreviation and has only three letters. Answer: SUV, i.e., sports utility vehicle. Another one. Clue: Span. Four letters. Now the word "span" could refer to: tip of thumb to tip of little finger; common span of 9 inches; a small distance, like a span of lace; the distance between two supports of a bridge or other structure; the full extent of something, like a span of memory. But none of this fits into four letters. Answer: Team (as in a team, i.e., span, of oxen). In each of these cases – Tucson or Santa Fe as an SUV or span as a team of oxen – the answer disrupts conventional semantic meanings. It ruptures signification, personal and cultural, with otherness. It is an *Enstellung*, a displacement. The language "means" autonomously. Doing crossword puzzles makes one alert to the other in the language. In Freudian terms, it is to be alert to the switch word, the bridge term, or the nodal point. It trains one to listen to the other in the saying of what one says rather than to what one thinks something means.

For psychotherapeutic practice, this implies listening to the language, not to the meaning. Not listening to the patient, but to the language the patient uses. Or better: listen to the language that uses the patient. As if the soul, the psyche is in the language, and not in the semantic meaning, which the individual ego or the cultural ego has assigned to the language. As Heidegger said: "Language speaks. A person speaks in responding to language. This responding is a hearing.... What is important is learning to live in the speaking of language."[14] That's where the other is. Some would say: That's where soul is. Not ego. As Heidegger said: "What is spoken is never, and in no language, what is said."[15]

Preparing the mind to discern the presence of soul is also explored by James Hillman as inhabiting a particular stance in relation to the world he describes as the aesthetic response of the heart, or "the heart of beauty."[16] Such a witnessing is receptive rather than projective; the phenomenon is invited to disclose its own inherent truth. The absence of projections evokes a vision of stillness, a calm clarity of perception. One is now open to beholding and communing with the inner truth of the phenomenon, which can only be apprehended at the level of the objective psyche, as experienced when greeted from the heart of beauty or "organ of truth."[17] Hillman appeals to Henri Corbin's rendering of beauty as "the supreme theophany, divine self-revelation," in that beauty is present in the very manifestation of the thing in itself. Such soul-making happens in the receiving, the taking in of an object, "so that it shows its heart and reveals its soul."[18]

Attunement (*melos*)

The capacity to listen beyond apparent meaning to true meaning finds a parallel in music:

> In his seminal essay "On Conducting," the 19th century composer Richard Wagner wrote of the *melos*, the melodic theme that underlies all great music. Wagner urged conductors to listen to this inner melody ... when they conducted, otherwise they would miss the heart of the music that transcended the specific notes and harmonies.... He urged conductors not to be "time-beaters," for "great music ... cannot be expressed in words and concepts, nor in arithmetical figures." Instead, he urged them to ... understand its "true spirit." Post-Wagnerian musicians have similarly commented on the need to listen for this soul of music. For example, violinist Isaac Stern spoke of the need to hear the silence between the notes, while composer-conductor Gustav Mahler said that what is best in music is not to be found in the notes.[19]

Psychoanalyst Allen Bishop, in his paper titled, "Hope and Forgiveness in Psychoanalysis,"[20] cites the poignant example of Beethoven, struggling desperately with the inexorable loss of his hearing, and explores the connection between relinquishing hope and transformation. Beethoven writes of being "to the verge of despair when I could not hear the bird sing or the shepherd's song.... The beloved hope, which I brought with me when I came here ... I must totally abandon." When Beethoven subsequently returned to Vienna, he had eight of his most productive years. Bishop posits that "[r]elinquishing hope involves an act of forgiveness/resignation in the internal world which paradoxically spurs the greatest growth." (Such sacrifice of hope is related to the "readiness" to receive a truth event in critical theory, which I will discuss further ahead).

According to British musicologist Marion Scott, Beethoven's body of work, consisting of three periods (early, middle, and late), can be characterized in the following way:

> In the first, Beethoven saw the material world from the material standpoint; in the second he saw the material world from the spiritual standpoint; in the third he saw the spiritual world from the spiritual standpoint.[21]
> (Beethoven, Pellegrini and Cudahy, New York: 1949, p. 79)

Similarly, psychologist Kenneth Wapnick dialectically speculates that Beethoven experienced the pain of his deafness in order better to "hear" the inner sounds so powerfully and beautifully depicted in the music of his later life.

In his important notion of psychoanalytic companioning, psychoanalyst Robert Grossmark describes the importance of an exquisite attunement to such a *melos* – or "register" of the patient. He writes,

> When we are working well with a patient, there is implicitly a sense of rhythmic synchronicity and mutual affective regulation and containment. When working with regressed states the features of companionship, proto-conversations and rhythmic engagement, are fore-grounded. When the verbal is stripped of its meaning, we are left with the vocal. The **sound, harmony, and rhythm predominate**. It is our work to stay as attuned as possible to the patient in this register and to not ask him or her to shift to a more verbal and intellectual register. Even when a patient is in the verbal/intellectual register, it is often the vocal and rhythmic domain that holds the affect and potential engagement."[22]

Here we observe the need to stay attuned to form (the "sound, harmony, and rhythm" of the interaction) above content (its verbal/intellectual register) to hear the truth of the encounter.

Readiness and Subjectivization

In order for one to be ready to recognize the dialectic, one already has to have been able to recognize it. Giegerich writes:

> [T]he psychologist is only a psychologist to the extent that he is already pregnant with the psychological I from the outset. He as civil man [sic] and ordinary consciousness already has to be reached by it, in the grip of it, so that it is the true subject that does the thinking in him, if through the opus he wants to arrive at it."[23]

What are the conditions for such 'fertilization' or readiness to occur?

In critical theory, we find the notion of a Truth Event (Alain Badiou), describing a rupture in the fabric of everyday life where an underlying truth may be glimpsed or discerned under certain conditions. Such an event represents that which is outside ontology, belonging to a wholly different dimension – that, precisely, of *non*-Being. "The Event is the Truth of the situation, that which renders visible/readable what the 'official' state of the situation had to 'repress,' but it is also always localized, that is, the Truth is always the Truth of a specific situation."[24] This aligns with the condition of a soul event, which has eachness character, that is, it is associated with a particular phenomenon wedded to its historical context; nor is it discernable as a positivity, being absolutely negative.

Psychology relates to "all actual occurrences of soul as being present only *as absent*.... It is precisely their intrinsic departedness (their presence as absent) that identifies them as events of *soul* (in contrast to "*psychic*" experiences of the human animal)."[25] The ability to hold in mind the dialectical contradiction-and-union of both presence and absence together resides within a particular quality of consciousness. Frank Ruda calls being able to receive a Truth Event "becoming a subject proper," or "subjectivization." Such becoming corresponds to the being of the psychologist who "becomes" the place for soul as Subject to make an appearance.[26]

In addition to the consciousness of the Psychological I, an example of subjectivization might be the description of "true prayer" as "only a true prayer if it is already God who through one's human praying is speaking the prayer to God, in other words, *not* the human person per se – not the ego."[27] Here we might say that true prayer was made possible through the subjectivization of the worshipper, whose status *as* subject is reinstated through the event of true prayer.

Subjectivization can only happen when there is externalization.[28] What does this mean? The word Hegel uses for 'externalization' in German is "Entlassen," which has multiple meanings, including *to let something go* (for example, one can say that one "entlässt" one's child into the world), *to relieve something of its function* (for example, to dismiss someone from a job), and also *the act of letting things be*. Giegerich reminds us of this when he writes, "We have to learn to suffer our hands to be empty, in the fullest sense of the word suffer. No image. No symbols. No meaning. No Gods: No religion. For is it not the empty hand, and the empty hand alone, that can be filled?"[29]

Capturing the contradiction and impossibility inherent in subjectivization, Ruda states that,

> only by fully sacrificing, i.e. *entlassen* what I am, by fully subscribing to the idea that I have nothing in my power, can one generate the condition [for receiving a Truth event].... To say it another way, as long as one thinks that there is something internal that should be treated as if it is unsacrificeable, there never will be emancipation. [Ultimately] One needs to assume that one cannot sacrifice and this is the greatest sacrifice. This is a sacrifice [the truth] demands. Its mode is what Hegel calls *Entlassen* and its slogans may be: act as if you are not free; act as if you are dead."[30]

These slogans have everything in common with Giegerich's observation of the sacrificial ego "death" required for psychological consciousness. The degree of sacrifice Hegel implies with *entlassen* could be compared to what the ego experiences when confronted with the need to sacrifice the wholeness and harmony of the highest principle itself. "If this *exclusive* goodness and consequently the entire highest principle as it had been understood have to be sacrificed, this requires the *katastrophê*, the going under, of the anthropological ego."[31]

Entlassen means the absolute negation of the false ego and a release of the self into its true identity: the conscious recipient of soul events.

On the other hand (of course!) "We must not try to get away from the ego, not fight the ego attitude: because this fighting would only be the confirmation of the ego! ...We will never get rid of the ego and will not even have to. We have to accept it, live with it, allow it to be, knowing that we are already surrounded by psyche on all sides. Hegel knew: The absolute is already there, and we are already where we ought to be. We just do not see it. This not seeing is the ego."[32] What must be sacrificed then is the hope of ever overcoming over the ego.

Critical theorists identify three ways to *betray* an event of Truth: (1) The first is a simple disavowal, with a corresponding attempt to follow old patterns as if nothing had happened, as if it were just a minor disturbance (an example for us would be the denial of soul in psychology altogether, or ignoring the phenomenon of Nina Simone's signing dancer); (2) the second betrayal is the false imitation of the event of Truth (e.g., new-age re-enactment of an ancient mythological ritual as a pseudo-event, or the priest insisting on the literal ritual of the Eucharist); and (3) a direct positivization or ontologization of the Truth event, with its reduction to a new positive order of Being (e.g., the wholesale reduction of psychology as the discipline of interiority to a branch of depth psychology called "PDI").

A Recognition that Compels Transformation

Giegerich describes Heraclitus' recognition of the vastness of the soul, "so deep a logos does it have" as analogous to the psalmist's transformative experience of divine knowledge. In Psalm 139, we read:

> O Lord, you have searched me and you know me.
> You know when I sit and when I rise; you perceive my thoughts from afar.
> You discern my going out and my lying down; you are familiar with all my
>   ways.
> Before a word is on my tongue you know it completely, O Lord.
> You hem me in – behind and before; you have laid your hand upon me.
> Such knowledge is too wonderful for me, too lofty for me to attain.
> Where can I go from your Spirit? Where can I flee from your presence?
> If I go up to the heavens, you are there; if I make my bed in the depths,
>   you are there.

Such knowledge "too wonderful for me, too lofty for me to attain" signifies the first emergence of the conscious awareness of this "unheard dimension of absolute interiority or internal infinity."[33] The sense from the psalmist is that such knowledge is incomprehensible, utterly irrational, and therefore unknowable, but Giegerich makes the argument that in reality it is merely *unimaginable.* "It is that new form of consciousness that ... orients itself in life by means of the abstractness of rigorous thought and conceptual comprehension, because it has sublated the modes of sensory intuition and imagination. It cannot be imagined any more."[34] The horizon of the imagination has been "exploded" into an infinite landscape of thought.

In contrast to "seeing through," what Giegerich here describes is seeing *more* – of gaining perspective, of radically expanding the horizon. Dialectical thinking is "a stepping backwards so as to *widen* the horizon before oneself."[35]

Once consciousness has seen a glimpse of the new logic, the old logic is compelled to give way. Glimpsed from within the limited perceiving and imagining consciousness, the radical "seed" ignites the destruction of that mode. The cat is out of the bag; "You cannot have an inkling of the inescapability of reflection without having fallen under an obligation: to allow the new 'content' to alchemically decompose your old frame of mind and the old logical constitution of your world." New wine can't be poured into old wineskins. The decomposition does away with the old wineskin, making way for a new wineskin – a new frame of mind and logical constitution of one's world – to receive the new wine. "What at first appears as a content *of* consciousness is in truth the seed of what wants to become a radically new *form* of consciousness at large."[36] This form of consciousness readily comprehends the true meaning of communion, the art of the signing dancer, the being *as* my father's treasure, companioning a patient, that is, recognizes a soul event.

Giegerich warns of "a black hole that swallows within it all precise thinking. It is the name for ... the refusal to allow it to work on our consciousness."[37] One must take care that such a radical new content is not defused or weakened by reintegrating it into the old status of consciousness. The new wine cannot go into the old wineskin. It must not be "deprived of its logical, notional, intellectual claims," thereby "translat[ed] into the harmlessness and fussiness of a mere romantic *feeling*."[38] That the director was compelled to make a film of her experience rather than just allow it to be neutralized by sharing it could be an example of letting the experience work on her prior consciousness. In this, she does not "betray" the event of truth she glimpsed.

Psychological Faith

For Jung, soul was *real*; it had an actual living quality – it was not merely an abstract idea. Jung was not a "tourist" in the land of soul but had taken up residence, so to speak. Giegerich notes that "Jung had been reached and touched, indeed 'gripped,' by the notion of the soul. And because he had been touched and gripped by it, ... he could grasp it."[39] One's having been reached, touched, and gripped by the notion of soul enables one to *perceive* it (and vice versa). Nor did Jung "allow the inherent pull of phenomena to seduce him into looking at them in the light of perspectives that they might suggest.... He remained *faithful* to his one thought, the Notion of soul."[40]

Where does one place their faith? Does one identify with the ego or with soul? Because the ego "wants to insist on what the eyes can see, on obvious positive empirical facts ... and on preserving the ontology of what we call 'objective reality' or everyday world, the whole common-sense sphere of daily life."[41] To not insist on what the eyes can see means *having faith in something else*.[42] So here it becomes apparent that anxiety – or the absence of psychological faith – is an obstacle to discerning a soul movement.

To conclude, we have looked at some of the qualities of consciousness that accompany the discernment of the dialectic: mental training needed to perform interiorization, exquisite attunement to the *melos* of the phenomenon, the sacrifice of sacrifice, an acceptance of imperfection, a willingness not to betray soul, and psychological faith. And though we have often heard that when the soul makes itself present, the ego suffers ("the experience of the Self is always a defeat for the ego"), it does seem that a deep joy tends to accompany the new horizon recognition of the dialectic brings to awareness, a logical joy that accompanies the receipt of a truth event. Ultimately, "if the soul is to come to life, [it] needs to be awakened through the act of appreciation."[43]

A final example of elucidating the soul's dialectic can be found in the following story:

My Father once told me a story about a small town in Minnesota that was situated on a hill. At the top of the hill was a hospital with a maternity ward. At the bottom of the hill was the town cemetery. *That was the whole story.* No further details forthcoming. I thought about this little town. What was it like? I could see toddlers dancing and playing about at the top of the hill. There was music in the air. A little further along, the children were older as they began to descend the hill. The music was fainter now. Soon the children began school at the little school house. Further down the hill, some went to college, and some went off to war and some never came back. They formed families and had children of their own. Some were musicians and some worked with their hands. Some were successful and some failed. As the years went by, some fell to disease and poverty – some slowed their pace and helped those who were falling behind. Near the bottom of the hill, they came to a small meadow. As they gathered around for one last time, old friends embraced. They forgave each other for any grief they might have caused and were forgiven in turn. In the east, behind them, the sun shone bright and warm on the children at the top of the hill.[44]

Notes

1 The psychological difference is defined as the difference between the semantic, worldly, or egoic realm and the syntactic, invisible, or soul realm.
2 Sigmund Freud, *The Interpretation of Dreams* (Harmondsworth: Penguin Books, 1976), 446.
3 Freud, *The Interpretation of Dreams*, 589n.

4 Slavoj Zizek, *Absolute Recoil: Towards a New Foundation of Dialectical Materialism* (London New York: Verso, 2015), 176.
5 See *Dialectics & Analytical Psychology* (2005), 6. for Giegerich's explanation of the dialectic.
6 Ibram X. Kendi, *How to Be an Antiracist*, 1st ed. (New York: One World, 2019), 20.
7 Kendi, *How to Be an Antiracist*, 20.
8 Kendi, *How to Be an Antiracist*, 20.
9 Kendi, *How to Be an Antiracist*, 20.
10 Kendi, *How to Be an Antiracist*, 18.
11 Wolfgang Giegerich, *The Soul's Logical Life: Towards a Rigorous Notion of Psychology* (Frankfurt am Main; New York: Peter Lang, 1998), 277.
12 Jacques Lacan, *Écrits* (New York: Norton, 2006), 220.
13 Personal communication (2020).
14 Martin Heidegger, *Poetry, Language, Thought* (New York: Harper, 1971), 210. (German: *Unterwegs zur Sprache* [Pfullingen: Neske, 1959], 33: "Die Sprache spricht. Der Mensch spricht, insofern er der Sprache entspricht. Das Entsprechen ist Hören.... Alles beruht darin, das Wohnen im Sprechen Der Sprache zu lernen.")
15 Heidegger, *Poetry, Language, Thought*, 11.
16 James Hillman, *The Thought of the Heart; [and] The Soul of the World* (Spring Publications, 1998), 40.
17 Hillman, *The Thought of the Heart*, 40.
18 Hillman, *The Thought of the Heart*, 36.
19 Kenneth Wapnick, *Touching the Heart of God-Psychoanalysis, Psychotherapy, and A Course in Miracles-An Unfinished Manuscript, Volume One: Into the Depths-From Light to Darkness* (Foundation for "A Course in Miracles," 2021), 37.
20 Unpublished paper.
21 Wapnick, *Touching the Heart of God*, 37.
22 Robert Grossmark, "Psychoanalytic Companioning," *Psychoanalytic Dialogues* 26, no. 6 (December 11, 2016): 698–712, https://doi.org/10.1080/10481885.2016.1235447, 702.
23 Wolfgang Giegerich, *What is Soul?* (New Orleans, LA: Spring Journal, Inc., 2012), 304.
24 http://www.lacan.com/zizek-badiou.htm
25 Wolfgang Giegerich, "Geist," in *Psychology as the Discipline of Interiority*, 1 ed., eds. Jennifer M. Sandoval and John C. Knapp (London ; New York, NY: Routledge, 2017), 41–42. Giegerich continues, "If and where psychology nevertheless insists on their having to be a present reality or immediate presence—as, for example, in the form of peak experiences, 'high' feelings, the emotion of numinosity, the veneration of 'the imaginal', the presence of 'the sacred', 'the Gods', 'Angels', or the discovery of 'one's personal myth'—there it would turn into kitsch, and soul into a consumer good for the gratification of the greedy ego."
26 Frank Ruda, "Entlassen. Remarks on Hegel, Sacrifice and Liberation," *Crisis and Critique* 1, no. 2 (June 14, 2014): 126.
27 Giegerich, *What Is Soul?* 125.
28 Ruda, "Entlassen," 126.
29 Wolfgang Giegerich, "Rupture, or: Psychology and Religion," in *The Neurosis of Psychology (Collected English Papers, Vol. I)* (New Orleans, LA: Spring Journal, Inc., 2005), 231.
30 Ruda, "Entlassen," 127–128.
31 Wolfgang Giegerich, "First Shadow, then Anima, or The Advent of the Guest" in *Soul Violence (Collected English Papers, Vol. III)* (New Orleans, LA: Spring Journal, Inc., 2008), 104.
32 Wolfgang Giegerich, *Working with Dreams*, 1st ed. (London; New York: Routledge, 2020), 88.

33 Wolfgang Giegerich, *The Soul Always Thinks (Collected English Papers, Vol. IV)* (Woodstock, Conn.; Lancaster: Spring Journal, Inc., 2010), 148.

34 Giegerich, *The Soul Always Thinks*, 149.

35 Wolfgang Giegerich, David L. Miller, and Greg Mogenson, *Dialectics & Analytical Psychology: The El Capitan Canyon Seminar* (New Orleans, La.: Spring Journal, Inc., 2005), 3.

36 Giegerich, *The Soul Always Thinks*, 149.

37 Giegerich, *The Soul Always Thinks*, 150.

38 Giegerich, *The Soul Always Thinks*, 149.

39 Giegerich, *The Soul's Logical Life*, 41.

40 Giegerich, *The Soul's Logical Life*, 43, my italics.

41 Giegerich, *Working With Dreams*, 83.

42 I.e., "Not what the eyes can see, but what opens the eyes…" from the *Kena Upanishad.*

43 Giegerich, *What Is Soul?* 50.

44 This was contributed by the author's father, Edward J. Dunvan.

Chapter 4

Returning to the Wilderness

Jung, Giegerich and the Infinite Task of Interiority

George B. Hogenson

When I was invited to keynote this conference,[1] my familiarity with the work of Wolfgang Giegerich was broad but not as deep as I would have liked. I first encountered Giegerich in 1988 when his paper, "The invention of explosive power and the blueprint of the bomb,"[2] appeared in *Spring*, then edited by James Hillman. Without going into too much personal history, I was, at the time, the associate director of the MacArthur Foundation's program on Peace and International Security. I had by then been directly involved with the issues surrounding nuclear weapons for over 15 years. Giegerich's paper was startling in its grasp of deeper aspects of the nature of the age of nuclear weapons than I had found in many "psychological" commentaries. I read his other papers on the subject with interest. Much later, I found his commentary[3] on Robert Romanyshyn's paper[4] on climate change similarly insightful, not least because of his critique of Romanyshyn's romantic anti-modernism; the discovery of perspective by Alberti was not going to carry the load of today's climate crisis when the much less romantic industrial revolution is the culprit. In both instances, Giegerich was addressing issues where I had done considerable work outside the confines of analytical psychology—indeed, in what is generally referred to as the world of public policy and politics—and Giegerich's hardheaded, while still psychologically insightful, approach was refreshing.

On the other hand, these same qualities were conspicuously on display in several other debates Giegerich carried on within the world of analytical psychology, broadly construed, with, among others, Stanton Marlin, Mark Saban, and Warren Colman, in the latter of which I managed briefly to get caught in the crossfire as well.[5] Each debate had its distinct qualities, but overall, Giegerich distinguished himself by his fierce combativeness coupled with truly powerful arguments, whether you agree with him or not. It was clear that one did not engage Giegerich lightly if one valued their intellectual limbs. Later, I will be turning to some aspects of *The Soul's Logical Life* that present, I will argue, a problematic aspect of the text and the overall meaning of analytical psychology's relation to theory in general and the use of myth.

DOI: 10.4324/9781003381150-5

I first encountered *The Soul's Logical Life*[6] upon its publication, and I remember reading through it rather in haste on a train trip, I believe it was from Zurich to Milan. I say in haste because until I returned to it to prepare this paper, I had not adequately registered the many nuances and intricacies of Giegerich's argument. As I had never written anything about Giegerich or otherwise had much to do with psychology as the disciple of interiority, I was also surprised when Greg Mogenson asked me to write a jacket blurb for *What Is Soul.*[7] I asked Greg why he wanted me to write such a comment, and he replied that he thought it would be interesting to have a comment from someone whose work was known to be different from Giegerich's. Greg's reference, of course, was to my work over the last 20 years on complex systems, emergence, and the mathematics of symbol systems, but what may not have been clear to Greg was that my philosophical training was divided into two principal areas—East Asian, particularly Buddhist, philosophy, which I had studied in Kyoto, Japan and at Yale, and on the other side, German philosophy from Leibniz through Kant and Hegel to Husserl and Heidegger. *What Is Soul?* was, therefore, more familiar territory than might have been evident from my more recent work, and I was delighted to offer a comment, which, to my surprise, found its way to the back cover of the book in its entirety. The invitation to give this talk carried an extra surprise when John specifically highlighted my book on Jung and Freud as one of the reasons for extending the invitation. I am always surprised when someone remarks on that book, now nearly 40 years after its original publication. But here it was again, and I will have occasion to refer to it in this paper.

The invitation to speak here, however, required a much deeper dive into Giegerich. I confess that I came to the project with hesitation, based first on a long-standing skepticism about the role Hegel plays in Giegerich's thinking. I was also rather distant from the world of archetypal psychology as developed by James Hillman, which seemed to be the focus of much of the discussion and controversy surrounding Giegerich. The only personal encounters I had had with Hillman ended badly from my point of view due to Hillman's seeming inability to recognize the shadow side of listening to one's "daemon," at least when directly challenged on the matter. On the other hand, my theoretical work over the last 20 years has emphasized elementary patterns of structure drawn from complexity theory in the analysis of Jungian categories like archetypes, but I do not view those structures as agents directing the individual's life. My hesitation was also grounded in what appeared to me to be a somewhat insular point of view on Jung and the development of Jung's theories captured best by David Miller's characterization of Hillman and archetypal psychology as "second wave Jungianism" and the work of Giegerich as a further successor state or "third wave Jungianism."[8] This characterization seemed to consign any other work on Jung to some remote and inconsequential island where, evidently, the waves never break.

These hesitations notwithstanding, I returned to Geigerich's work, particularly *The Soul's Logical Life*, but also the various debates he has had with other Jungians, most notably Stan Marlin and Marc Saban. I find Giegerich's general critique of contemporary psychology as, in many cases, a little deeper than the pages of *Psychology Today*, telling and important. Much the same goes for analytic training programs, which I fear are increasingly viewed as opportunities to pick up a few additional technical skills and the title of analyst—either Freudian or Jungian. On the other hand, Geigerich's deep and genuine commitment to rigorous and systematic thought is invigorating amid so much fuzzy thinking both within and outside the Jungian community.

But the purpose of this conference is to focus attention on *The Soul's Logical Life*. The intent, when originally scheduled, was to celebrate the 20th anniversary of the book's publication, and as is characteristic of such inflection points in the life of a major thinker, to offer some reflections on the work after the passage of time. Giegerich presents a particularly daunting challenge in this regard, given the extraordinary extent of his scholarly production and the array of topics he has addressed. To fully assess his work requires not only the persistence to make one's way through his writings but also the ability to assess the sources of his argument critically and the framing of his position. Even within the confines of *The Soul's Logical Life*, it is difficult to see where one starts and what elements within the text are most salient to an assessment. Much of the body of the text is devoted to Giegerich's critique of imaginal or archetypal psychology and its major practitioners, and while I find much of that discussion compelling, I believe there is much to be said about the status of the image that is not encompassed in Hillman's archetypal psychology. But I will dodge that question for now and offer only a promissory note to say I will take it up another time. But looking at the book from the standpoint of its structure, we have that complex and detailed critique of archetypal psychology bookended by two myths—and at least one parable—and I want to argue that these myths, Thor's journey to Utgard and Artemis and Actaion cast different lights on Giegerich's project, and on our relationship to it. I will focus primarily on Thor and bring in Actaion in my conclusion.

I was struck when I first saw the logo selected for this conference, Thor attempting to lift Utgard Loki's cat. I was surprised, however, that Giegerich gives us only this moment in the entire tale, given the detailed sophistication with which he interprets the myth of Actaion and Artemis, weaving its elements together into a single seamless fabric taking up 25 percent of the book. Added to this was Giegerich's admonition that:

> Every reader's task is to be Thor and to try with all his might to lift what at first appears to be an ordinary cat and experience the incredible weight holding it down—until, finally, he becomes aware of the fact that in reality he is dealing with a section of the world serpent, with a visible shape in which the invisible horizon of everything becomes accessible. If he reads in this way, he is able to see what is truly great in the seemingly insignificant, to sense the miracle of the ordinary, the secret in the manifest, the "unconscious" in the conscious, or, more logically speaking the "universal' in the "singular."[9]

I want to be clear that I find this passage and Giegerich's comments on the loss of textual integrity to the "world wide web" on the following page both stimulating and admirable. Close reading has fallen out of favor in too many instances, including the reading of Jung. But I must challenge Giegerich at this point by arguing that in the case of Thor's encounter with the cat in the myth of his journey to Utgard, Giegerich has failed to follow his admonition. This is in contrast to his reading of Artemis and Actaion at the conclusion of the book. While you can find versions of the story of Thor in any number of sources, ranging from children's books to scholarly tomes, they are usually truncated renderings, lacking the context provided by the original source, the *Prose Edda* of Snorri Sturluson. In the *Edda*, the story of Thor's journey to Utgard follows a series of other accounts of Thor's prowess and is cast as the one example where Thor's strength fails him. The story is told by three strange figures in Asgard—the home of the gods—to Gangleri, who is, in fact, the Swedish King Gylfe, disguised as a poor peasant. The three strange figures, Har, Jafnhar, and Thride, usually translated as High, Just-as-High, and Third, are identified elsewhere in the Edda as epithets for different manifestations of Odin. The other stories are suffused not only with Thor's physical strength but also with his magical qualities reflecting the shamanic foundations of Norse mythology. But in the case of the journey to Utgard, Ganglere finally asks the decisive question:

> "Tell me, has Thor never been in a situation where he encountered so much strength and power that he was overwhelmed by might or magic superior to his own?"
>
> High replied "I expect that there are few others who could answer your question, even though many situations have seemed difficult to Thor. Although some things, because of their power or their strength have prevented Thor from being victorious, there is no need to tell about them, not least because everybody ought to keep in mind that there are so many examples where Thor was the mightiest."
>
> Then Gangleri said "It seems to me that this time I have asked something that no one can answer."
>
> Just-as-high replied, "We have heard reports that seem unreliable to us, yet here, close by sits the man who can give a true account. You can trust what he says because he has never spoken falsely, and he may not and he will not start now."
>
> Then Gangleri responded: "I will stand here and listen for a solution. Otherwise I call you beaten, because you are unable to answer my question."
>
> Third then spoke, "It is obvious that he wants to know these tales, even though we take no pleasure in telling them. You, however, must now keep quiet."[10]

Thor's adventure in Utgard is an embarrassment to the gods. It is something one should not speak of. There are other peculiarities to the story. We should first note that Ganglier-Gylfe's question poses two issues, Thor's physical strength and his skills in magic. Additionally, the various myths of Thor's engagement with the giants are usually motivated by revenge for some slight or protection of one or another of the Aesir or Vanir goddesses whom Odin has managed to auction off by mistake, and they are invariably about his physical strength and rage. But in this tale, there is no apparent motivation for Thor's journey. He is simply going, as Giegerich correctly writes, "to the world or realm without" "the beyond: the sphere of the demons and giants." He travels accompanied first by Loki, then adds two human children, Thjalfe and Roskva, acquired from a poor peasant as he leaves Midgard in compensation for the boy's laming one of the goats that pull his chariot. Thor must leave his chariot behind and proceed on foot. It is then, as they wander in the wilderness, that they almost immediately meet Utgard Loki, at first disguised as the giant Skrymer. They sleep in his glove, thinking it a cave, and on successive nights, Skrymer's snoring so enrages Thor that he throws his hammer at the giant's head with no apparent conse-quence—"Was that an acorn that fell on my head?" Skrymer asks. Skrymer offers to carry Thor's provisions in his pack but ties it so tightly that not even Thor can open it. They now wander hungry as well as sleepless. All of this, of course, is being done through Utgard Loki's magic—none of it has to do with Thor's strength; rather contrary, at every turn, Thor's strength is defeated, and he has no insight into the magic that Utgard Loki uses to deceive him. Returning to the original question posed by Ganglier, this is not a story about Thor's strength being overwhelmed. It is, I would suggest, a story about his deficient understanding of magic or illusion, the very stuff of Utgard, the wilderness.

Giegerich characterizes this as "trickery," but it seems to me it is something more than that. The giants are astonished by Thor's strength, but Utgard Loki is confident that he can protect himself and his group from Thor's wrath through the power of his magic. Indeed, in the account of Thor's activities that immediately follow this narrative, Thor does set out on a characteristic effort to revenge himself, but not on Utgard Loki as one might expect, given his other vendettas against the giants. Rather, having deceived another giant, Hymar, into thinking he was a "young man" or even a boy, Thor sets out on a fishing expedition to catch none other than the Midgard Serpent itself, using the head of Hymar's largest ox as bait. The serpent only escapes Thor's hammer because Hymar, terrified by the ferocity of the struggle between Thor and the Serpent, cuts Thor's fishing line.

In my early reflections about this paper and the story of Thor and Utgard Loki, I initially thought that an apt title would be "Thor never thinks." He may as well be just "some dude,"[11] as Giegerich characterizes many interpretations of Actaion in his reading of that myth, stumbling through the forest. But thought does play a role in the narrative, in the form of one of the giants in

Utgard Loki's retinue, Huge, who runs a series of races with the human boy, Thjalfe. Thjalfe is extremely fast, but as Utgard Loki remarks, nothing is faster than thought – Huge. "Thought," it appears, does find its "natural location in the primal wilderness, where" Giegerich tells us, "Actaion is hunting for it."[12] But in the case of Thor and his companions – who are all oblivious to what is going on around them – thought finds its natural location in the primal wilderness, and it is the province of the natural inhabitants of that wilderness, not the interlopers from the domains of the gods or humans.

These considerations call into question Giegerich's admonition that "Every reader's task is to be Thor and to try with all his might to lift what at first appears to be an ordinary cat and experience the incredible weight holding it down." The problem is that Thor does not become aware of his situation until Utgard Loki explains things to him. After three trials—the cat is only the second—he is downcast, agreeing that perhaps he has overestimated his strength. More to the point, not only does he fail to see through the cat to the serpent, but he also fails to see through first Skrymer and then Utgard Loki. Compare this to Actaion, who, "as a true hunter has the capacity of 'seeing through' the empirical stag and through the factual wound to the Hunting Goddess, the Goddess of the untouched wilderness, as the killed stag's inner image."[13] Actaion's ability to "see through," however, is the result of his willingness to engage in the violence of killing the stag. As Giegerich writes, "Without this 'violence,' there would be no successful penetration into the heart of the wilderness and to the Untouched and no facing 'the whole.' The ruthlessness of Artemis' untouched nature and the ruthlessness of the hunter instinct are perfect equivalents."[14] I don't know whether Giegerich has ever read Jon Krakauer's book, *Into the Wild*,[15] or seen the movie, but if anyone has any questions about the real nature of the wilderness, I recommend one or both.

My title is "Returning to the Wilderness: Jung, Giegerich and the infinite task of interiority." I could have put this better as a question: How do we return to the wilderness after Jung and Giegerich? Giegerich begins *Logical Life* with a call for genuine theory in psychology, in some sense commensurate with the sophisticated theorizing that underpins the natural sciences. Such theorizing would move psychology away from the simplistic version Giegerich correctly sees in much of today's psychological discourse. Giegerich's theory has the form of logic, specifically the logic of Hegel. Where Jung is concerned, I would say, theory is finally grounded in the notion—to be Hegelian for a moment—of the archetype-in-itself. My concern regarding Hegel is that he occupies a rather unusual place in the history of philosophy, perhaps equaled only by Plato and Aristotle, in that he seems inescapable after his thinking enters the arena. Every philosopher since Hegel, at least in the European continental tradition, has had to deal with Hegel and usually ends up enveloped in some form of the master's system. Jung, as Giegerich, has masterfully cataloged in the essays Greg Mogenson collected in volume VI of the English papers, as well as elsewhere, resists the embrace of Hegel in what Giegerich characterizes in one paper as "Jung's betrayal of his truth."[16] Strong words!

Another moment of autobiography. My original field of study was Buddhist philosophy, beginning as an undergraduate and continuing for one year of graduate study before active duty in the Air Force. Shortly before leaving Yale, I picked up Paul Ricoeur's monumental *Freud and Philosophy*[17] and read it through while also learning the intricacies of nuclear weapons design and the attendant strategies that go with them. Ricoeur's book changed my life, and upon returning to Yale, I soon found myself taking up the work that would lead to *Jung's Struggle with Freud*. I bring this up here because Ricoeur's reading of Freud is shaped in many ways by his engagement with Hegel's system as a hermeneutical guide. It would seem if we put Giegerich and Ricoeur together that Hegel is the universal solvent for psychoanalysis in all its forms. Under the rule of Hegel's logic, does Jung become Freud and vice versa, or do they both turn into "Hegelians" like so many before them?

I have not gone through all of Giegerich's commentaries on Jung and Hegel, but there are enough places that point to Giegerich's sense that Jung was put off by Hegel for more personal than systematic reasons—not unlike his disdain for Heidegger, who he also compared to a psychotic patient—that Giegerich views Jung's response as a missed opportunity on Jung's part. I hope to go through more of this material and revise this characterization. But at this point, I want to suggest a different framework for Jung's response to Hegel, one based on his experience with Freud, which will return us to the question of entry into the wilderness.

In *Jung's Struggle*,[18] I argued that Freud's system was encompassing in ways that made it impossible to extricate oneself from the hermeneutical enclosure of psychoanalysis, its Midgard, as defined by Freud. The most conspicuous form of this enclosure was Freud's often repeated claim that the objections of his critics only proved the truth of his position because criticism was a manifestation of resistance, which was accounted for by the theory. This is a mode of argument that the philosopher, Hans Blumenberg, has referred to as a paratheory, an element within a larger theory that is intended to turn criticism of the theory into a proof for the accuracy of the theory. As Blumenberg writes in his monumental *The Genesis of the Copernican Revolution*:

> The advantages of such a paratheory are of incomparable value rhetorically (or, many people would like to say here, "strategically"): Internally, it protects one from doubts, and externally it destroys the resistance, by categorizing assent to the theory as a symptom of rationality and inner freedom, as an ethical accomplishment, and putting the reasons for resistance to it beyond the pale, as extratheoretical and scientifically and morally indefensible.[19]

In *Jung's Struggle with Freud*, I constructed a similar argument from the specific elements of Freud's theorizing. Regardless of how one specifically formulates the idea, as I put it then, stepping outside the boundaries of psychoanalysis, as defined by Freud, left one without an interpretative framework with which to understand one's psychological status. To put it a bit more dramatically, having once become enmeshed in Freud's system, to leave meant to stand naked in the face of all the unconscious could throw at you. There was safety within Freud's system, albeit at the expense of one's autonomy. In the history of psychoanalysis, Jung was not the first to confront this situation, nor would he be the last. But an argument can be made that he was the most successful in finding a way to establish his ground while remaining in touch with the depths of the unconscious. In moving away from Freud's enchantment, however, Jung would have had to come to terms with the power of all-encompassing systems. Jung may have been a less than exemplary reader of Hegel, but he had an intuition about the totalizing nature of Hegel's system, something he had encountered in Freud, that put up warning signs of the risk of enclosure. Enclosures, of course, are what farmers built around their buildings and fields, thereby defining the Midgard and demarcating it from the Utgard. Systems invariably define boundaries, and if thinking takes place in Utgard, it is incumbent on the thinker to step outside the enclosure to enter the wilderness of giants and demons, as Jung did after the break with Freud.

Giegerich asks near the beginning of *Logical Life* whether:

> [I]t is feasible that psychology could ignore the tremendous logical complication, differentiation, sophistication that the Western mind has gone through and simply stay intellectually beneath the niveau that has been reached in the Western soul's intellectual development—and truly get away with it? No chance. Psychology has to climb the mental peaks that have been reached, such as the peak, to mention only one example, represented by the logic of Hegel, and slowly learn to settle on those peaks.[20]

By way of conclusion, do we want to settle on those peaks? Is the temptation to find a peak, and build our enclosure, thus demarcating our little Midgard to shield us from the giants and demons, or must we, each time we find ourselves becoming a "stay-at-home," throw the spear and risk venturing down the mountain into the wilderness, possibly to climb the next peak? This, I take it, is the infinite task of interiority—to return to the wilderness when theory turns into domesticity. My earlier hesitations regarding Giegerich, if not Hegel, have abated while preparing for this conference, and I look forward to going deeper into the wilderness with Giegerich to learn more thereby, beginning with the papers we will hear in the next few days.

Notes

1 This paper was presented at the annual ISPDI conference, "The Soul's Logical Life," July 8–11, 2021.
2 Wolfgang Giegerich, "The Invention of Explosive Power Ad the Blueprint of the Bomb: A Chapter in the Pre-History of Our Nuclear Predicament," in *Spring: A Journal of Archetype and Culture* (Dallas, TX: Spring Publications, 1988), 1–14.

3 Wolfgang Giegerich, "The Psychologist as Repentence Preacher and Revivalist: Robert Romanyshyn on the Melting of the Polar Ice" in *Spring: A Journal of Archetype and Culture* 82 (Dallas, TX: Spring Publication, 2009), 193–221.

4 Robert Romanyshyn, "The Melting Polar Ice: Revisiting Technology as Symptom and Dream," in *Spring: A Journal of Archetype and Culture* (Dallas, TX: Spring Publication, 2008), 79–116.

5 Warren Colman, "Synchronicity and the Meaning-Making Psyche" in *Journal of Analytica Psychology* 56 (2011): 471–91; Warren Colman. "Reply to Wolfgang Giegerich's 'a Serious Misunderstanding: Synchronicity and the Generation of Meaning'." *Journal of Analytical Psychology* 57, no. 4 (2012): 512–16; Wolfgang Giegerich. "A Serious Misunderstanding: Synchronicity and the Generation of Meaning." *Journal of Analytical Psychology* 57, no. 4 (2012): 500–11; discussion 512; Wolfgang Giegerich. "Two Jungs. Apropos a Paper by Mark Saban." *Journal of Analytical Psychology* 60, no. 3 (2015): 303–15; Stanton Marlan. "The Philosophers' Stone as Chaosmos: The Self and the Dilemma of Diversity." *Jung Journal* 7, no. 2 (2013): 10–23; Stanton Marlan. "The Psychologist Who Is Not a Psychologist: A Deconstructive Reading of Wolfgang Giegerich's Idea of Psychology Proper." *Journal of Analytical Psychology* 61, no. 2 (2016): 223–38.; Mark Saban. "Some Reflections on Barreto's Response." *Journal of Analytical Psychology* 60, no. 1 (2015): 122–25.; Mark Saban. "Two in One or One in Two? Pushing Off from Jung With Wolfgang Giegerich." *Journal of Analytical Psychology* 60, no. 5 (2015): 679–97.

6 Wolfgang Giegerich, *The Soul's Logical Life: Towards a Rigorous Notion of Psychology* (Frankfort am Main: Peter Lang Publishing, 1998).

7 Wolfgang Giegerich, *What Is Soul?* (New Orleans: Spring Journal Books, 2020).

8 David Miller, "Introduction." in *Dialectics & Analytical Psychology*, edited by G Mogenson (New Orleans: Spring Journal Books, 2005), vii–xxi.

9 Giegerich, *The Soul's Logical Life*, 57.

10 Snorri Sturluson, *The Prose Edda* (New York: Penguin, 2005), 53–56.

11 Giegerich, *The Soul's Logical Life*, 233.

12 Giegerich, *The Soul's Logical Life*, 117.

13 Giegerich, *The Soul's Logical Life*, 236.

14 Giegerich, *The Soul's Logical Life*, 237.

15 Jon Krakauer, *Into the Wild* (New York Villard, 1996).

16 Wolfgang Giegerich, *Dreaming the Myth Onwards C. G. Jung on Christianity and on Hegel Part 2 of the Flight into the Unconscious* (New Orleans: Spring Journal Books. 2013), 289

17 Paul Ricoeur, *Freud and Philosophy: An Essay on Interpretation*. Translated by D Savage. (New Haven: Yale University Press, 1970).

18 George Hogenson, *Jung's Struggle with Freud* (Wilmette: Chiron Publications, 1994), 29.

19 Hans Blumenberg, *The Genesis of the Copernican World* (Cambridge: MIT Press, 1987), 657.

20 Geigerich, *The Soul's Logical Life*, 29

Chapter 5

Mandamin "Food of Wonder"

Peter White

Mandamin is a story in *Ojibway Heritage* by Anishnaabe author Basil John-ston. It is one of a group and he introduces it by saying, "There is another tale entitled "Corn" that is no less striking. But the story is not really about corn or its origins."[1] Though of course he doesn't use such terminology, Johnston with these words presents what we in psychology as the discipline of interiority (hereafter referred to as PDI), call "the psychological difference," the differ-ence between man and soul or the empirical and logical life. Johnston is letting us know that this is a soul matter we are delving into and that the Western scientific perspective that prevails all around him will fail to reach its meaning. He then makes this difference explicit, saying that one of the story's themes is, "… the continuation of life in a new form in the Land of the Living after death."[2] Here we can see a dividing line appear between Johnston's and psy-chology's style or method of interpretation. For the author, the corn myth is allegorical of the literal afterlife whereas for PDI it is allegorical of logical negativity, a phrase that will remain without meaning until the end of our dis-cussion when the story and all of its internal complexities have come to light. And while we can see connections between the author's commentary and psy-chology, it is important to make clear that our discussion will make no claim as to the story's meaning for traditional Anishnaabe. Having determined that the Anishnaabe perspective is outside our task of a psychological interpretation, a return to the psychological difference will underscore the contrast between the "man" and "soul" perspectives. On the "man" or "human" side, interpretations of phenomena are produced by reasoning causes and effects in a reality where up is up and down is down. On the soul side, the side where psychology finds its task, reality is inverted; it is a perspective where up actually *is* down, where opposites are shown to share an identity with each other, and where negations mark the path to a most strange corn plant, a corn plant that is not a corn plant, but a figuration of the soul's logical life.

I will begin with a summary of the myth:

An orphan by the name of Zhowmin or "grape" was raised by his grand-mother Zhaw-b'noh-quae and it was she who gave him his spiritual educa-tion by him telling stories that evoked characteristics such as patience and

DOI: 10.4324/9781003381150-6

courage and principles such as, "always be thankful for what you have," and "someday do something for your people." Shortly before she died, Zhaw-b'noh-quae said to Zhowmin, "One day, a stranger will come. Do what he says." Soon after her death, a surly, petulant stranger arrived at the village inquiring as to whether there was one good man among the people there. The elders selected Zhowmin, and because he and the stranger were of the same totem, the youth was bound by tradition to treat him as a brother and provide hospitality of food and tobacco. Only after they ate and smoked did Zhowmin ask the stranger the purpose of his visit, and the latter replied, "I have been sent to find a good man ... I hope for your sake and for the good of your people that you are a good man." Angrily, Zhowmin demanded that the stranger identify himself, and so he did, saying, "I am Mandamin, (food of wonder), sent by the great spirit Kitche Manitou ... Zhowmin! You must fight me to prove your merit. If you win, you live; if you lose, you die." When Zhowmin rejected the challenge, Mandamin said, "If you do not wish to fight me, I will take your refusal as cowardice. Cowardice is tantamount to defeat. In either case, there is death, and it matters little whether you refuse or accept the challenge." Remembering his grandmother's words and with the reputation of his people put in question, Zhowmin agreed to fight. For three nights, they fought from dusk until dawn, neither one able to get an advantage over the other. During each day, they slept and ate together as if there were no enmity between them. Finally, at the end of the third night, Zhowmin saw his opportunity and, after striking Mandamin with his war club, he stabbed him in the back, killing him. After the death, Zhowmin felt remorse and, after weeping and singing a song in his honour, buried the stranger next to his grandmother. He then went to a medicine man who instructed him, saying, "Look after Mandamin's grave just as you would your grandmother's." After some time, a strange new plant appeared that neither Zhowmin nor the village medicine man had ever seen before. The medicine man took and ate a kernel of the corn, saying, "It is sweet; it is good." The medicine man continued, saying the plant was Mandamin, food of wonder; that Zhowmin had done a great service for his people; that the youth had not killed Mandamin but given him life in a new form and that by his death, the Anishnabeg were given life.

Zhowmin the Boy

Zhowmin is not an ordinary boy. His identity with the spirit messenger Mandamin is evident in the correspondence of his name, which means "grape," and the word "meen" meaning seed or berry, from the word Mandamin.[3] Also, his status as an orphan suggests that he is marked from birth for a unique soul purpose. His lack of earthly parents suggests that his true parent is Kitche Manitou, the great spirit. At seven, Zhowmin reaches the age for education. In the practical matters of hunting, fishing, and being a good warrior, he is taught by the men while his grandmother Zhaw-b'noh-quae provides his spiritual education and in her teachings, she is the voice of his spiritual father Kitche Manitou. We begin to see that Zhowmin, rather than just being another boy in the village, is different. In fact, he is not a person at all in the individualistic sense. He is the aspect of human-ness that can and must expose itself to the soul and prove its devotion through a violent battle, becoming the lightning rod of contact between the positivity of ordinary human existence and the negativity, the logically real and empirically un-real soul.

Regarding Zhowmin's spiritual education, we are told that, for his grandmother Zhaw-b'noh-quae, "... the good life was not less important than the practical." For the Anishnaabe, the phrase *mino bimaadiziwin* or "the good life" is a stance toward life that is centered in respect, gratitude, and the mutual helping and sharing that was the natural consequence of traditional activities like moose hunting or making maple sugar. In "the good life," the individual knows and affirms that his value and worth are in the community and are not in himself as an individual.[4] Zhowmin is an enthusiastic devotee of "the good life," of being the very definition of the values and principles taught by Zhaw-b'noh-quae, lessons such as "Always tell the truth"; "always be thankful for your powers, great and small"; "seek peace"; "listen to your elders and you will learn something"; and "someday do something for your people." These are all principles and, in light of the soul moment at the heart of this story, principles are what we might call "dead soul," soul food to be sure but not at all the point of contact between soul and human, the event conveyed later in the story. We might even call these principles "harvested soul," in that they have resulted from the immanent critique of reflection that the image of harvested corn is allegorical of. It is a source of nourishment for the maintaining of one's knowledge of the soul to be sure, but nothing like the murderous planting that created them.

Zhowmin the Man

The birth of Zhowmin's manhood signals the death of Zhaw-b'noh-quae, or to say it psychologically, the arrival of Zhowmin's manhood *is* the death of Zhaw-b'noh-quae, though the narrative is not quite so explicit. The story tells us there is a boy who grows to manhood and a grandmother who happens to die at that time. Viewing this narration from the standpoint of PDI invites us to see not two events here but one. Zhaw-b'noh-quae is the spiritual aspect of Zhowmin in the first stage or determination of what Zhowmin is. As soon as the next determination presents itself, she simply no longer exists. Here we have a reminder of the interpretive principle that characters in myth are nothing more than the personified essence of their role. In *The Soul's Logical Life*, Giegerich explains this in his description of Actaion as the hunter:

> Actaion is not, as he would be in ordinary reality, first of all a human being, who then among many other things also likes to go hunting now and then. If we thought so, we would still be *imagining* Actaion rather than

thinking him. The characters in myth live in the realm of "pre-existence." Therefore, the separation between existence and essence which character-izes our ordinary reality does not apply.... The figures of myth are totally subjected to their essence, and their behavior as described in myth is their only raison d'être.[5]

When Zhowmin reaches manhood, Zhaw-b'noh-quae cannot retire and have a nice life among friends and relations, experiencing the respect given to elders that is such a prominent feature of Anishnaabe culture still today. She is solely an archetypal figure, an archetypal role, and when that is complete, she no longer exists. Zhaw-b'noh-quae is, and is only, the manifestation of the soul as teacher. As such, she has been Zhowmin's *external* experience of the realness of the soul, relating it to him through the picture-language of stories filled with the images of his everyday reality. The arrival of his manhood, which heralds his interiorization of the realness of the soul, is her death. This is the logic on the soul side of the psychological difference we mentioned earlier. On the human side, where up is up and down is down, Zhowmin's reaching manhood and Zhaw-b'noh-quae's death would simply be a predictable coincidence; to see a link between them would be illogical. On the soul side, the identity of these characters and events is the very essence of its logic. The point of seeing the identity in opposites does not have the purpose of just being contrary to traditional reasoning, nor is it an attempt to be mysteriously esoteric, but rather it is essential to comprehending the narrative as the unfolding of a single notion or concept whose separate parts or "moments" are all interrelated and even identical with each other. The notion at the heart of this myth is: The simultaneity or mutual mediation of the soul's desire to become real in this world and its devotee's coming of age. The devotee, meanwhile, is not to be understood as an individual person but as man in his role as the vessel of soul.

The Identity of Zhowmin and the Stranger

Zhaw-b'noh-quae announces the next determination or unfolding of what Zhowmin is when she says, "After I leave, a stranger will come to you. Do what he says."[6] In this statement we have another instance of the logical identity of that which is narratively separated, in that, in her foreknowledge of the arrival of Mandamin, Zhaw-b'noh-quae reveals her identity with him. Here we have an example of the tautological presupposition of myth interpretation that Giegerich introduced in *The Soul's Logical Life*:

The temporal element in the story with its succession of events is due merely to the narrative *medium*. A story cannot say everything at once, it has to go through its truth discursively, one aspect after another. In the "message," i.e., in the single archetypal, psychological or logical moment described here, everything is "simultaneous" and all parts of the story tautologically talk only about strictly the same situation, one and the same truth.[7]

In the first part of the story, Zhaw-b'noh-quae exists as the spiritual aspect of Zhowmin and with the arrival of his manhood, Mandamin is now that same aspect. In this next determination, however, the experience of soul for Zhowmin has gone from corporeal to incorporeal, from the earthly figure of his grandmother to a spirit being, or expressed psychologically, from the positivity of the empirical world to the negativity of the soul.

By linking herself to the stranger, and thus the further determination of Zhowmin's spiritual aspect, Zhaw-b'noh-quae identified Mandamin as Zhowmin's own Other, the soul aspect of him as man. However, even though their identity is indicated by their sharing the same totem, Zhowmin is irritated and thoroughly unimpressed by the stranger.[8] One could be tempted to explain the youth's annoyance as his resistance to transformative change, a very reasonable psychological argument but for the fact that it misses the dialectic at play; that what appears to be a contradiction is a dialectical unity, a unity that contains within itself both unity and difference. The key to Mandamin is that he is the unity of 1) his identity with Zhowmin, as portrayed in Zhaw-b'noh-quae's foreknowledge and their sharing a totem, and 2) his difference from the youth, his utter otherness, as displayed in his temperament being all that Zhowmin is not.

Who and What Is Zhowmin?

Now that Zhowmin has reached manhood we can ask once again who he is. Earlier we noted that, in his name's correlation to the word "meen" of Mandamin and in his status as an orphan, that he was no ordinary boy but one marked for a particular soul task. Having seen his enthusiasm for his grandmother's spiritual teachings we can see that he is the devotee, the student with an especially intense need to fulfill his task of learning. In the text we are told that, "No matter how often Zhowmin heard these principles, he never tired of them. And because they were delivered with love, Zhowmin determined to live by these laws."[9] In this last sentence Johnston, in his translation from Anishnaabe to English, omitted the word "was" that is typically idiomatic for English speakers of this phrase, that is, Zhowmin *was* determined to live by those laws. This, I believe, is no mistake but rather a rendering that is closer to the kind of moment being described. If the phrase had been "Zhowmin was determined," one would interpret it as his decision to really put his shoulder into it and to earnestly do his very best. The phrase, "Zhowmin determined" is different. There is no distance between the noun and the verb, no escape hatch or reservation. There is a finality to it, a sense of total commitment that the word "was," had it been used, would not have conveyed. There is soberness to the phrase. It is not heated with emotion but rather has a certain sense of coldness in its quiet resolve.

The Soul Disguises Itself

When Mandamin appears as the stranger in the village, Zhowmin does not recognize him as the messenger of Kitche Manitou. He does not "clue in" to the likelihood of this stranger being the one his dying grandmother had so recently predicted. The soul in its guise as Mandamin has truly disguised itself. Had Mandamin, when he appeared, evoked the characteristics affirmed in Zhowmin's spiritual education such as, "courage, generosity, fortitude, resourcefulness, patience, endurance and perseverance,"[10] he would have instantly recognized him as identical with himself, a fellow Anishnaabe. Instead, Mandamin is described as surly, petulant, and demanding. He is the negation of mino bimaadiziwin or, "the good life," that Zhowmin has devoted himself to. One is led to ask, "What is the purpose of such a disguise? Would it not make more sense for the messenger of Kitche Manitou to appear as the embodiment of the values celebrated in the stories Zhowmin had heard?"

The answer is that the soul, in its moment of self-renewal, moves forward in the "backward" act of canceling or negating itself. The picture-language of myth is conveying the self-negating nature of interiorization, a self-negating that is also its self-generation, as we will see. Zhowmin's first spiritual teacher was the embodiment of care and love. His second spiritual teacher, the further determination of the devotee, is the inner contradiction of the first. One might say that the attitude presented by Mandamin is the prelude of the negation which continues to build and whose fullness is reached in the killing of the soul as messenger.

What Is At Stake for the "Good Man"

When the stranger reveals himself as Mandamin, food of wonder, he repeats that he is an emissary in search of a good man who will prove his inner worth and strength. Then he says, "Zhowmin! You must fight me to prove your merit. If you win, you live; if you lose, you die."[11] Now the negation that first appeared as the stranger's off-putting manner at their first meeting has intensified. It is the same negation but the challenge has further determined it and made it explicit. With this statement of "good man," any remainders of the moral sense of the word "good" fall away and the self-contradictory language of myth comes to the fore, presenting a very different notion of what it means in the myth of Mandamin. The proof of a "good man" here is that he can fight the messenger of the god and kill him. Blood has to be spilled. There has to be death for the negativity of the soul to become real. The soul's realization of itself is a negation of life, not in the sense of literal death but in the sense of a reconstitution of the logic of consciousness which is nevertheless a very real death. We may note that the deed demanded seems to bear no relation to the lessons from the stories told to Zhowmin by his grandmother. If those lessons are to become real within Zhowmin, a reversal must take place; he must transgress all of them by murdering the god who inspired them. On the "human" side of the psychological difference this does not make sense. A youth, for instance, who has grown up in a strict religious environment who later murders someone is simply a criminal, a good man gone bad. On the "soul" side, killing is not killing but is allegorical. It is "... a concrete visual and emotion-laden *image* for a non-visual, (in a certain sense of the word) 'abstract,' invisible psychological reality."[12] Killing is a transgression, a negation of all that had made reality real. Why is transgression crucial?

> We have to realize that it is the very nature of cognition to be a transgression and violation. But this transgression is not an offense in our moralistic or juridical sense. The word 'transgression' expresses only the shocking, awe-inspiring character of this archetypal moment of the soul's "killing" recognition of itself.[13]

Mandamin's demand for a fight to the death is the indicator of the soul's desire for a new cognition of itself, a re-cognition that is not the passive reception of information but rather the reconstitution of the logic of its knowing.

One Becomes Two

We claimed earlier that Zhaw-b'noh-quae and her teachings represented the first form taken by Zhowmin's spiritual aspect, and it was a human form. Mandamin, the second figuration of his soul aspect, still retains a human form, but is explicitly "not of this world," as his being a messenger from Kitche Manitou shows. Moreover, his name, "food of wonder," is a negation of the anthropological form in which he appears. Mandamin is spirit food, which is to say, thought. By partaking of this food in the transgression of killing, the soul can manifest itself as logical negativity, that is, as the way that Zhowmin thinks the thinking he figures forth, the logic of his people's being-in-the-world.

After Mandamin's declaration of his true identity and purpose there is a back and forth between the two as Zhowmin resists the invitation of his own Other. The situation recalls the following statement by Jung:

> When a summit of life is reached, when the bud unfolds and from the lesser the greater emerges, then as Nietzsche says, 'One becomes Two,' and the greater figure, which one always was but which remained invisible, appears to the lesser personality with the force of a revelation. He who is truly and hopelessly little will always drag the revelation of the greater down to the level of his littleness, and will never understand that the day of judgement for his littleness has dawned. But the man who is inwardly great will know that the long expected friend of his soul, the immortal one, has now really come, 'to lead captivity captive,' that is, to seize hold of him by whom this immortal had always been confined and held prisoner, and to make his life flow into the greater life—a moment of deadliest peril![14]

Zhowmin ultimately rises to the occasion when he recalls his grandmother's words, "After I leave a stranger will come to you. Do what he says," and he accepts the challenge to fight.

Negation As Protecting Distance, Day-world and Night-world

Through his antagonism toward Mandamin, Zhowmin the devotee creates an objective distance between himself and Mandamin. I spoke of Zhowmin earlier as having the task to serve as a lightning rod in the contact between human and soul. The lightning rod, typically placed on the top of tall structures such as barns, was able to absorb the force of the lightning bolt and conduct the energy safely to the ground, negating its destructive power which otherwise would start a fire that would burn up the barn, destroying it. In order to serve as this lighting rod, Zhowmin has to establish a distance, an objectivity vis-a-vis the soul. If there is nothing to relativize or neutralize the contact with soul, the humanness of the human side of the psychological difference is lost and thus the soul as well. This is so because if the human side of the syzygy is not maintained, the soul's desire to make itself real in the world, expressed in the story as the search for "a good man," is undone. The narrative pictures this protecting objective distance in Zhowmin's antagonism.

In this archetypal moment of the soul's logical life, the moment of making itself real in this world, the soul as human must not be destroyed. By contrast, in the Greek myth of Semele, discussed by Giegerich in *Dialectics and Analytical Psychology*, she as the human figure is completely consumed in her contact with Zeus, the lightning bolt. Giegerich explains that, "If the soul wants to portray its own need of absolute devotedness and self-abandonment to itself as its other, it chooses a feminine figure."[15] With its masculine warring brothers, the myth of Mandamin demonstrates the moment of devotion where two animus figures perfectly negate each other. As Mandamin, the soul is negating itself as the current logical form of human consciousness. Zhowmin, as human consciousness, is negating the killing reconstitution of itself. And so it goes in the story as Zhowmin and Mandamin begin to fight:

> Equal in determination and strength they fought on equal terms; wrestling, punching, pounding, and twisting in order to gain advantage. One moment Zhowmin would knock Mandamin to the ground; the next, Mandamin would hurl Zhowmin to the earth. So the battle went all night until both warriors fell exhausted to the soil.[16]

In the battle, Zhowmin and Mandamin are both "lightning rods," neutralizing each other. Every attempt to perform the negation of killing by one is met by an equal response from the other. Despite being in the night-world of the soul, Zhowmin is able to maintain himself and despite being in his own realm, Mandamin is unable to kill. Here we see the soul's interiorization into itself as the identity of identity and difference. Mandamin and Zhowmin, soul and man, who were earlier shown to be identical as totem brothers, are here one in their passionate commitment to negate each other. And yet their difference is sharply drawn as earthly and divine, human and spirit, man and soul. Each of them constitutes the existence of the other. At the end of each of the three nights of battle, the day-world returns where there is no animosity between them and they eat and smoke together as brothers.

At the end of the third night, at the moment when the night-world and the day-world meet together, the negation that has been made more explicit with each further determination finds itself in the hand of Zhowmin as he plunges his knife into Mandamin's back. And yet in another sense, the negation via the kill already took place in the moment of Zhowmin's agreement to fight Mandamin, and the three nights of battle could be interpreted as the imaginal portrayal of the wound itself seen from within. This, of course, follows the approach that Giegerich presented in his interpretation of the myth of Actaion, where he contrasts a psychological interpretation of the pond in which Artemis is beheld by the hunter with the rendering by the Roman poet whose version was the source for the analysis:

> ... OVID's idyllic 'familiar pond' must not be imagined as a literal pond situated somewhere out in the forest, separate from the killed quarry; it *is* the deadly wound. In the bleeding wound the tall Goddess and her nymphs have their epiphany or revelation, which is pictorially portrayed in our story as their bathing in the nude in the pond.[17]

There the goddess represented Actaion's encounter with the naked truth and the hunter's fate of being torn to pieces by his own dogs as a picturing of the real negative violence of the cognition of truth where the logic of one's being is dismembered and reconstituted in a new form. What, then, might we find in this wound with its perfectly matched adversaries of man and soul, where the devotee's only way to prove his worth and "goodness" is to kill his own spiritual aspect, the spirit that had inspired the devotion that brought him to this moment? The conclusion is: Devotion is murder. True devotion is the absolute cognition of the object of one's worship. The object is utterly destroyed but the moment of its destruction is simultaneously the full flowering of the object *as* the internal nature of the subject.

The Sacrifice

The soul does not want to be observed with reverence or taken as a model of proper principles but wants to be known in its truth, a moment that is its own death, where death is the realization of itself as thought. In his paper, "Killings," Giegerich describes the ritual of big game hunting as the origin of soul, the moment where man was able to experience the absolute negativity of death in life, having become identical with his prey in the thrust of the spear. The complex interrelationship between hunting, sacrifice and myth is captured in the following statement:

> We also know that for the early hunter the hunted *animal*, too, was not biological animal, mere meat supply, but man's close relative, his "brother" or "father," indeed, the god. What does it mean that the hunter sees in the hunted animal his brother or father? *In the hunted or immolated animal man knows himself.* Via his killing the animal (or a human, in the case of human sacrifices), man gained his initial self-knowledge, his first awareness of himself, a self-knowledge that would later *articulate* itself in his images and stories of gods.[18]

In "Mandamin" the god in effect offers himself in sacrifice in order to become a new life-source for the Anishnaabe: Corn, if we take the narrative literally, or a new logical form of consciousness if we read the images allegorically. And through this act of devotion, the soul's death in the form of the spirit messenger Mandamin, the soul is made real in the world. This is because in the moment of real contact between the soul as human and the soul as god, a moment perfectly pictured in the struggle between life and death, the god Mandamin who had existed until then as an object appearing external to Zhowmin is interiorized into him. And in this moment Zhowmin too is "killed" as the form or logic of his thinking is sublated, giving way to a new form of knowing where the object of his devotion has become the nature of his own thinking and being. Such a transformation cannot be pictured and yet in the tale of Mandamin it must be because the image is the only means by which myth can convey the non-existing reality of the negativity of the soul.

In this story, the negation of Mandamin is itself negated by the appearance of the corn plant. The earth in which Mandamin is planted, meanwhile, is allegorically Zhowmin himself, and the interiorization of the soul is pictured in the corn plant, the "food of wonder" that requires his constant care and attention to be a reality in this world. This determination that cancels the death of Mandamin is what Giegerich, drawing upon Hegelian terms, calls the negation of the negation, a moment in the soul's self-relation, also called sublation, where what has been negated is rescued and continues to have a role within a new form of consciousness or thinking. A contemporary example of this would be our own psychological method which negates the images of myth as being archetypal "entities" but then negates its negation of those same images by interiorizing them into themselves such that they form the framework for thinking them as both the identity of themselves and the identity of themselves *and* their opposite. This is psychology's "food of wonder."

The Logical Kill

Despite not being able to complete the task of the kill after a short battle, Zhowmin and Mandamin do not give up but fight on and on and on. In this way the notion of killing is applied to itself as the negation of the kill is itself negated. If the killing was completed in the moment that Mandamin and Zhowmin started to fight, the soul level in which the victim is offering himself up as sacrifice in the fatal blow would not be reached. It would be a positive killing appropriate to a murder mystery or thriller movie, an imitation of the positive killings that happen each day on battlefields or in street violence. The soul killing has to be a logical one, where the death is of the logical constitution of consciousness, one's way of being-in-the-world. The negation of the "positive" kill in the battle lasting for three nights is what makes the knife blow finally thrust into Mandamin a logical killing. The reconstitution of Zhowmin's consciousness that is pictured in the rising of the corn plant, even though it is narratively separated as happening later in time, is really simultaneous with the wound inflicted on Mandamin. The bleeding out of Mandamin is the influx of soul into the consciousness of Zhowmin and thus the fulfillment of the devotee's task of making the soul real in this world. Each constitutes the other and each *is* the other even as their difference is maintained. The moment of contact between soul and human is the identity of the identity and difference of 1) Mandamin as the dying god and 2) the "food of wonder" growing up and into the consciousness of Zhowmin. In short, it is the identity of the identity and difference of soul and human.

The Soul Catches Up with Itself

The indicator that Zhowmin's task was successful is shown narratively in his genuine surprise at the corn plant that emerges from the grave of Mandamin. The images of the myth here display what Giegerich calls absolute-negative interiorization, a moment where what has been there all along suddenly "dawns on you, 'comes home' to you, reconstitutes your own mind. *My* catching up with *it* means *its* imperceptibly catching up with *me*, but as if from behind or *from within* myself. It means my being contaminated with or infected by it."[19] The moment of Zhowmin's knife blow is the moment of Zhowmin's "contamination" or "infection" and its result is pictured in the "food of wonder." Finally, what we have in the summation of the myth of Mandamin and all of its moments is one definition of the indecipherable phrase presented at the beginning of our journey together, logical negativity.

Notes

1 Basil Johnston, *Ojibway Heritage: The Ceremonies, Rituals, Songs, Dances, Prayers and Legends of the Ojibway* (Toronto: McClelland and Stewart, 1976), 34.
2 Johnston, *Ojibway Heritage*, 34.

3 Johnston, *Ojibway Heritage*, 34.
4 Animikiibineshiins, (Traditional Knowledge Keeper), in discussion with the author, July 2020.
5 Wolfgang Giegerich, *The Soul's Logical Life: Towards a Rigorous Notion of Psychology* (Frankfurt am Main: Peter Lang, 1998), 232–233.
6 Basil Johnston, *Ojibway Heritage*, 35.
7 Giegerich, *The Soul's Logical Life*, 120.
8 Some explanation of the totem or clan system in Anishnaabe culture is helpful to understanding the kind of identity that is being conveyed between Zhowmin and Mandamin. Johnston explains: "Each function in the Ojibway schemata of society, government, defense, provision of necessities, education, and medical practice, was discharged by a social unit whose members were born into the unit and especially trained. Each social unit represented one form or aspect of public duty which was symbolized by an emblem, known as a totem. The totem was probably the most important social unity taking precedence over the tribe, community and the immediate family…. Men and women preferred to regard themselves as members of a totem and then a community. Strangers, when they met, always asked one another, 'Waenash k'dodaem?' (What is your totem?); only afterwards did they ask, 'Waenaesh keen?' (Who are you?)" (Basil Johnston, *Ojibway Heritage*, 59). What is most important for our present discussion is that members of the same totem were considered blood relatives, regardless of their not all being genetically related. The seriousness with which this tradition was taken can be seen in the fact that marriage between members of the same totem was considered incest and strictly forbidden.
9 Johnston, *Ojibway Heritage*, 35.
10 Johnston, *Ojibway Heritage*, 35.
11 Johnston, *Ojibway Heritage*, 35.
12 Giegerich, *The Soul's Logical Life*, 109.
13 Giegerich, *The Soul's Logical Life*, 248.
14 C. G. Jung, *The Archetypes and the Collective Unconscious*, CW 9i: 217.
15 Wolfgang Giegerich, David L. Miller and Greg Mogenson, *Dialectics and Analytical Psychology*, 29.
16 Johnston, *Ojibway Heritage*, 36.
17 Giegerich, *The Soul's Logical Life*, 234.
18 Wolfgang Giegerich, "Killings," in *Soul Violence, Collected English Papers. Vol. 3* (New Orleans: Spring Journal Books, 2008), 201.
19 Giegerich, *The Soul's Logical Life*, 147.

Chapter 6

The Difficulty of Encountering One's Own Other in a Clinical Case of a Young Adult in Japan

Nanae Takenaka

Young Adults Today in Japan and the Non-attendance of University Students

It has been one of the biggest concerns in Japanese universities that there are some students who do not get credits and postpone their graduation for years, without doing anything in particular. The first report on this type of student can be identified with what Paul A. Walters, an American psychologist, named as "Student Apathy" in 1961.[1] In Japan, it also began to be reported in the 1960s.[2] Although it was not discussed further in the United States, it continues to draw attention in Japan until today, where the number of this type of student has constantly been increasing.[3] In this chapter, a clinical case of a student who stayed in university for eight years without attending classes will be introduced and the psychology of this type of student will be discussed further.

First, I would like to explain the actual situation that surrounds Japanese young adults, especially university students today. One of the features of Japanese society is that the straightforward career course weighs the most. Today, more than half of eighteen-year-olds who graduate from high school straightly enter universities. After they enter university, in the first and second year they often have enough time to enjoy their student life with club activities, part-time jobs, or the like. Being expected to graduate at the end of their fourth year, they begin their job hunting in the third year. The belief that students should start to work as a full-time employee right after their graduation is so common in Japanese society that the students in the third and the last year are put under the enormous stress of finding a job for themselves. If one fails job hunting in the third or the last year, his or her opportunity to start their career as a full-time worker becomes very limited. Moreover, it is expected that they stay with the company they choose until their retirement. Every year in winter, when the companies all at once begin their recruitment processes for future graduates, we find on campuses the students who have recently dyed their hair back to their original black—of which before they might have had in their favorite colors—and are wearing plain black uniform-like suits for job interviews.

DOI: 10.4324/9781003381150-7

In general, for job hunting in Japan, students should erase their individuality as much as possible. Companies tend to look for the fresh, obedient generalists.

In contrast to the uniformity and restlessness that surround Japanese university students, the non-attendant students stand out. While most students try very hard to catch up with the rapid flow from their entrance toward graduation, those students of non-attendance somehow stop participating in the flow. They often stay awake till midnight or early morning, browsing social networking services (SNS) or the internet on their smartphones or playing video games. It is common that non-attendant students keep their social activities such as part-time jobs, club activities, or hanging out with friends. However, they often do not have close friends. It can be said that the non-attendant students are psychologically isolated from society.

As a psychotherapist at the student counseling office, I have been working with a relative number of students who do not attend classes for more than months. Most of them started to come to us because their parents or their supervisors pushed them to do so. They are often very inexperienced at talking with others, especially about themselves. Of course, there are talkative ones, but I have rarely heard their introspective thoughts about their non-attendance. In general, I can point out that they have difficulties facing the situation they have set up by themselves, having a sense of urgency to do something about it, and thinking through their own lives. While the triggers of their non-attendance may vary, they give me exactly the same reason for their non-attendance: they say that they are demotivated because they do not know what they want to do in the future. Nevertheless, I always have difficulty being fully convinced by it. The students who have difficulties with their job hunting also say that they do not know what they want to do in society, but they are actually looking for something ideal for themselves though unsuccessfully. Even if it is true that the non-attendant students do not know what they want to do in the future, there must be other reasons why they cannot fulfill their tasks here and now. I have been attempting to find a more convincing explanation for the non-attendance from a psychological point of view. With the word "explanation," I do not mean something like that this personality correlates with the phenomenon, or that these students tend to have a strong tie with their mother, and so on. I am not looking for explanations from outside the phenomenon. My interest lies in what the psyche is expressing by the non-attendance. In order to understand that, I need to get into the phenomenon and gain an explanation from within.

Attitude Toward Dreams

In this chapter, I would like to examine the dreams reported by one of my patients, whom for the purposes of this chapter will be referred to as Dan. As I will explain more in detail, he had not regularly attended classes for four years. Trying to understand his dreams, this chapter aims at exploring what the psyche of the Japanese young adult experiences today. Before stepping forward into the case description, I would like to clarify my attitude toward dreams briefly.

To begin with, quotations from Jung's later works, on which Wolfgang Giegerich puts great importance, need to be introduced.

> In myths and fairytales, as in dreams, the psyche tells its own story, and the interplay of the archetypes is revealed in its natural setting as "formation, transformation / the eternal Mind's eternal recreation."[4]
>
> Above all, don't let anything from outside, that does not belong, get into it, for the fantasy-image has "everything it needs."[5]

First of all, we need to make it clear that the dream is *not* about the dreamer. Because the dream-I in each dream is a construction of the soul, we cannot take it as being identical with the dreamer. This means that the personal association about the dream or the dream elements should not be considered as essential for the dream interpretation. On the contrary, it can be even erroneous, because it could easily lead us to the *too personalistic* way of working with dreams. The dream does not belong to the dreamer. He or she is nothing but *the medium*, through which the soul expresses itself. For the *psychological* attitude toward the dream, we can never forget that "the dream exists for its own sake".[6]

The dream interpretation is, thus, to make the soul's speaking about oneself more accessible for us. Giegerich says,

> In the course of one's patient, step-by-step, word-for-word immersion into a dream, the dream's own teleology, its spirit, or the logical life that it is, as well as its imaginal content and substance, slowly take over.[7]

In this chapter, I would like to try to see the soul's logical movement within each dream Dan has reported, hoping that the work will "let the dreams—indirectly, unintendedly—reflect the psychology of the patient",[8] and moreover, the psychology of the contemporary young adult in Japan.

Case Description

Dan was a twenty-three-year-old male student who studied at a college of science when we first met. He lived by himself, financially supported by his parents. He came in to talk just before starting his sixth academic year. Although he had no problems acquiring credits during his first academic year, after entering his second year, he gradually began to miss classes. From his second year, he acquired zero credits. He would attend classes at the very beginning of the semesters, yet always would start missing classes before a month went by. Even though he would continually attend laboratory classes and the like, so as not to cause trouble for groupmates, he would not get course credit due to not handing in reports.

During the week, while he was not attending classes, he came to campus around noontime, showed up in his music club, took his meal in the school cafeterias and such. During nights and evenings, he continued the part-time job that he began in his first academic year. There were times he joined his fellow club members out when they called on him, but he did not talk much to anyone about his situation and had no true close friends. At home, he mostly watched animation videos or played smartphone games.

He was continually evasive with his parents about his situation, though he had eventually come to end of his allowed number of academic years[9] and the pressure from his parents had been mounting. On the suggestion of his parents, he came to my student counseling office. Upon talking about his situation, he had difficulty conveying his sense of urgency. He said, "I don't feel as though I can graduate. I'm thinking of just dropping out." However, he did not seem to have any kind of concrete plans for his future.

There was no apparent sign that he had any kind of developmental or mental problems, though the conversation with him was far from fluent. He seemed to be very inexperienced at talking with others. For every session, he brought a topic to talk about—for which he made much effort—but it was hard for me to maintain and deepen the conversation with him. The topic he brought up was always daily-life–based, for example, what he cooked during the week or what he played in his music club. Moreover, when I asked him questions about his topic, he always seemed to get flustered about the questions. It made me feel uncomfortable and hesitant to talk with him.

While Dan kept coming to the counseling, he started to re-attend classes. Although he thought that things were going well, it turned out that he did not get the credits as he expected at the end of his seventh academic year. This meant that he had to work even harder in his eighth and last year if he wanted to graduate. He began to think of leaving university more seriously. He chose to take a leave of absence for one year. In the first month after he took his leave of absence, he just returned to his former lifestyle, namely, waking up around noon, idling time away, and going out for his club activities and a part-time job. I pushed him to do anything he could. Although he was very reluctant, he talked with a career counselor at the university whom I had introduced to him. She found a small IT company for Dan. He started to work there a few times a week as an intern. Also, he started a new part-time job. Somehow these actions woke him up to reality. While his parents (especially his mother) were of the strong opinion that Dan had to graduate from university, it became clear to Dan that he did not have any motivation for it. After five months of working for the IT company as an intern, he agreed with the company to join as a full-time worker and forgo graduation.

Dreams and Interpretations

He reported sixty-four dreams through our counseling sessions. I would like to take up six of them, focusing upon "the tension between the dream-I and some

Other",[10] of which Giegerich identifies as a common theme of many dreams. I would like to begin with a dream in which we can see a clear clash between the dream-I and the Other.[11]

The Direct Contact with the Other

Dream 11 (Session No. 39)
   My family is going to barbecue in our yard. Strangely, I am completely naked. My mother asks me to get some nori seaweed from our neighbor. I go out without wearing any clothes. The neighbor and an old man on the street see me naked. When I come back home, my mother asks me to wake my brother up. I go upstairs for that. I think I will put on some clothes while I am at it. My mother said that I should wear the pants she has washed, but I refuse them and take different ones. (A long explanation about the conversation with his brother.) I go back downstairs. Food for the barbecue is left at the entrance. A cat comes in. It is a big cat about 80 cm long. It seems to be after the food. I say, "Get away!" and try to shut it out, but it is too slippery. It snitches a piece of salmon. My mother says that cats are so strong that you cannot do anything if you allow them to come in. I go to the back door to check and see if another cat has already gotten in. There is another fairly big cat, about 120 cm in length. Moreover, it is standing on its two hind legs. I slam myself against it and try to kick it out, but it keeps its footing firmly. I say, "You must have already eaten something!" It says, "Are you OK with touching me, such a dirty cat?" and "you can't push me out, it's freezing outside!" I reply, "It's none of my business!" I shut the cat out.

The dream shows the dream-I as a child of his mother. His being naked suggests that he feels completely protected by her. He can even go out without wearing anything. The dream-I seems to be an innocent child who does not have a borderline between inside and outside, who does not know shame or fear yet. He believes in his safety in his environment.

The mother gives the dream-I orders. At first, he obeys his mother, but when he chooses his clothes, he rejects his mother's choice. It seems that with the vertical movement of the dream-I going upstairs, his consciousness changes its level. He gains self-awareness. He is no longer a naked baby. He wears what he wants. He becomes the one who decides his own action.

Then, the cats appear. Cats often represent femininity. It is interesting that right after the dream-I said "No" to his mother, cats as the wilder femininity appear with unordinary large size. They want to steal food, the origin of energy, from the dream-I. Fighting with this cat and the next one makes the dream-I stronger. It is remarkable how seriously the dream-I throws himself into the situation. We see here the one who actively fights for himself and talks with its Other. The real contact with his own Other takes place in this dream. Finally, the dream-I **"shut(s) the cat out."** He makes a clear distinction between inside and outside.

Among all the dreams Dan reported, this is in fact the only one dream in which the face-to-face collision between the dream-I and the Other is observed. Most dreams are rather characterized as *passing by the Other*. The following are three examples of such dreams.

Passing By the Other

Dream 2 (session No. 35)
   I am going up a narrow street at night. Passing by the people going down, I notice that I am also going down. Among those going up the street, I see a person who is wearing a Hannya mask of a female demon on his/her face and has swords in each of his/her hands. Passing each other, I sense this must be a very dangerous person. As expected, I am cut in my back by her. I am almost dying and cannot do anything. There is a group of people that fights with the female demon. At first, they use laser beams, which turn out to be ineffective. Finally, using a magic bomb, they beat the demon.

First, **"a narrow street"** and **"at night"** are mentioned. This may indicate that the consciousness is not fully awake and clear. The consciousness does not have access to wider views. Instead, the dim consciousness at night is able to encounter something which is unknown or uncanny for the daytime consciousness. At first the dream-I is **"going up"**, but seeing other people going down, **"I am also going down"**. The dream-I does not have any direction of his own. He is dependent on others.

Then **"I see a person who is wearing the Hannya mask."** The Hannya mask is used in *Noh*, a traditional Japanese performing art, when a woman gets furious because her lover does not give her enough love back (Figure 6.1). It has to be noted that she is not just angry. Her anger is because of her love. It is so deep as to turn her into a demon. Here appears the femininity characterized by other-worldly passionate love.

The female demon and the dream-I **"pass each other"** at first. The dream-I wants to go by without any complications, but it would not happen like that. Soon after the dream-I passed by her, her anger climaxes and **"I am cut in my back by her."** This may indicate that she is furious because the dream-I has ignored her. It is the dream-I who is expected to appreciate her passion. She is the Other for him. Slashing him in the back is her cry for love.

Then, all of sudden, **"a group of people who fights with the female demon"** appears and **"using a magic bomb, they beat the demon."** Instead of the dream-I, *they* face the demon. Further, the love and the anger the female demon desperately wanted to deliver are forgotten. She turns into just a target for *their* attack. It can be said that the magical power is the child-like resolution for difficulties.

There are feelings of love and hatred and images of killing and cutting in this dream, which imply the intense encounter of the dream-I and the Other.

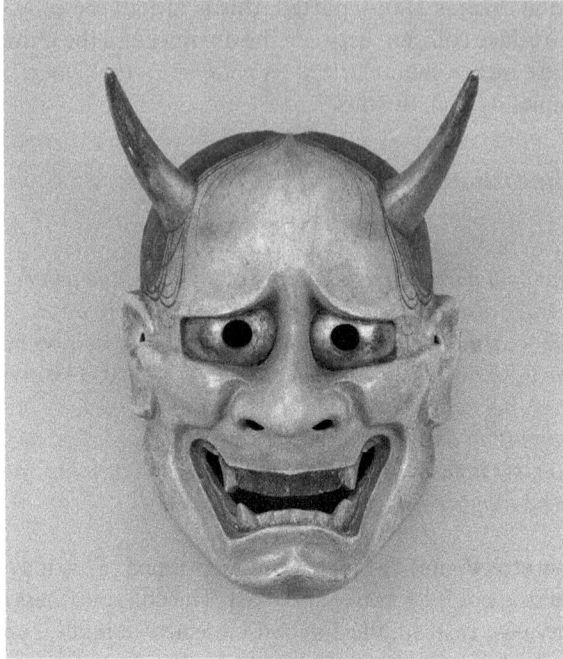

Figure 6.1 Hannya (Noh-Mask).
Source: ColBase (https://colbase.nich.go.jp/collection_items/tnm/C-1554?locale-ja=&locale=jp)

However, the entrance of *they* and their magical power prevents their confrontation. To be more exact, the encounter has happened to the dream-I, when the female demon slashed him. He has been touched by his own Other. But the dream creates a magical flight from what has already happened to the dream-I. The encounter attempted by the female demon remains unrequited.

The next dream I picked up goes as follows:

Dream 27 (session No. 50)
I am being chased on a charge of murder. I left my mother's house and hide myself in an abandoned house. My pursuer finds me and arrests me. I am sentenced to the death penalty and will be executed tomorrow morning at six. Four bullets will be put in my head. If I survive after that, I will be found not guilty and released. Since I still have time till then, I go buy a custard pudding at a store. The TV there is showing the news which reports that a man who was possessed by a monster in his head has just recovered consciousness. Watching this news, it becomes clear to me that the monster will possess me, too. I am certain that when my head is possessed by a monster, it will get strong enough to survive being shot by bullet shots. I feel relieved that I will be found not guilty.

Here again, we see the theme of *a serious encounter has already happened* and *being almost killed, but saved by a magical power.* At the beginning of the dream, it is made clear that the dream-I has already committed a serious crime and "the death penalty" as the Other is chasing the dream-I. It demands his life. Although at first glance, the dream-I accepts what he has done and its result, all of a sudden, a strange idea of **"if I survive after that, I will be found not guilty and released"** comes up. This idea distorts the concept of the death penalty. The death penalty cannot be a game that predicts whether the suspect was guilty or not guilty. Once it is executed, he has to die. The dream-I in this dream *is* a murderer and the penalty *is* the charge for what he has already done. But the seriousness of committing murder has been forgotten. Moreover, the strange idea of **"a monster"** which helps the dream-I appears. The issue is completely replaced from a serious crime and the death penalty to surviving with the help of magical power. The facts that the dream-I is a murderer and that he is about to be killed are going to be canceled.

The last one I chose under the theme of passing by is as follows:

Dream 44 (session No. 55)

Ms. S invites me to a party. I say, "I'm not available on Monday and Tuesday due to my part-time job, but I can come after that if it is not too late." She picks me up by car. I take the passenger seat. We drive down a dark road. I see two deer ahead. Instead of running away, they run towards us. One of the deer passes us. The other one keeps coming straight towards our car. Right before hitting the deer, Ms. S loses control of the wheel, and our car dashes head-on onto a side road. A car comes up from behind and passes by.

(Ms. S is his senior at his club.)

"Ms. S invites me to a party," and after some hesitations, the dream-I accepts the invitation from her. **"She picks me up by car. I take the passenger seat."** Now the dream-I is in a car with the woman. Since a car gives a protected and private space, the closeness between the femininity and the dream-I is observable. Also, the passiveness of the dream-I can be noted. He is invited to the party and he is in the passenger seat. The woman handles the situation. The description that **"we drive down a dark road"** may indicate the uncertainty that the dream-I experiences about his current situation. He does not know to where he is heading. He gives the woman free rein.

Then, **"I see two deer ahead."** The deer is often said to represent death and rebirth because of its antlers. In Japan, there is a well-known image in which a god traveled with a white deer (Figure 6.2). In the Japanese myth, *Kojiki*, the deer also appears as a messenger of God (*Amenokaku*). There is an interpretation that *Amenokaku* might have something to do with swords because the deerskin was used for a bellow in smithing.[12] Taking into consideration that swords can be connected with masculinity, the deer in this dream appears as the opposite of the female driver. Such deer as a messenger of God and masculinity **"runs towards us."** They desperately want to make contact.

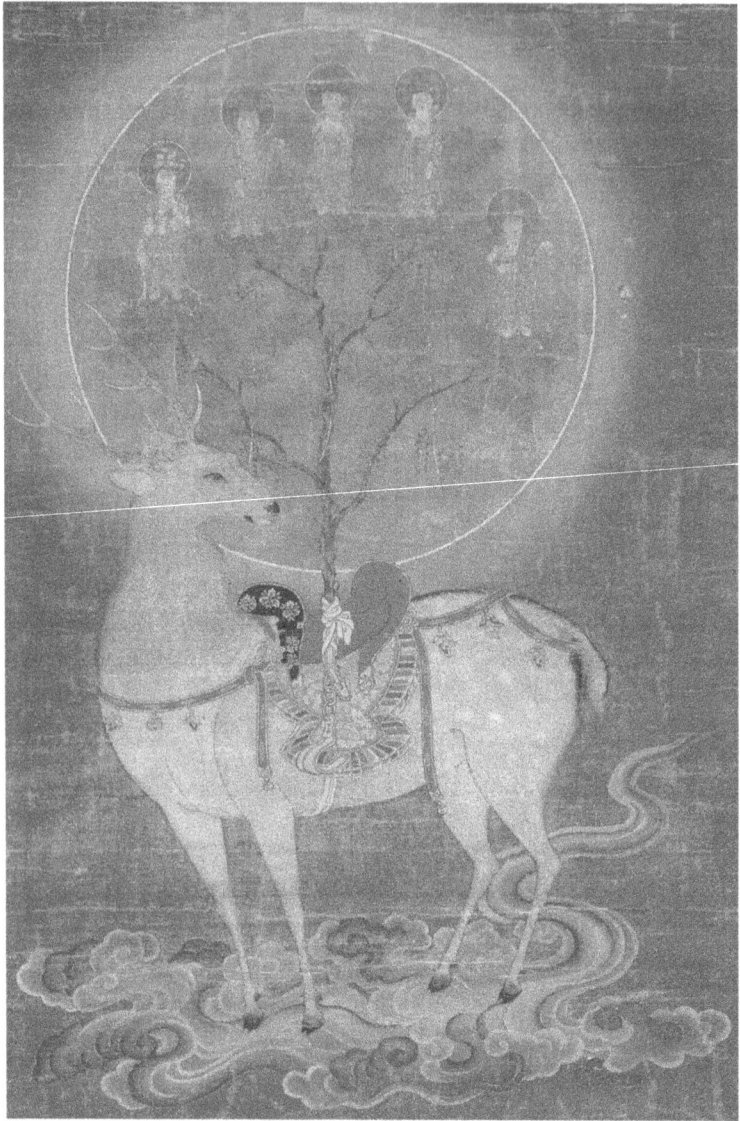

Figure 6.2 Kasuga Deer-Mandala.

Source: ColBase (https://colbase.nich.go.jp/collection_items/tnm/A-11696?locale=ja)

However, a collision between the deer and the car does not take place. The deer sidesteps the car, and so does the woman. It looks as if the original intention of the deer has not been fulfilled in this dream. Then, the dream refers to **"a car comes up from behind and passes by."** Although at first glance it does not seem to be such important information, this remark may suggest that it is *passing by*, rather than a real collision of two, that the dream wants to say. We tend to think that an encounter is how two different elements make a collision, but no matter how strange it may sound, I assume that this dream depicts the encounter as only realized by *passing by*. It could be the way how the dream-I experiences its own Other.

The Commitment through Someone Else

The dreams that Dan reported in the final phase of our counseling process felt somehow new to me. They did not seem to be the dreams of passing by nor the direct contact with the Other. Some of them are examined below.

First, it is a very short, but intense dream.

Dream 52 (session No. 64)
   My younger brother dashes into my apartment, saying that he has killed our parents.

Psychologically, killing one's parents is a very important theme, especially in the case of adolescents and young adults. They are psychologically tasked to go beyond their parents. The killing of parents in the dream shows a big developmental challenge for the psyche.

What draws our attention is that the deed is done by the brother of the dream-I, while the dream-I stays in his own cozy space. The dream-I himself did not know anything. He remains innocent until his brother tells him what has happened. *Through the brother*, the dream-I is involved in the event of killing his parents.

Following is another dream in the final phase of our sessions.

Dream 53 (session No. 64)
   We are playing a final game of a basketball tournament. Each team has twenty players and we are using four balls. The court is crowded. I pass a ball to Y who is free right under the hoop. He is going to pass the ball to another because he is not confident about shooting a basket. I say to him with a loud voice, "Don't do that! Do it by yourself!" Y tries to shoot a basket, but fails. I encourage him, saying, "Nice try!"
                                                    (Mr. Y is one of his friends from high school.)

"A final game of a basketball tournament." In addition to the basketball game itself, a final match implies the strong tension between two groups. It is a serious collision with enemies both physically and mentally. The game seems to be more complicated than an ordinary one because **"each team has twenty players and we are using four balls."** Forty players with four balls can be simply divided into four games, but there is no such differentiated structure in the dream. However, the dream-I looks so focused upon the match, that it does not seem to matter to him. **"I pass a ball to Y who is free right under the hoop."** He finds someone who can move freely in the crowded court.

Although Y is not confident in himself and wants to avoid the challenge, the dream-I encourages him. The one who shoots a basket tends to attract the attention of the audience. He is often admired as a hero. However, one does not become a hero without the passes and the defense of other teammates. It requires strong team unity. The dream-I is not the one who directly gets the point, but he plays an important role in the game. He watches, passes balls, and encourages.

What is interesting in Dream 52 and 53 is that the decisive act is done by someone other than the dream-I, and *through* that person, a strong commitment to the event is evoked in the dream-I. We can also see the same tendency in Dream 44, the dream of the deer. The driver, who decides the action, was not the dream-I, but through the action, the dream-I became more aware of what was going on in front of him.

Discussion

The Particular Relationship between the I and the Internal Other

As I said before, the conversation with Dan was somehow odd to me. He talked like a one-man show. In the course of therapy, I began to assume that he might not have established his self-relation within himself. This seemed to explain the fact that he did not seem to have conflicts, for example, between attending classes and not, or between his reluctance and his parents' trust. My question was then: if he has not established his self-relation, is it because of the lack of his own inner other, as often observed in the case of autistic persons, or because of the lack of the internal dialog between the I and its own other?

Listening to his dreams, it gradually dawned on me that there was the internal other in Dan's psyche and that the difficulty of our conversation might come from the particular relation between the I and the other. As I mentioned earlier, most dreams did not show the face-to-face encounter between the dream-I and the Other. In contrast with the Other that straightly approached the dream-I, the intentionality of the dream-I was too weak. Faced with this type of dream, one may feel that something remains uncompleted.

Here, we have to be reminded that, as Giegerich stresses, "there should not be any 'shoulds'" in dreams.[13] We need to think that the face-to-face encounter between the dream-I and the Other may not be its interest. Instead, the uncompletedness, the passing by *is* what the soul depicts again and again. The critical situations such as being cut (Dream 2: the dream of the female demon), being shot (Dream 27: the dream of the death sentence and a monster), being attacked (Dream 44: the dream of the deer) do not actually aim at the direct clash of the two, but at waking the consciousness (the dream-I) up to reality. In Dream 2 and 27, instead of being truly threatened by the Other, he flies away from the situation by means of a magical power. In Dream 44, however, the dream-I keeps his eyes open and witnesses the following car pass by them. Why was this possible? The difference between Dream 44 and the other two dreams is that the dream-I was not alone, but with a woman, enclosed in a car. The woman and the car prevent him from flying away from the situation. This hints at the importance of someone neither the dream-I nor the Other. We have seen the dreams in which the decisive action is done by someone else, such as his brother (Dream 52) or his friend (Dream 53). *Via the someone else*, the dream-I can be involved in the situation and experiences its seriousness.

The Psychology of the Young Adult in Japan

This reflection reminds me of the fact that Dan attended laboratory classes, so that he did not cause trouble for his group mates. This is one of the typical attitudes among non-attendant students. Taking into consideration what I discussed before, it can be pointed out as a characteristic of non-attendant students that the I needs someone else to relate itself to the event going on in front of it, or psychologically to its own other. If the I has only weak intentionality of its own, it is easily alienated from the world both internally and externally. By standing in between, the *someone else* plays the role of connecting the I with the other. This means, instead of the dyadic relationship between the I and the other, we may need to take into consideration the triadic relationship among the I, the other, and the third party, namely *someone else*. By this, I do not mean anything transcendent in Jungian psychology. The third here needs to exist on the same horizontal level as the I and the other.

The young adult is usually supposed to go through conflicts and overcome various difficulties, which strengthen the I. Through the process, he or she gains his/her individuality and gets ready for living as an adult in society. However, the examination of Dan's case suggests that whoever confronts the situation does not always have to be the I who speaks in front of the therapist. Instead, the therapist needs to be attentive to the presence of *someone else*. In dreams, the someone else may appear as we have seen above. What else could the *someone else* appear in? Lastly, I would like to refer to my idea about that.

At the beginning of this chapter, I mentioned that the non-attendant students say that they are demotivated because they do not know what they want to do in the future, while there are other students who struggle with their job hunting saying the same thing. Even if one does not know what to do, he/she can graduate from university and start to work. In Japanese society, where the ability to adapt can be more important than the intentionality of the I, it is true that, more or less, university students *are driven* by society to find a job and graduate from university. Here I would like to remind you of the image in Dan's dream of *the dream-I sitting in the passenger seat of a car driven by a woman*. When the I identifies itself with the idea of a university student as their *persona*, it can drive the car, even if in fact it is society who drives the car. However, non-attendant students fail to identify themselves as university students, because they know that they do not fulfill the requirements of university students. They believe that they failed to belong to the university and that they are not worth wearing a mask of the university student. They think that they are no one. As a result, it may feel as if the car and the driver are missing in their psyche. But it is not right. The beliefs are their flying away from reality. In reality, they cannot stay behind a mask of no one. The fact is that they *are* university students who do not attend classes, who do not fulfill the requirements of university students. When they are confronted with the fact and accept the reality, the awareness would let them get in the car. As long as they get in the car, who drives the car does not matter so much. As I have already discussed, in Japan where the collective is given more importance than individuals, the car is driven by society. Moreover, it can be in the passenger seat in which the I can become active and relate itself to its own other.

The dreams I introduced may be interpreted to display an awkward way of the soul to relate to itself. It seems as if the soul lacks its own internal other and thus cannot relate to itself, come home to itself. However, we need to consider the possibility that the soul insists on relating itself indirectly (having) rather than (being) itself.

Notes

1 Paul A. Walters, "Student Apathy," in *Emotional Problems of the Student*, ed. Graham Burt Blaine and Charles Campbell McArthur (New York: Appleton-Century Crofts, 1961), 129–147.
2 See Yomishi Kasahara, *Apathy Syndrome* (Tokyo: Iwanami-shoten, 1984). (In Japanese).
3 In another occasion I have also discussed this phenomenon. See Nanae Takenaka, "Voices from Nature and Withdrawal (*Hikikomori*) in Japanese Culture," in *Cultural Complex in China, Japan, Korea and Taiwan*, ed. Thomas Singer (London: Routledge, 2010), 181–198.
4 C. G. Jung, "The phenomenology of the spirit in fairytales." 1940. *CW* 9i, para. 400.
5 C. G. Jung, *Mysterium Coniunctionis*. 1955. *CW* 14. para. 749.
6 Wolfgang Giegerich, *Working With Dreams—Initiation into the Soul's Speaking About Itself* (Oxon and New York: Routledge, 2021), 35.
7 Giegerich, *Working With Dreams*, 72.
8 Giegerich, *Working With Dreams*, 65.
9 In Japanese universities, normally the student needs four years for his/her graduation, but if one fails to get enough credits it can be extended up to eight years. Also, one can take a leave of absence for a maximum four years. During the leave, he/she does not need to pay the tuition at most public universities.
10 Giegerich, *Working With Dreams*, 137.
11 For better understanding the Other, see Wolfgang Giegerich, "6. Actaion and Artemis: The *Pictorial* Representation of the Notion and the (Psycho-) *Logical* Interpretation of the Myth," in *The Soul's Logical Life* (Frankfurt am Main: Peter Lang, 1998), 203–275, or Giegerich, "Introduction: Psychology and the Other," in *Collected English Papers Volume III Soul-Violence* (New Orleans, Louisiana: Spring Journal Books, 2008), 1–41.
12 Kenji Kurano, *Kojiki* (Tokyo: Iwanami-Shoten, 1991), 60. (in Japanese)
13 Giegerich, *Working With Dreams*, 148.

Chapter 7

You Are Here (Now)

Psyche's Logic or Sense of Soul in Jung, Hillman, and Giegerich

Michael R. Caplan

Two Guides ("admired colleague and well-loved friend")

An anecdote conveyed by Wolfgang Giegerich about a minor incident involving his friend and senior colleague, James Hillman, sets us on our path:

> At a time when "spraying graffiti" was still unknown in Europe, there all of a sudden appeared in Zurich someone who soon became known as "the Zurich sprayer." In a spontaneous reaction, Hillman with his martial, somewhat youthful anti-authority bent found this great, because the sprayer "put a face on" naked, blank walls. This was for me a very revealing response, because it is antiphenomenological: putting something on a blank surface to give it a face versus letting the phenomena show their actual face or non-face, here: letting precisely the emptiness and barrenness of a concrete wall speak.[1]

Hillman and Giegerich always acknowledged each other's contributions toward the advancement of what both considered foundational to psychologist C.G. Jung's project, and to psychology as such, in its revolutionary potential. (I use their own words as often as possible in what follows, both to establish a sort of conversation between them, and to emphasize a certain duality that is characteristic of psychological thinking, as I hope will become clear.) Hillman called Giegerich's "the most important Jungian thought now going on – maybe the only consistent Jungian thought at all,"[2] while Giegerich declared that Hillman's "has no peers among the other types of psychology in the Jungian tradition," because through it "psychology became conscious of itself ...."[3] Hillman spoke warmly of Giegerich as an "admired colleague and well-loved friend," while after Hillman's death Giegerich remembered him

> with deep gratitude, both for the enormous inspiration I received from his insights through his writings and for the personal support during my early years as a Jungian .... I also stayed internally in intensive close connection with him at those later times when our views began, I use his words, to "diverge" ....[4]

DOI: 10.4324/9781003381150-8

This divergence, although going back to the late 1980s, was firmly established with Giegerich's presentation of "Killings: Psychology's Platonism and the Missing Link to Reality" at the Festival of Archetypal Psychology in 1992, which I was fortunate to witness. I was struck by its uncompromising criticisms, but also by its consistency with everything I'd been learning from Hillman's work. Indeed, as Giegerich had earlier put it, "With my critique I mobilize Hillman against Hillman"[5] (as they each often mobilize Jung against Jung, distilling the essential from the conventional in his thinking).

Among those familiar with both writers, the conflict led predictably to either taking one side or the other, or to attempted balancing acts. And many readers do only tackle one of the two. Hillman afficionados tend to favor his words echoing the "pop" Jung, with talk of myth and imagination, over his more demanding formulations. Those who begin with Giegerich tend to assume his self-declared move beyond Hillman means Hillman's "archetypal," "imaginal" psychology holds no further lessons or discoveries. Then there are those who started with Hillman and went on to Giegerich, more or less my own trajectory, but who no longer look back because Giegerich's work is so genuinely advanced.

Hillman also admired how Giegerich "stares into the face of the shadow in our times and offers no false hopes."[6] The shadow is a Jungian concept, but Jungian too is this sense for the meaning of our current collective reality: "The great problem of our time," Jung had written, "is that we don't understand what is happening to the world."[7] Hillman had in fact begun to speak of "an imagination of extraversion"[8] oriented toward technology and the public realm. Attracting Giegerich's own penetrating gaze, this shift from what he called "the narrow confines of the consulting room" was, Giegerich continued, "not completely surprising, but rather a consistent development of the germinal ideas of archetypal psychology ...."[9] In the end, however, he determined that Hillman settled for a merely "nostalgic, romantic position."[10] Refuting as psychologically defensive Hillman's most treasured responses to modernity, like the aesthetic "animal sense" and the antique *anima mundi* trope ("soul of the world"), he showed how Hillman's unwillingness to stare "into the face of the shadow in our times" compromised his very conception of psychology. My own answer to the issue, in 2013, was to compare Hillman's still-limited "revolt" – abandoning psychological thinking where it is needed most – with Giegerich's more complete "revolution."[11] (This figure of revolution keeps returning.)

They never did settle their divergence, nor was it resolved by others in terms of a preference for image over concept, fantasy over logic, personal over cultural, or of Hillman's penchant for *anima* versus Giegerich's *animus* – although these terms do color their work, respectively. Yet Giegerich and Hillman truly follow Jung, who, in the words of historian Sonu Shamdasani, "did not intend to form a particular school of psychotherapy, but, in line with the unitary conceptions of psychology in the late nineteenth century, intended to establish psychology in general."[12] And Giegerich is categorical: psychology "is not such that there could be several varieties of it."[13] Some conflicts will consequently require definitive resolution. But there are others that remain instructive precisely in their divergence, asking us to occupy first one, then another position as the only way to comprehend (Latin *comprehendere* – to take together) psyche's self-contradictory logic. "This initiation does not make us whole," proclaims Hillman, it points (revolutionarily, one might say) toward "a hermetic duplicity and aphroditic coupling going on in every instant."[14]

Setting Out ("our real situation")

Psychology is a professional field, a domain of contending theories and claims and standards. I'm not a psychologist. My interest in psyche (from ancient Greek *psyché* – departed soul, animating breath, spirit, mind) is at once more general, in the grand questions of history and consciousness; more specific, in Jung's identification of what seems to me the single basic principle for interpreting psyche's sense (uroboric motion – from the Greek Uroboros, the serpent eating its own tail); and more personal, because in my late teens, I went through a nine-month period of paranoid, obsessive thinking and depersonalization. I felt like I was floating behind myself, and couldn't conceive how, given my body's materiality, there was any room for "me." Taking up no physical space, "I" could just as readily not exist (and I remember a nightmare of facing a mirror and dissolving).

A few years later, acute crisis over, I started reading Hillman – *Re-Visioning Psychology* and soon everything else I could put my hands on. I'd come across him earlier but, desperate as I'd been for solid ground, found his inversions of perspective too unsettling. Now, though, I felt instantly at home. His writing animated as if from within each topic he addressed (an astonishing range: war, panic, masturbation, ceilings, color terms, the paranormal ...), respecting both its mysteries and its necessities. Making my way hungrily through the Hillman-edited back issues of *Spring Journal*, I then discovered Giegerich's essays on techno-modernity and immediately recognized a profound kinship, along with a challenge that tipped into full motion the revolution Hillman had inaugurated for me.

Building on key insights from Jung, their shared approach seemed capable not only of drawing out the deeper sense in human culture, which I'd always found fascinating. It proposed as well that there could be sense even in my strange breakdown. Hillman had coined the term "pathologizing" to honor Jung's principle that such crises might offer "purposes which we have misperceived and values which must present themselves necessarily in a distorted form ...."[15] This sentiment is expressed also in Giegerich's avowal that, specifically as "a Jungian," he must "trust that even in a despicable symptom there is some soul substance .... Some seed, some meaning or telos."[16] Had some purpose, some value been presenting itself in my pathologizing? If so, could theorizing strictly in terms of the *logos* of *psyché*, the logic – the language, speech, intelligible pattern, *sense* – of soul, perhaps bring my thinking to its senses?

Setting out to address such a question, it will be supremely useful to note first these remarks of philosopher John Sallis:

> In itself the word *sense* houses the most gigantic ambivalence, indifferently coupling the difference between what is called the sensible, things of sense apprehended perceptually, *and* signification, meaning, a signified or intended sense. One will speak of course of the two senses of sense, not without marking in the very phrase the abysmal character of the differentiation: to differentiate between the two senses of sense presupposes the very differentiation that it would effect. In dealing with sense one will never have gotten to the bottom of things.[17]

In dealing with "soul" in Giegerich and Hillman one will never have gotten to the bottom of things either. Our real lives are first and final – the territory from which our understanding may be mined, as well as the concrete domain of our activity, "the vale of soul-making," as Hillman often quoted Keats. Psychology is hopelessly, indeed constitutively entangled with the real – real thoughts, feelings, dreams, actions, events. Even Dr. Phil says the process begins with "owning" one's actual situation – with what Dr. Giegerich spells out as "the necessity to commit oneself unrelentingly to life on this earth as it really is (and not as it might be wished to be)."[18] Yet we must also understand that, as Giegerich spins this elementary contradiction, "Psychology is not about life and life phenomena, not about people and their development or behavior, but it is about 'the soul,' the 'logical life,' the dialectics operative *within* such life phenomena, *within* people's behavior."[19]

Although psychology may be "a speculation in the service of, and thus rigorously bound by, the real phenomenon,"[20] its concern is the soul, which is "the inner of every real"[21] and "the truth of our real situation."[22] For psychology, "soul and truth are correlates."[23] The soul/truth of a phenomenon is thus to be found only through an acknowledgment of the real, including its contradictions – and including *ourselves*, because for psychology, reality is that complex which appears *to us* and *as us*. As a *contra*-natural realism, psychology trains us in the revolutionary motion required to make sense of our being here, now.

Setting out to explicate such a possibility will, however, require first a break from everyday sense in favor of what Hillman spoke of as the "underworld" – pure meaning disguised as image, pure signification cloaked in sensual form:

> a wholly psychic perspective, where one's entire mode of being has been desubstantialized, killed of natural life, and yet is in every shape and sense and size the exact replica of natural life. The underworld Ba of Egypt and the underworld *psyché* of Homeric Greece was the whole person as in life but devoid of life.[24]

Sense of Psyche ("the notion of soul")

Psychology may conventionally designate a field of competing theories, claims, and standards, but to embrace its originary mandate means, according to Giegerich, that it "has no choice … its name has always already given it its first principle, soul."[25] He underlines the continuity with Jung: "it is a unique feature of Jungian psychology that it makes serious use of the term soul."[26] Hillman said that he too was "trying to restore to psyche (and psychology) its ancient sense akin to soul …,"[27] and Giegerich endorsed him on just this basis: "re-visioning psychology was an attempt to construe psychology as one integral whole … rooted in and derived from one center or ground, the notion of soul."[28] But psychology is a modern enterprise, and since modernity is built upon the obsolescence of a sacred dimension and shuns any hint of supernaturalism, it is hardly surprising that some pioneers in the field put forward a "psychology without soul,"[29] or that the very term is dismissed by serious contemporary theorizing.

The word only survives at all thanks to the endurance (in, let us say, the human soul) of its folk-sense. Everyone will at some point have recourse to talk of "soul" (even as they disavow literalism: "Of course, I don't *believe* …") or "soullessness" (and without any hint of mystification). It is perfectly non-controversial to speak of "the soul" of some situation or activity – its meaningful core, inner life, animating logic. "Soul" is perhaps the only word that modernity *cannot* fully "de-soul" – empty of mystery, flatten out; it can only be dismissed as outmoded. Yet its archaism (*arche*-ism) is the living thread that connects us with all that comes before the rupture that is modernity. It still breathes with what Hillman called an "ancient sense" thanks to its ineradicable ties to religion, mythology, and folklore, and not despite but because of its connotations of spiritualism and sentimentalism. Giegerich: "The word soul cannot be divorced from the notion of soulfulness."[30]

If we, as moderns, may no longer define soul as mystic substance or immaterial being, we can, as human folk concerned with profound questions, nevertheless think in terms of what Giegerich refers to above as "the notion of soul" – an *idea*. And this, Giegerich has articulated better than anyone. The word "soul" – that which is at once most meaningful and most mysterious – directs thinking where no other idea can anymore: toward the attribution of, at once, the deepest human significance and an absolutely uncanny otherness. Yet this sense of "soul" is both humble and prosaic, and functionally secular in our resolutely post-metaphysical intellectual climate. Giegerich instructs us soberly that "The psychological sense of soul is only a methodological one, a way of looking at things …,"[31] and that

> a "method" (which contains Greek *hodós*, way, road), [is only] an approach, a style of thinking, *with which* one can study the objects of one's study, in the case of psychology all sorts of phenomena: dreams, myths, symbols, psychological symptoms just as well as, e.g., our modern technological civilization.[32]

The psychological sense of soul can, like the sense of balance, be improved with methodical practice because it is not mystical, but rather *a sense for the center of gravity of sense*. And only a psychology with such a notion of soul would "deserve its name,"[33] would be a "true psychology"[34] – unlike empirical psychology (taken up, we might say, with the human animal), academic (the human subject conceived philosophically, socially, politically), scientific (the brain), or personalistic (the betterment of the ego). It would be a *psychological psychology* – noun and adjective reflexively forcing thought back upon itself, continually putting into question just what "psychological" *means* and hence what psychology *is*. "We are thinking about thoughts, not about things," said Hillman, "or about the effect of thoughts upon our experience of things."[35]

Psyche's Sense ("that in itself moves in opposite directions")

It seems telling that a contentious relationship between two practitioners brought psychology's singular nature into focus for me, and in my thinking, their characteristic preferences and signature moves never cease to question, correct, and complement each other. "Could it be," asks Giegerich, "that it is the syzygy that manifests itself in our strife, at once uniting and dividing us with and from each other?"[36] For despite their individual inclinations and limitations, both do comprehend psychology as syzygy, comprising in its fullness "the entire dialectic of imagining (personifying, objectifying, reifying, ontologizing) *and* de-imagining (sublation, dissolution, putrefaction into logical movement)."[37] Hillman wrote, for example, that "just as a *psychological* intellect requires anima consciousness, anima consciousness requires psychological *intellect*."[38] Most importantly, both attest to psychology's utter uniqueness: of all approaches to interpreting our personal and cultural realities, whether traditional or modern, *psychology alone is uroboric* – as Jung, at his most uncompromising, had realized:

> It seems as if we were just waking up to this fact, and that the dawn is still too dim for us to realize in full what it means that the psyche, being the *object* of … observation and judgment, is at the same time its *subject*, the *means* by which you make such observations.[39]

Jung saw that psychology "lacks the immense advantage of an Archimedean point such as physics enjoys."[40] There is no more ostensibly objective reality "outside" psyche upon which we can base our self-understanding. Giegerich's resultant verdict is conclusive: "If we long for an Archimedean point outside of psychology … then this is not psychology at all."[41]

Hillman often quoted Jung's statement, "The psyche creates reality every day. The only expression I can say for this activity is *fantasy*."[42] Again, Giegerich concurs: "Jung's insight that the psyche as fantasy creates reality every day is the premise from which my thought proceeds, just as is the other idea of Jung's that we are surrounded by psyche on all sides, and inescapably so. Up to this point there is no difference between Hillman and me."[43] Let us continue to follow this thread, this shared basis, while understanding that "Both soul and psychology follow a 'uroboric' logic"[44] – that is, the domain of *psyche* and likewise the interpretation of its *logos* are constituted by "one single act or attitude that in itself moves in opposite directions and thus is self-contradictory."[45]

To successfully think "inside" and "outside" uroborically, however, to conceive "soul" and "truth" in the "real," we will have to retreat before advancing. We must first restrict ourselves to the *inside* and to that indisputably "subjectivity-*internal* other," the dream, so plainly "consciousness's own."[46] For as Hillman counsels, "only separated things can join" (my youthful dissociation bore the seed of a truer association between matter and my "self" than I'd been able to conceive prior), or else, according to alchemy, "a *monstrum* is born of a premature conjunction."

> To go through the world seeing its one underlying truth …, that nature and spirit, body and mind, are two aspects of the same invisible energy or implicate order, thereby neglects the acute distinctions joined by these conjunctions, so that our consciousness, no matter how wise and wondrous, is therefore both premature and monstrous.[47]

Psychological Fidelity ("saying … again")

If, per the subtitle of Giegerich's book, *Working With Dreams: An Initiation into the Soul's Speaking about Itself*, dreams are but initiatory to psychological thinking, we should keep in mind Hillman's counsel: "Do what we will, the dream presents itself in the robes of duplicity, stating simply that an ambiguity of significance is its habitual presentation. If dreams are the teachers of the waking-ego, this *duplicity is the essential instruction they impart*."[48] Dreams are affecting, yet elusive; common, yet private; lived through, yet only grasped in memory. Dreams are pure signification (the one side of what Sallis called "the gigantic difference within sense"[49]), yet this *logos* is wholly embodied in sensual imagery (the other).

The dream is necessarily meaningful because it is composed of nothing but meaning; and, at least when one is within it, even the strangest things make sense because everything is *made of sense* (including the dream-I). "The statement 'the dream *is* consciousness' is," writes Giegerich, "… analogous to 'this mountain range consists of lime-stone."[50] Freud recognized as much: "Not until we wake up does the critical comment arise that we have not experienced anything but have merely been thinking in a peculiar way, or in other words, dreaming."[51] This is why putting the dream into words allows us to *think through* the thought which *appears* in/as the dream's imaginal form: it is a homeopathic process of like curing like, distinguished only (though really) by their *apparent* difference. Jung: "We have simply got to listen to what the psyche spontaneously says to us. What the dream, which is not manufactured by us, says is *just so*. Say it again as well as you can."[52] Giegerich elucidates:

> The dream is speaking, not we. We only have to listen. But the detailed work with the individual words and images of the dream ... is itself nothing but the way of listening. Listening is thus also an intensive activity. Jung called it "saying again." The word "saying" in this phrase refers to the active side, the "again" to the passive side ....[53]

The process externalizes the dream into language but stays resolutely faithful to it, our words forming its "living periphery."[54] Through the mundane magic of verbalization, we may eventually arrive at a moment of truth, of its truth, *the dream's* truth; and the sense of the dream may thereby come to affect our sense of things, including ourselves. Thus could Jung declare, "Image and meaning are identical; and as the first takes shape, the latter becomes clear."[55] How?

Psychological Vision ("everything necessary is there")

To answer, we must further arrest our forward motion to focus systematically on Hillman's watchword, *image*, and his imagistic approach to dreams – for, as he says in language reminiscent of Sallis, "We get more sense (significance) from an image the more we note its sense (data) ...."[56] His primary injunction: "stick to the image" in its precise givenness, just as it appears. "Simply: the actual qualities of the image. Vagueness, dullness, indifference – and imprecision, too – are also qualities. ... The more precision, the more actual insight."[57]

Although he doesn't simply mean "picture," and our vision of it is not with the eyes, Hillman's idea of "image" is *like* a picture in important ways:

> What makes images like pictures is just this independent presence of the image that seems to stand still, or at least stands me still, before it .... As the eye watching a picture both concentrates and darts, so the mind confronted with an image starts racing even as it stands still. This double action discloses levels and builds complexities without ever leaving the scene, without ever going beyond the ... object with which it is presented. Like a picture, an image too has borders. It sticks to itself, inheres within itself. It doesn't lead somewhere else, as does a story. Thus the mind's activity can find nowhere to go but more deeply into the image. Time doesn't enter pictures. ... All the parts are happening at once ... When a dream is written out as a story, the end comes after the beginning and is its result. But when we take the same dream as an image, then the last sentence can be heard in terms of the first (or any other) and can result in the first (or any other).[58]

So, first, an image both arrests and engages our thinking, which is restricted by the image's borders. Next, the image – and the dream taken as image – "inheres within itself": its disparate elements together form a whole, each playing its role in the overall meaning such that none can be changed without changing the meaning itself; and they are related according to "the logic or syntax of it, to the logical structure of the dream, to the abstract formal relation of its individual elements."[59] The elements of the image – and of the dream-as-image – "gain their sense from where, when, and which way they stand"[60] (and Hillman shows how the simplest prepositions – on, over, after, beside, within – "are the subtle joints which articulate the internal positioning of the image, how it knits together"[61]).

"Time doesn't enter pictures," Hillman says above; all elements of an image are simultaneously present. To view a dream as image means that, in Giegerich's words, "Beginning and end as well as everything in between must be brought into vibration."[62] This represents "the move from a mentality that reads events as narrative (a series of successive developments in time leading to an end-result) to one that views the same events imaginally."[63] A dream thus interpreted becomes "a closed, self-contained Now. ... All past and future that still exist are the *internal* past and future of the dream itself."[64] The dream is "infinite. A totality. A world unto itself."[65]

The classicist Gerald Else describes two core principles of Aristotle's *Poetics*: "Wholeness guarantees that no part is missing which should be there; unity, that nothing is there which belongs somewhere else."[66] In the same spirit, Hillman instructs us to assume that in the image "everything there is necessary," which "further suggests that everything necessary is there."[67] But, he asks, "What sort of necessity is this ...?"

> Imagistic necessity ... need not be taken literally, as a kind of *kismet*, as if fantasies were implacable forces and dream images determined fate. Rather, "it could not be otherwise" is a psychological rule of thumb, saying that one works with what is given and only with that, and even if insufficient it is necessary and cannot be wished into something other than it is, either by explanation, by reduction, or by association.[68]

What is given may be unsettling or may seem inadequate; our minds may be undisciplined: "We each would escape the necessity of the image, whether it be dreams, fantasies, or the images in which we find ourselves behaving."[69] The preceding series of indications – precision, arrest, limit, inherence, logical structure, simultaneity, necessity – thwart our escape attempts, and together comprise a *discipline of interiority*, to use Giegerich's language, rules of thumb for *interiorizing the image (dream, phenomenon) into itself*. Jung adopted the alchemical injunction about the importance of a sealed vessel: "Above all, don't let anything from outside, that does not belong, get into it, for the fantasy-image has 'everything it needs' within itself."[70] So, says Hillman, there is nowhere else to look but further at or into the image. It holds our attention – and what is attention but a primary definition of consciousness? And our attention is held in the present; so an image makes us present to ourselves, convocates consciousness to be all present and at attention.[71]

Psychological Material ("what our real behavior thinks")

Hillman's reference to "the images in which we find ourselves behaving" brings us at last to the question of everyday reality (and eventually to the issue of modernity – "the present"), after our preparatory separation by way of the idea of soul (and its uroboric motion), of the phenomenon of the dream (and its uroboric interpretation), and of the discipline of image (as entry to the uroboric). Psychological thinking can bring us home to our very nature and our actual lives, but not without first subverting our every natural habit of thought and alienating us from the day-world perspective. Most egregious to this viewpoint is that, in Giegerich's unequivocal phrasing, "Psychological truth is the truth of the *appearance*, a truth irrespective of the difference between 'fact' and 'illusion' (or 'delusion') ...."[72] (My near-delusional experience long ago contained a truth I continue to draw upon.) Yet we also know, from Giegerich's many such assurances, that "the logic that psychology is concerned with is the logic of the real."[73] How do we parse this disjunction, now that we're squarely up against it?

Hillman said that for psychology, "'fantasy' and 'reality' change places and values. First, they are no longer opposed. Second, fantasy is never merely mentally subjective but is always being enacted and embodied .... Third, whatever is physically or literally 'real' is always also a fantasy image."[74] Thus, we "solve the matter at hand, not by resolving it, but by dissolving the problem into the fantasy that is congealed into a 'problem.'"[75] Through a psychological perspective, even phenomena that encompass concretely external reality may be "regarded from a dream-viewpoint, as if they were images, metaphorical expressions."[76] Then, as we interiorize a dream into itself by taking it as image and thinking through its logic, we take the day-world phenomenon as dream, and do the same. "Fantasy" is but Hillman's preferred term for the *logos* (internally coherent like any logic) informing our actual lives, the "images" shaping reality into the phenomenon as which it appears, and shaping us into *those to whom* it appears.

Psychological interpretation is constrained by the facts of the case; for they, like the dream's specific elements, are all we have and, theoretically, all we need. We are bound by and beholden to what appears in the real, including ourselves, and "the only thing that really counts is what our real behavior thinks."[77] The *logos* of *psyche*, the meaning of our deepest sense of things, the sense in/of our deepest meaning, the soul/truth of the real, becomes accessible only through what Giegerich calls a "devotion to the present and its hidden presence, its face and voice ..."[78]

Psychological Ethos ("It has a right to come.")

From the Proto-Indo-European root *bha* "to shine," and the Greek *phain-esthai* "to appear," the *phainomenon* – "that which appears" – is psychology's prime matter. Dreams, of course, are pure appearing, even the "I" making an appearance only so that everything else might appear along with it – uroborically related sides of a single moment of meaning, their very duality constituting the one phenomenon. And dreams appear to the dreamer ("the moon in my dream is exclusively my own moon. Nobody else could possibly see *this* moon"[79]) – another phenomenon constituted by its two uroborically related aspects. But all psychological phenomena appear *to* someone, *at* some time; indeed, a "psychological phenomenon" is nothing other than this appearing. It may initially appear in pathologized and distorted form (affected, too, by our own attitude toward it), but for a Jungian-based approach, it is ultimately otherwise. Hillman:

> The supposed creative pandaemonium of the teeming imagination is limited to its phenomenal appearance in a particular image, that specific one which has come to me pregnant with significance and intention, a necessary angel as it appears here and now and which teaches the hand to represent it, the ear to hear, and the heart how to respond.[80]

That which "has come to me" – from where? What uroboric relation entails in real life? Inside and outside *are* concretely separate, no matter how we may regard them "from a dream-viewpoint" when practicing this discipline, methodologically treating real exteriority *as if* it were, like the dream's, subjectivity-internal. There is a maxim from the 18th century theologian, J.G. Hamann, that we might usefully adapt, although psychology's version is slipperier. Religious prophecy, he said, was "a speech to the creature through the creature"[81] – in other words, from God to humanity through the prophets. We need add a uroboric enclosure and a movement of return: from the soul, through the human, *back to soul.* By means of this word, "soul," we can learn to recognize meaning as it forges itself in the medium of our existence, establishing what therefore, for us, means and matters the most. The underworld lends its sense to the day-world, shapes it, shapes *us,* peopling and emplotting the life-situation that finds itself "on the analytical couch," so to speak. Our discipline of interiorization is nothing other than the interiorizing of the phenomenon into itself, because it turns the phenomenon to face *its own image* through the medium of our speculations.

But, as Hillman had cautioned, we would each "escape the necessity of the image." Even Dr. Phil knows that psychological denial is a rejection of what is manifest in those images of our own reality that we sometimes suddenly catch, exposed. This is why Giegerich speaks of "the debt we owe to what actually presents itself ... including all its ultimate consequences."[82] The psychological task is to catch up with the thinking that manifests in and as the real – for the "soul of the matter is the thought that animates it, the thought as whose external manifestation or embodiment ... the psychological phenomenon exists."[83] As for interpretation, Hillman recommended "the imagistic way, the phenomenological way," that we "take a thing for what it is and let it talk"[84] – recalling, of course, Jung's "Say it again as well as you can." And Giegerich: "A genuine interpretation is not our personal opinion about a phenomenon; rather, it merely states what the latter shows."[85] Whether we're analyzing what Giegerich calls the *opus parvum*, the "small work" of our personal lives, or the *opus magnum*, the "great work" of historical consciousness, our approach must be "taught by the Real ...."[86]

Wondering with Giegerich about "the particular direction in which a psychological investigation would have to move in order to become psychological in the first place"[87] (in other words, here near the end of my essay, addressing *how we begin*), we find that we must move into the phenomenon that has come or is coming toward us. That which appears and our receptivity to its appearing are two sides of one uroboric figure – like the dream-I and the dream's events, like the dream itself and the dreamer upon waking. For psychology, "soul" is what holds the subject and object of the psychological gaze together, because *it is regarding itself* in the given.

"Psychological phenomena are *events of meaning*,"[88] Giegerich tells us, and "events of meaning ... have *logos*-character .... They *speak*."[89] We are being addressed by a necessary angel. And as the sense of the dream may come to affect our sense of things (including of ourselves), so the meaning *as which* we exist may enter into dialogue with the meaning that we are not (yet), by means of the phenomenon that presents itself to us. The "necessary angel" and "I" are mutually defining. It's what Hillman called "soul-making."

A true psychology would attest, with Hillman, that "in my disturbances there really are forces I cannot control and yet which want something from me and intend something with me."[90] Speaking of any "arriving new reality" – however discomfiting – as a "guest," Giegerich says that, for Jung, "What is coming is not viewed as enemy, senseless, and utterly alien, totally unrelated. Although as yet unknown, it is nevertheless a priori connected to us. There is an intrinsic bond between what is coming and us. It belongs. It has a right to come."[91] From *intelligibility* ("What does it mean?") to *intentionality* ("What does it mean with me?"), from how the phenomenon *appears* to what the phenomenon *wants* – such is our revolutionary road.

Psychological Conclusion ("not how to get out")

Psychology is revolutionary, not only in the modern sense as *the overturning of an existing order* (although this was very much the intent of the early psychologists[92]), but also in the ancient one as *the eternal rotation of heavenly bodies* (hence Jung's interest in the archetypal and the alchemical); revolution interiorized into itself, both thoroughgoing and ongoing. It is not just a matter of perspective turned upside down, but of an incessant conceptual activity like gyroscopic in-flight adjustments oriented toward truth, that center of gravity of sense. The wager of psychology is that what is *made of* sense *makes* sense – whether in the dream or in the waking dream at work in reality. To look *with soul, for truth* is a practice of *making sense* of what's given in and as the real, including ourselves. And its validity is dependent not on any kind of external verification – for psyche "is reinstated in its hereditary rank as that which surrounds us on all sides and has nothing outside of itself"[93] – but arises out of interpretive fidelity to the phenomenon's own internal coherence, whether that of the dream or across domains and encompassing concrete reality as well.

Hillman had described the underworld as a perspective "where one's entire mode of being has been desubstantialized, killed of natural life, and yet is in every shape and sense and size the exact replica of natural life": such was my mercifully brief experience of depersonalization. Initially decisive in my turnaround was a rediscovery of faith in communication through the physical, an affirmation of meaning's non-verbal expression (for which I'll always be grateful to a friend who reached out with a simple hug at a pivotal moment). But the crisis eventually did give way to a stable self-conception, thanks in no small part to the uroboric idea of psyche. I was torn away from, but eventually returned to, what natural consciousness takes for granted, and what I could now grasp in its contradictory, *contra* natural finality – that we are *fully both senses of sense* (although one or the other may dominate, situationally): 100% sensible, belonging to the positive, material world, and 100% signification, made of meaning, utterly immaterial (not unlike the miracle of Catholic math, in which Christ is 100% human + 100% divine).

Revisiting true psychology's fount in Jung, Giegerich writes:

> We have our identity as Jungians (or should I say: as psychologists, which would be the same thing) if in everything we experience One changes to Two for us; if we experience not only ourselves, our patients, and Jungian psychology, but also every particular phenomenon and each individual statement as double-bottomed, bottomless. But then the reverse applies too: each person, no matter of what psychological school, for whom One has changed to Two in the way he sees the world, each person who on his own theoretical base penetrates so consistently into the depths that he plunges into the bottomlessness of his own ground, is *ipso facto* a "Jungian" even if he has never heard of Jung. [94]

So, any unity to be achieved between Hillman and Giegerich – beyond adjudicating their quarrel over the proper response to modernity (in which Giegerich clearly prevails) – will be no static thing. As Hillman wrote of alchemy's goal, "The conjunction is not a balanced mixture, a composite adding this to that; it is not a blending of substantial differences into a compromise, an arrangement; it is not a symbolic putting together of two halves or two things into a third."[95] It is, in Giegerich's words quoted earlier, "one single act or attitude that in itself moves in opposite directions and thus is self-contradictory." Our guides must unbalance each other rightly, to keep the investigation in uroboric motion and our aim true.

For as Giegerich says, "What matters therapeutically is not how to get out of a distressing situation, but, on the contrary, how to get properly into it ...."[96] Of course! Each present is all we've got. And we must "let ourselves be placed by the soul's process into the situation that is."[97] Hillman admitted that Giegerich was "justified in claiming ... that I am nostalgic and escapist from the actual historical present,"[98] that to him, "Time was psychologically of no interest ...."[99] But how can a *phainomenon* appear (without ravaging us unnecessarily) if we avert our gaze from "here and now"? And should our "necessary angel" take the form of a blank wall, how would we address it, if we immediately covered over its "emptiness and barrenness"? Those Giegerich essays I read early on, especially the nuclear bomb papers, completed for me Hillman's revolutionizing move because they showed it was possible to soulfully face today's constructed world in all its seeming soullessness, from which Hillman had recoiled despite a few inspired gestures.

Return ("something will start to move")

Circling back now to our opening anecdote, here is James, looking at the wall in Zurich, and Wolfgang, critical of his friend's impulse to change what he sees before him. To Giegerich this is, while here merely casual and offhand, still emblematic of Hillman's larger theoretical failure. Hillman should have remembered his own adage, that "Our surface presents our depth."[100] Rather than proposing corrective responses – moralistic, activist, aesthetic – to our most distressing phenomena, to today's presenting problems, he should have trusted in psychology's uroboric methodology, for he himself acknowledged the supreme value of "staying with what is happening, staying in the mess ... Deepening insists: no avoidance and no escape."[101] In general, outside this issue, he would certainly agree with Giegerich (and with Jung's famous admonition about *holding the tension of the opposites*), that "if we do not try to steal away from this hopeless situation by means of some defense mechanisms, if instead we honestly endure our being stuck, paradoxically something will start to move. A reversal takes place."[102] Here, he ignored his own better sense. Jung himself said, "I am convinced that the growing impoverishment of symbols has a meaning."[103] Giegerich, thankfully, took up the challenge of that meaning.[104]

If the outline of psychological movement was complete with Jung's insight into its uroboric nature, it requires only the ongoing elaboration of its intricacies, a willingness to accept its revolutionary implications, and the courage to stick to the phenomena. And if Giegerich takes Jung further than Hillman did, any move beyond Giegerich can only be, ever and anew, more deeply into here and now.

My deepest thanks to Wolfgang Giegerich, Gilles Goyette, John Robertson, and the editors.

Notes

1 Wolfgang Giegerich, "James Hillman. An Assessment," (unpublished, unpaginated manuscript, 2012), PDF; quoted by permission.
2 James Hillman, "Once More into the Fray: A Response to Wolfgang Giegerich's 'Killings'." *Spring 56: A Journal of Archetype and Culture* (1994): 2.
3 Giegerich, "James Hillman. An Assessment."
4 Giegerich, "James Hillman. An Assessment."
5 Wolfgang Giegerich, "Shalt thou build me an house for me to dwell in? Or: Anima mundi and Time. A response to Hillman's 'Cosmology for Soul. From Universe to Cosmos'," in *The Soul Always Thinks – Collected English Papers, Vol. 4* (New Orleans: Spring Journal Books, 2010), 114.
6 Hillman, "Once More into the Fray," 2.
7 Quoted in Wolfgang Giegerich, "C. G. Jung's Psychology Project as a Response to the Condition of the World," in *The Flight into the Unconscious – An Analysis of C.G. Jung's Psychology Project: Collected English Papers, Vol. 5* (New Orleans: Spring Journal Books, 2013), 2.
8 James Hillman, "The Imagination of Air and the Collapse of Alchemy." *Eranos Jahrbuch 50 – 1981*: 332. This paper presents one of Hillman's most insightful, radical explorations of the direction Giegerich would continue to pursue.
9 Wolfgang Giegerich, *The Soul Always Thinks Collected English Papers, Vol. IV* (Woodstock, Conn.; Lancaster: Spring Journal, Inc., 2010), 73.
10 Giegerich, *The Soul Always Thinks*, 77.
11 "In July 1789, ... the king's aide, the Duke of Rochefoucauld-Liancourt, arrived to inform Louis of the fall of the Bastille. 'Is this a revolt?' the king asked. Rochefoucauld answered, 'No, sire, it is a revolution.' ... Louis XVI could have suppressed a revolt; after the *revolution*, however, nothing can ever be the same again." Michael R. Caplan, "Revolt or Revolution? Hillman, Giegerich and the Completion of the Psychological Move," *ISPDI Newsletter* (August, 2013).
12 Sonu Shamdasani, *Jung and the Making of Modern Psychology: The Dream of a Science* (Cambridge: Cambridge University Press, 2003), 15.
13 Wolfgang Giegerich, *The Soul's Logical Life: Towards a Rigorous Notion of Psychology* (Frankfurt a/M: Peter Lang GmbH, 1998), 278.
14 James Hillman, *Loose Ends: Primary Papers in Archetypal Psychology* (Dallas: Spring Publications, 1975), 60.
15 James Hillman, *Re-Visioning Psychology* (New York: Harper & Row, 1977), 57.
16 Wolfgang Giegerich, "The Opposition of Individual and Collective," C.G. Jung Page online seminar (Oct. 5, 1998, 18:56:34), accessed 1998, URL unavailable.
17 John Sallis, *Stone* (Bloomington: Indiana University Press, 1994), 14.
18 Wolfgang Giegerich, "Deliverance from the Stream of Events: Okeanos and the Circulation of the Blood," in *The Neurosis of Psychology: Primary Papers Towards a Critical Psychology – Collected English Papers, Vol. 1* (New Orleans: Spring Journal Books, 2005), 241.
19 Wolfgang Giegerich in Giegerich, David L. Miller and Greg Mogenson, *Dialectics and Analytical Psychology: The El Capitan Canyon Seminar* (New Orleans, LA: Spring Journal Inc., 2005), 2.
20 Wolfgang Giegerich, "Jungian Psychology as Metaphysics? A response to Sean McGrath," *International Journal of Jungian Studies* 7:3 (September 2015): 248.
21 Wolfgang Giegerich "The Flight into the Unconscious: C.G. Jung's Psychology Project," in *The Flight into the Unconscious*, 177–78.
22 Wolfgang Giegerich, "Soul and World" (unpublished, unpaginated paper from 2012 Conference of the ISPDI); quoted by permission of the author.
23 Giegerich, *The Soul's Logical Life*, 231.
24 James Hillman, *The Dream and the Underworld* (New York: Harper & Row, 1979), 46.

25 Giegerich, "James Hillman. An Assessment."
26 Wolfgang Giegerich, *What Is Soul?* (New Orleans, LA: Spring Journal Inc., 2012), 5–6.
27 Hillman, *The Dream and the Underworld*, 213 n. 48.
28 Giegerich, "James Hillman. An Assessment."
29 See Chapter 1 of Giegerich's *What Is Soul?* for a discussion of this topic.
30 Wolfgang Giegerich, "Introduction: Psychology and the Other," in *Soul-Violence – Collected English Papers, Vol. 3* (New Orleans: Spring Journal Books, 2008), 1.
31 Giegerich, *What Is Soul?* 83.
32 Wolfgang Giegerich, "Introduction: The Object of Psychology," in *Technology and the Soul: From the Nuclear Bomb to the World Wide Web – Collected English Papers, Vol. 2* (New Orleans: Spring Journal Books, 2007), 12.
33 Wolfgang Giegerich, "Introduction," in *The Neurosis of Psychology*, 8.
34 Wolfgang Giegerich, "'Irrelevantification' or: On the Death of Nature, the Construction of 'the Archetype,' and the Birth of Man," in *The Soul Always Thinks*, 413.
35 James Hillman, *Anima: An Anatomy of a Personified Notion* (Dallas, Texas: Spring Publications, 1985), 149.
36 Wolfgang Giegerich, "Once More, the Reality/Irreality Issue: A Reply to Hillman's Reply," in *Soul-Violence*, 335.
37 Giegerich, *The Soul's Logical Life*, 274, on the "Notion" or "Truth" in his reading of the Actaion/Artemis myth.
38 James Hillman, *Anima*, 143.
39 C.G. Jung, *Analytical Psychology: Its Theory and Practice: The Tavistock Lectures* (New York, NY: Vintage Books, 1970), 5.
40 Quoted in Wolfgang Giegerich, *Neurosis: The Logic of a Metaphysical Illness* (New Orleans, LA: Spring Journal Inc., 2013), 10.
41 Wolfgang Giegerich, "Jungian Psychology: A Baseless Enterprise – Reflections on our Identity as Jungians," in *The Neurosis of Psychology*, 168.
42 Quoted in James Hillman, *Archetypal Psychology: A Brief Account* (Dallas: Spring Publications, Inc., 1983), 23.
43 Giegerich, *Soul-Violence*, 319.
44 Giegerich, *The Neurosis of Psychology*, 3.
45 Giegerich, *The Soul's Logical Life*, 237: "Such is the Notion, and such is the logical life of the soul."
46 Wolfgang Giegerich, *Working With Dreams: Initiation into the Soul's Speaking About Itself* (New York: Routledge, 2021), 21.
47 James Hillman, "Silver and the White Earth (Part 2)." *Spring: An Annual of Archetypal Psychology and Jungian Thought* (1981): 56–57.
48 Hillman, *The Dream and the Underworld*, 127.
49 John Sallis, *Double Truth* (Albany, NY: State University of New York Press. 1995), 206.
50 Giegerich, *Working With Dreams*, 21.
51 Quoted in Herbert Blau, *The Dubious Spectacle: Extremities of Theater, 1976–2000* (Minneapolis: University of Minnesota Press, 2002), 310.
52 Giegerich, *Working With Dreams*, 127.
53 Giegerich, *Working With Dreams*, 120.
54 Giegerich, *Working With Dreams*, 108.
55 Quoted in James Hillman, "An Inquiry into Image." *Spring: An Annual of Archetypal Psychology and Jungian Thought* (1977): 75.
56 James Hillman, "Image-Sense." *Spring: An Annual of Archetypal Psychology and Jungian Thought* (1979): 139.
57 Hillman, "An Inquiry into Image," 68–69.
58 James Hillman, "Further Notes on Images." *Spring: An Annual of Archetypal Psychology and Jungian Thought* (1978): 160.

59 Wolfgang Giegerich, "The Smuggling Inherent in the Logic of the 'Psychology of the Unconscious,'" in *The Flight into the Unconscious*, 155.
60 Hillman, "Further Notes on Images," 172.
61 Hillman, "Image-Sense," 134.
62 Giegerich, *The Soul's Logical Life*, 273.
63 Wolfgang Giegerich, "Hospitality towards the Gods in an Ungodly Age: Philemon–Faust–Jung," in *The Neurosis of Psychology*, 203.
64 Giegerich, *Working With Dreams*, 110.
65 Giegerich, *Working With Dreams*, 111.
66 Quoted in George Whalley, *Commentary on Aristotle's Poetics* (Montreal & Kingston: McGill-Queen's University Press, 1997), 80 n. 66.
67 Hillman, "An Inquiry into Image," 69.
68 James Hillman, "Back to Beyond: On Cosmology," in *Archetypal Process: Self and Divine in White, Jung, and Hillman*, ed. David Ray Griffin (Evanston, Illinois: Northwestern University Press, 1989), 252.
69 Hillman, "Back to Beyond," 252.
70 Quoted in Wolfgang Giegerich, "Closure and Setting Free or, The Bottled Spirit of Alchemy and Psychology," in *The Flight into the Unconscious*, 391.
71 Hillman, "Further Notes on Images," 161.
72 Giegerich, *The Neurosis of Psychology*, 12.
73 Wolfgang Giegerich, "The Lesson of the Mask," in *The Neurosis of Psychology*, 257.
74 Hillman, *Archetypal Psychology: A Brief Account*, 23.
75 Hillman, *Re-Visioning Psychology*, 135.
76 Hillman, *Archetypal Psychology: A Brief Account*, 45.
77 Wolfgang Giegerich, "The Burial of the Soul in Technological Civilization," in *Technology and the Soul*, 204.
78 Giegerich, *The Neurosis of Psychology*, 203.
79 Giegerich, *Working With Dreams*, 15.
80 James Hillman, *Healing Fiction* (Woodstock, CT: Spring Publications, Inc., 1983), 4.
81 John R. Betz, *After Enlightenment: The Post-Secular Vision of J.G. Hamann* (West Sussex, UK: Wiley-Blackwell, 2012), xii.
82 Wolfgang Giegerich, "The Alchemy of History," in *Soul-Violence*, 395.
83 Giegerich, *Technology and the Soul*, 16.
84 James Hillman, *Inter Views: Conversations between James Hillman and Laura Pozzo on Therapy, Biography, Love, Soul, Dreams, Work, Imagination and the State of the Culture* (New York: Harper & Row, 1983), 14.
85 Wolfgang Giegerich, "The Leap after the Throw: On 'Catching Up With' Projections and the Origin of Psychology," in *The Neurosis of Psychology*, 71.
86 Wolfgang Giegerich, "The Opposition of 'Individual' and 'Collective': Psychology's Basic Fault – Reflections on Today's Magnum Opus of the Soul," in *The Flight into the Unconscious*, 353: "This is why I want to mine the objective phenomena (for example, the phenomena of Globalization, Profit Maximation, etc.) for soul ... I want to listen to what the real process is telling me; I want to be taught by the Real how I have to think ...."
87 Wolfgang Giegerich, "The Present as Dimension of the Soul: 'Actual Conflict' and Archetypal Psychology," in *The Neurosis of Psychology*, 104.
88 Wolfgang Giegerich, "The Sacrifice of Isaac and the Watershed of History: Preparatory and Methodological Remarks Concerning the Topic of Ritual Killings," in *Soul-Violence*, 175.
89 Giegerich, *What Is Soul?* 93.
90 Hillman, *Re-Visioning Psychology*, 105.
91 Wolfgang Giegerich, "*Psychologie Larmoyante*: Glen Slater, for example. On Psychology's Failure to Face the Modern World," in *The Soul Always Thinks*, 509.

92 "At the end of the nineteenth century, many figures in the West sought to establish a scientific psychology that would be independent of philosophy, theology, biology, anthropology, literature, medicine, and neurology, whilst taking over their traditional subject matters." Shamdasani, *Jung and the Making of Modern Psychology*, 4.
93 Wolfgang Giegerich, "The Nuclear Bomb and the Fate of God: On the *First Nuclear Fission*," in *Technology and the Soul*, 98.
94 Giegerich, *The Neurosis of Psychology*, 170.
95 Hillman, "Silver and the White Earth (Part 2)," 57.
96 Wolfgang Giegerich, "The Rescued Child, or the Misappropriation of Time: On the Search for Meaning," in *Soul-Violence*, 47.
97 Wolfgang Giegerich, "The End of Meaning and the Birth of Man: An essay about the state reached in the history of consciousness and an analysis of C.G. Jung's psychology project," in *The Soul Always Thinks*, 205.
98 James Hillman, "Divergences," unpublished paper from the Thiasos seminar on Giegerich/Hillman (2008); quoted by permission of Marcus Quintaes.
99 Giegerich, "James Hillman. An Assessment."
100 James Hillman, *Egalitarian Typologies versus the Perception of the Unique* (Dallas: Spring Publications, 1986), 21.
101 James Hillman, *Kinds of Power: A Guide to Its Intelligent Uses* (New York: Doubleday, 1995), 51.
102 Giegerich, *The Neurosis of Psychology*, 155.
103 Quoted in Giegerich, *The Flight into the Unconscious*, 14.
104 I have my own interpretation of what today's "nothing is sacred" means, related to my very particular and limited criticisms of Giegerich, but I cannot address that here.

Chapter 8

Vicarius I-Statement
From Substance to Subject

Greg Mogenson

Some Words to Begin with from Jung and Hegel

In a passage of great importance to psychology as the discipline of interiority, C.G. Jung highlights the *subjectivity* of psychology. In contrast to the other sciences, each of which is devoted to the study of objects construed as external to themselves, "the psychology of complex phenomena,"

> ... lacks a point which is distinct from [its] objects, ... [From this it follows that] psychology inevitably merges with the psychic process itself. It can no longer be distinguished from the latter, and so turns into it. ... the effect of this is that the process attains to consciousness. In this way, psychology actualizes the unconscious urge to consciousness. It is, in fact, the coming to consciousness of the psychic process, but it is not, in the deeper sense, an explanation of this process, for no explanation of the psychic can be anything other than the living process of the psyche itself.[1]

Dovetailing nicely with the dialectic of archimedeanlessness that Jung here describes is a statement from Hegel:

> ... everything turns on grasping and expressing the True, not only as *Substance*, but equally as *Subject*.[2]

In this essay, I shall be discussing a kind of interpretative statement that analysts may be inspired to make from time to time when working from the analytic attitude that these passages imply. Throughout the whole of what follows, the reader is invited to bear them in mind.

The Analyst's Saying "I ..." On Behalf of the Patient

In *As You Like It*, through the mouthpiece of one of his characters, Shakespeare declares "... the world's a stage ... all ... men and women merely Players."[3] Now, if this be so does it also mean that analysts, too, will be cast at

DOI: 10.4324/9781003381150-9

times, not merely as one or another of the supporting characters of that familiar play called Transference, but at once both less than this and more, as the *understudies* or *stunt doubles* of the men and women who are their patients?

I raise this question because of a mode of expression that I have become increasingly aware of using in my practice. In barest description, it amounts to this. After attentively listening to some matter of interest—be it a life situation or a dream, a symptom or an emotional experience—I am astonished to realize, "breaking a leg," as it were, that the interpretive comment I have then given voice to has the form of an I-statement said on behalf of the patient.

Now I hasten to emphasize that such utterances on my part, as effective and furthering as they typically are, have little or nothing to do with technique. I do not with artful intent set out to present my interpretations in this manner. Nor is it my intention, as I reflect upon this mode of expression, to put a new tool in anyone's toolkit. My interest, rather, is wholly limited to the phenomenality of such vicarius soliloquizing. Out of the mouths of babes and analysts alike, my speaking in this way—both as the patient and for him—has phenomenon character. An event of meaning has occurred, in part, through my giving voice to it. Anticipating a bit, it could even be said that such statements as these are but the further determination of the materials being interpreted, the topics discussed—their becoming subject, as it were. Which, of course, is pretty much what Jung was getting at with his essential insight that far from standing outside the psychic process as *explanation* of it, psychology is but the phenomenology-continuing *expression* of "the coming to consciousness of the psychic process" itself.[4] It only needs to be added that the same holds true for what the psychotherapist and analyst say. Their utterances, too, are not explanations of the patient's psychic situation or process, but rather and at best, the expression of "the coming to consciousness" of these.[5]

Simply, and yet not so simply, it happens like this. Concurrent with listening to the case material, there is a reflective moment in which listening gives way to what might be described as a thoughtful overhearing of itself restating what's been heard, and this, moreover, in such a way that, relating itself to itself in the matter at hand, what I like to call the subject matter's I, gives rise to itself, voice to itself, as its own recursive and mercurial result.

Now, I say "the subject matter's I" to indicate occasions when the I that speaks is not the me that could be pointed at sitting vis-à-vis the patient in the consulting room, nor the patient, either, for that matter. While, of course, the two of us do sit there like that, speaking words for which we are separately responsible, the I that like some "third of the two" or "one for all" subsequently establishes itself,[6] far from existing beforehand, is only produced in the first place as the *mise en scène*–distilling result of its own saying[7]—hence its characterization as the subject matter's I.

But what does it mean, "produced as its own *mise en scène*–distilling result"? What kind of a subject is that? In the discussions that follow we shall be delving into this question. Here, at the outset, I would simply reply that just as one is not a listener before one listens or an interpreter before one interprets, so the subject is not truly that until, "breaking the fourth wall,"[8] so to speak, what can variously be called the concentrated result of the entirety of the material at hand, the distillate meaning of the setting and all the characters of the apperceptive surround, or again, the unity of the unity and difference of all the moments of the situation that has been "staged by the soul," has ventured to become conscious, ventured to say "I."

Objections and Clarifications

Now I can readily imagine that initial impressions will have already brought some objections to the fore. First among these might be the very reasonable concern that analysts speaking in the manner I have described may be doing too much of the patients' work for them. In psychotherapy and analysis patients have to invest themselves, apply themselves. Different from medical and dental treatment, the talking cure depends upon their work, too. Wouldn't those times when the analyst stands in for the patient, saying "I ..." on his or her behalf, undermine this requirement?

Another objection follows on the heels of this one. Would an analyst's speaking in this way not come across in a too-authoritative manner? Analysts and therapists, after all, as Lacan aptly observed, are already in the position of "the one supposed to know." Never mind that they may not know and may even be barking up the wrong tree. Surely, no licence should be issued for them to wildly act this out.

In response to these perfectly valid concerns, I can only reiterate what I said earlier about the phenomenon character of such interpretive statements. Far from being a technique that anyone should endeavor to apply, what I am here referring to as the analyst's speaking on behalf of the patient is just something that happens, if it happens at all. Having event character (or at least largely so), it is not authenticated by the analyst's authority, training, or skill, but only by its phenomenality as such.

Another, this time more sympathetic, first impression might be that statements said on behalf of the patient constitute a form of empathy. Having felt into the patient, the analyst in this way demonstrates attunement with him. In response to this, I would only say that the kinds of statements I have in mind have less to do with empathizing with patients (as important as this may simultaneously be) than with opening up the psychological difference. Jung famously said it is not the psyche that is in us, but we who are in the psyche.[9] Whereas empathy is usually focused upon the inner of the patient (upon his feelings and concerns at a personal or ego level), the vicarius I-statements that I have in mind are in each case the speculative or logic-speaking result of exposure to the entirety of the situation in which the (analyst as) patient finds himself.

It is a matter, then, not of "vicarious introspection,"[10] as empathy has sometimes been called (though this may find a place in it, too), but of a gesture wherein the subject or interpreter takes a step back, as it were, to widen the horizon in front of him. The horizon widened in front of the interpreter—in our context, in front of the analyst in his role as the understudy or stand-in for the patient—corresponds to that second sense of psyche that Jung distinguished, the psyche we are in. While we may, to be sure, have plenty of subjective psychic content in our inner, the psyche that we are in and that surrounds us outwardly to the very horizon, has, as our dreams and apperceptions attest, the objective character and veracity of a scene or landscape, which of course is what Shakespeare was getting at when he said the world's a stage.

Analyzing from the Self

There is yet another first impression to be noted and departed from. In the Jungian tradition a distinction is drawn between "analysing from the Self," on the one hand, and analyzing from the persona or the ego, on the other. With respect to the first-mentioned of these modes of interpretation, two anecdotes from former analysands of Jung's are especially pertinent. One of these, a recollection of Marvin Spiegelman, is from a final meeting that he as newly fledged analyst had had with Jung just after graduating from the Jung Institute.

Following upon an initial period of sitting together with it seemed nothing to say to one another, Jung, reports Spiegelman,

> began to speak, from out of himself somewhere. He spoke of his own life. Throughout all this apparent soliloquy, I was totally present too and I had the experience, subsequently reported by others also, that Jung was "speaking to my condition," and addressing himself to all my problems, fears, concerns, and deep desires. Most of all, it was an experience of Self speaking to Self.[11]

Another example of Jung "analyzing from the Self" is recounted by Jane Wheelwright. In her report Wheelwright speaks of how in Jung's presence "one felt as though all the surrounding matter had turned into whirling molecules."

> Everything there seemed to be moving, melting, changing forms. Everything stirred. Reality blurred, conversation happened unplanned. I felt someone, not me, spoke through me and someone not Jung was speaking through him. There was also the feeling of being swept into the depths of a perilous, dangerous underworld but since Jung had descended into this strange world and emerged so could I. In his presence I did not register on the difference of our statures! An archetype had taken over? Whatever it was, it seemed to be creating before my eyes and ears and senses, a model of the changed person I was meant finally to become. Trying the new me on, so to speak. Equally strange was Jung. Instead of being the doctor who cures you, he was allowing himself to be equally affected .... Two people were caught in a vise that was forcing them to undergo an important rearrangement of themselves that had significance—some meaning far beyond them.[12]

Although in neither of these recollections is Jung described as overtly saying "I" on behalf of the patient, there is much in them that is in accord with the account I have given of the analyst's voicing interpretations in this way. Both Spiegelman and Wheelwright remember Jung as having given voice to their soul situation, and this, moreover, not from some doctorly perch outside, but in the mediating manner of an intercessor, from out of their own depths. The only problem with these accounts is that without any discussion of the actual work that was conducted or of the truths discussed, they amount to little more than idealizing tributes to Jung as intuitively gifted analyst and mana-personality, on the one hand, and to the archetype of the Self, on the other.

Now it is true, of course, that Jung was a great man and master analyst. What is pertinent in our context, however, has more to do with the analyst's putting off *his* greatness, *his* brilliance, and letting the material at hand—in these cases, the soul situation of his patients—speak through him.[13] Though not explicitly indicated in these reports, this, I suspect, was very much in play in Jung's work as an analyst. Just as Mrs. Wheelwright recalls that she did not register the difference of stature between herself as Jung's patient and he as her doctor, neither, evidently, did Jung. On the contrary, his speaking as and for the patient was rooted in his having truly taken that old adage to heart, the one about nothing human being alien to me. And it follows from this that the speculative insight that the Jungian tradition has formulated as "Analyzing from the Self" is more humbly sourced than its usual, more idealized conceptualization suggests.

An Approximate Example

I can well imagine that an example of the therapist speaking in the first person vicarius would be welcome at this point. Surveying our literature for an approximation of this, I find myself thinking of Jung's essay, "Individual Dream Symbolism in Relation to Alchemy."[14] In that essay, Jung provides extensive commentary on the dream series of a dreamer about whom little more is indicated than that he was "a young man of excellent scientific education."[15] Now the odd, but in our context, interesting thing about this commentary is that it is adduced by Jung in a completely vicarius manner. Or better to say, in an *absolutely* vicarius manner, since the commentary and interpretations that Jung offers are absolute in the sense of their being *absolved* (= freed) from the difference between the dreamer and the analyst. The circumstance of this was that Jung did not want to influence the production and content of the dreams with his presence and so did not take the dreamer on as his patient. It was only after the dreams of this series were dreamt that Jung became their analyst. And how did he manage this—to interpret the dreams without the dreamer to provide them with context and associations? As questionable as this may be to some, Jung met this challenge by taking the series itself as the context of each particular dream and then "proceed[ing]," as he put it, "as if I had had the dreams myself and were thereby in a position to supply the context."[16]

Turning now to a dream of this series, let us observe as best we can its being interpretatively changed-up into the form of subject by the analyst's saying I in the patient's stead, or as Jung just worded this, by his approaching the dream as if he had dreamt it himself.

The twelfth dream of the dream series is presented in a single sentence:

> The dreamer finds himself with his father, mother, and sister in a very dangerous situation on the platform of a tram-car.[17]

Interiorizing himself into this dream, debuting upon its stage as if he were its dreamer, Jung declares with respect to the figure of the dreamer,

> He has fallen right back into childhood, a time when we are still a long way from wholeness. Wholeness is represented by the family, and its components are still projected upon the members of the family and personified by them. But this state is dangerous to the adult because regressive: It denotes a splitting of the personality which primitive man experiences as the perilous "loss of soul." In the break-up the personal components that have been integrated with such pains are once more sucked into the outside world. The individual loses his guilt and exchanges it for infantile innocence; once more he can blame the wicked father for this and the unloving mother for that, and all the time he is caught in this inescapable causal nexus like a fly in a spider's web, without noticing that he has lost his moral freedom. But no matter how much the parents and grandparents have sinned against the child, the man who is really adult will accept these sins as his own condition which has to be reckoned with. Only a fool is interested in other people's guilt, since he cannot alter it. The wise man learns only from his own guilt.[18]

I cite this passage for sake of the statement that Jung subsequently makes. Immediately following upon his saying that "The wise man learns only from his own guilt," Jung adds that rather than unravelling into blame, such a one will ask himself, "'Who am I that all this should happen to me?'," even as he looks into his own heart for the answer.[19] This, I would offer, is a fair approximation of what I am calling vicarius I-statement.

Now, of course, if the dreamer had been Jung's patient and this dream had been presented in an actual session, it would have been given in the first person, not the third. The dreamer would have stated, "*I find myself with my father, mother, and sister in a very dangerous situation on the platform of a tram-car.*" With this in mind, we can readily imagine how a more fulsome speculative interpretation could have unfolded. Just by restating the dream out loud, the analyst would become the speaker of its I. More boldly than the patient, perhaps, who most often cannot make head nor tail of his dreams, the analyst would then proceed to read and re-read it in a way that lets all the details that are predicated of the I come home to the I, even as, maintaining itself in the face of such self-othering negations, the I constitutes itself in the first place as their sublated result.

"I've fallen right back into my childhood," declares the analyst into the room. "I'm with my family in a dangerous situation, dangerous because regressive." "The integrated, self-responsible man that I am, has unravelled into mother, father, and sister." "But while this is so," we can imagine him then saying, "I do not succumb, but rather ask myself" (and with these words the aforementioned "fourth wall" is broken such that, applying itself to itself, consciousness becomes self-consciousness): "Who am I that all this should happen to me?"

The Speculative Subjectivity of the Self-Positing I

In the question Jung gave voice to on behalf of the dreamer, a speculative form of the I posits itself, establishes itself. By this I mean that the I referred to by Jung in his vicarius I-statement is not so much some already existing ego to which things have additionally happened, but the other way around, the result in the first place of the names it gives to the circumstances and contingencies that it sublatedly produces itself as the logical essence or knower of.

Now with this name-conferring, subjectivity-constituting turning of the tables upon circumstance and contingency in mind, let us delve a little deeper in to the absolute subjectivity of an I that, to say it with an expression of Hegel's, is as at home with itself on the object side of the ordinarily prevailing difference of consciousness as it is on the subject side.[20] The first thing to be noted with respect to this is that while "I" is simply a pronoun that designates the unique subjectivity of the me that each of us are, it is also and at the same time a universal that, in what might be called an "it takes one to know one" manner, produces itself as the knower of other universals and of universality as such.

"In thinking an object," writes Hegel,

> I make it into thought and deprive it of its sensuous aspect; I make it into something which is directly and essentially mine. Since it is in thought that I am first by myself, I do not penetrate an object until I understand it; it then ceases to stand over against me and I have taken from it the character of its own which it had in opposition to me. Just as Adam said to Eve: "Thou art flesh of my flesh and bone of my bone," so mind says: "This is mind of my mind and its foreign character has disappeared."[21]

This is an important statement. Updating that great speculative ur-statement of the bible, "flesh of my flesh and bone of my bone,"[22] Hegel well-conveys the difference-sublating "intentionality toward the other"[23] through which the logic that pervades both the subject side and the object side of the ordinarily prevailing difference of consciousness—let us call this, the rib that these both share![24]—gives voice to itself as I. And here it may be added that it is this I, which in another context Hegel has characterized as "an 'I' that is a 'We' and

a 'We' that is an 'I',"[25] that the analyst gives voice to on those vicariusly interpretive occasions we are concerned with in this chapter, "mind of my mind,"
indeed.

Variations on this Theme from Jung and Giegerich

A moment ago, I referred to our text from Hegel as an updating of Adam's
words to Eve in the bible. Updating these again, a passage from Jung and
another from Giegerich come to mind. In the first of these, Jung, speaking to
students of the Jung institute about the interpretation of dreams, encourages
them to expose themselves wholeheartedly to the material at hand, interpreting it boldly. The analyst, he declares, "must give credit to his own interpretation. He must have courage, he must help; [otherwise] it is as if a man is
bleeding to death and you *ponder!*"[26] Reading these words, we may be reminded
of the descriptions Spiegelman and Wheelwright gave of Jung's work with
them in analysis. Clearly, when offering interpretations to his patients, Jung
shared a rib with them, in the sense of this described. As for Jung's own further
account of the interpretive boldness he recommends, this he maintains can be
confidently ventured to the extent that the analyst is at the same time modest
enough to take correction from the further unfolding of the psychic process.
"You can only say, 'My God, I don't *know*, but if it is an error, the unconscious
will correct it."[27] It is by being faithfully rooted in such a conviction, at the
same time as he is immersed in the matter at hand, that the analyst is able to
come boldly forward with his (returning to Jung's wording), "'It seems to me
like this.' And stand for it!"

Turning to Giegerich, I am immediately reminded of his similarly "flesh of
my flesh" or "mind of my mind" interpretation-emboldening statement, "psychology begins where any phenomenon (whether physical or mental, 'real' or
fantasy image) is interiorized absolute-negatively into itself, and I find myself
in its internal infinity. This is what it takes; psychology cannot be had for
less."[28] Succinctly descriptive of the speculative turn in analytical psychology,
this is an important passage. And when cited in our context three of its words
are of especial importance—its author's bold declaration that "I find myself"
in the matter at hand. Restating this maxim with the emphasis placed upon
these words it may readily be added that on each interpretive occasion the kind
of insight that is deserving of the name "psychology," produces itself, freshly
and anew, via the analyst's giving voice to the phenomenon he is concerned
with (in the context of psychotherapy, to the patient's material) *as I*—which is
also to say, as or in the register of what we have been calling "the first person
vicarius." For the I that is referred to here is not the empirical subject, existing
beforehand, but rather, in the spirit of what Jung called "the coming to consciousness of the psychic process itself," the speculative subject that only gives
rise to itself as the result of the phenomenon at hand obtaining self-character
through its being interiorized into itself.

Imitative I-Statements and their Difference from Speculative Ones

In an earlier section of this essay, I briefly differentiated between occasions when the therapist says I on the patient's behalf and ordinary expressions of empathy. I want now to further elaborate upon this difference by contrasting what in the psychotherapy literature are called "imitative statements" with the kind of statement that is of concern to us here.

The term "imitative statement" comes from Leston Havens, who has discussed how an analytic therapist, drawing upon the feelings and impressions evoked in him by a patient, may venture to speak out on the patient's behalf. When with a doubtful person, for example, he may simply offer up the statement, "How can I decide?"; with a depressed one, "What hope is there?"; and when with a fearful one, "Where does one find courage."[29] The merit of this style of expression is readily appreciated when we stop to consider the extent to which empathic statements can tend to "force patients to feel what the therapist believes they feel or should feel."[30] Especially in our day, when psycho-educational counselling has so much replaced the interpretive effort to work things out from scratch, it is likely that a well-meaning therapist may have his thumb on the scale in this way. In view of this, a more neutral kind of empathy may be called for, one which "does not challenge, impress, or reach into what is private and defended," but rather, "increases or secures the other's self-possession," via the therapist's offering himself to the patient for the patient's purpose. And here I would add that a further merit of such imitative statements lies in the alternative they provide to the therapist's asking questions too frequently. When questions are repeatedly addressed to them, patients may feel put on the spot, their therapy like an interrogation.[31] What a relief, then, when the movement from consciousness to self-consciousness is instead mediated by means of comments and offerings of the imitative kind. All this, I believe, is evident in Havens's further examples. On behalf of a woman who, while confident in her beauty and desirous of getting married, was puzzled by a man who was highly inconsistent in the attention he showed her, Havens exclaimed at various points in the session, "Can he love me?" "Can I love Him?" "Why is he so elusive?" "*Aren't* I beautiful?" After capturing her interest with these statements, he then in closing returned to his position in the dyad saying, "I just hope he's worth your while."[32] In another case, this time with a male patient whose difficulties stemmed from his being in relation to others "either up front and naked or hidden away,"[33] Havens again found imitative statements to be helpful. "When I want something, it runs away," he was able to say for the patient with respect to one situation they had been discussing. "I have no rights," he said in another.[34]

This brief account of imitative statements is pretty much sufficient for our purposes here. It only needs to be added that while I hold such statements in high esteem and make frequent use of them in my work, their main importance in the present context is as a foil against which to throw into relief what is different about vicarius I-statements. We already know that vicarius I-statements have phenomenon character and are not, the way imitative ones are, a matter of technique. And to this it may be added that while in both kinds of statement the analyst speaks on behalf of the patient, the imitative and the vicarius ways of his doing so differ in that while the former mediates for the patient the taking up of a definite position, which of course is very important, the latter has rather to do with presenting such a position, not in terms of the difference of consciousness as which the ego exists, but from the viewpoint of the soul, or as this might also be expressed, in the light of the psychological difference. This is not to say that the psychological difference is not already opened up to at least a minimal extent in the case of imitative statements. Even with them the soul side of the psychological difference weighs in, if only very lightly, via the analyst's speaking in the manner of the aforementioned "'I' that is a 'We' and a 'We' that is an 'I'." Thus, in formal regards, if not yet concretely, the rapport of the "we" into which the patient is drawn is as much at odds with and negating of his stick-in-the-mud self-identicalness (even when content-wise it may seem to merely reiterate, mirror or redouble this) as it is with respect to the ordinarily prevailing subject-over-against-object, self-over-against-other difference of consciousness. But as I just said, all this is only a very minimal expression of the form of subject and the viewpoint of the soul. It is not yet wholeheartedly enough the voice of the objective soul situation to fully warrant the epithet "vicarius."

The Traditional Meaning of Vicarius and the Analyst as *Vicarius Animae*

I want now to touch upon the history of the word that I have been using to indicate the subject of this chapter. An old Latin term, "vicarius" means "substitute," "agent," "deputy." In Roman Catholicism it is used to indicate priests serving in one of the various ecclesiastical offices and of popes in their role as Vicars of Christ. In the Anglican Church the term is used for the clergy more generally, even the most undistinguished parish priest being called a vicar. In these institutional contexts, the idea is of a cleric who mediates for the people their highest values and principles by modeling for them the example of Christ. In olden days, by acting in this way the priest looked after the relationship with God, much as the cobbler looked after everyone's shoes. Sacred matters were his specialty. Individuals and peoples did not have to establish this themselves.

Of course, we analysts are also mediators. As a matter of routine, we are all the time mediating between the patient and his inner, on the one hand, and between the patient and other people, on the other. This very ordinary kind of mediation, however, is too horizontally oriented to warrant the term vicarius as its identifier. I say "horizontal" here because, for all their difference from each other, that which is intrapsychic (e.g., inner images, feelings, emotions) and that

which is interpersonal (i.e., people and their social dynamics) are alike in existing positively as things that can be pointed at on the horizontal plane of the
ordinary difference of consciousness. The vicarius mediation that an analyst
may additionally have to provide, by contrast, has a vertical character, as was
formerly the case with priestly mediators. Perpendicular to people and the psychology they have, it has to do with discerning, representing, and subjectively
giving voice to or speaking in the name, not of God any more or some religious
matter, but of the logically negative successor of these, the logic or concept that
invisibly and over our heads, so to speak, we live in and exist as in our times.
And here, further to this point, we may again recall Jung's teaching that it is not
so much that the psyche is in us, but rather we that are in the psyche.[35]

Now it is crucial to emphasize that the logic just spoken of, which can also
be referred to as "the soul of the real," has gone through enormous form
changes in the course of its history, as has the office of mediator in keeping
with these. Whereas formerly, in those times when religion dominated, the soul
had had the form of God, his mediator the form of priest, in our day, *post
mortem dei*, soul has the form of psychological phenomena, the mediator of
these the form of analyst.

Indicative of the movement from consciousness to self-consciousness, the
positivity of religion's substantiated form of thought has given way during the
last several centuries to the negativity of this come home to itself as the modern subject. Sweepingly illustrative of this movement is the contrast between,
on the one hand, the God in the Old Testament story who, upon appearing to
Moses as a bush that burned and yet was not consumed, identified himself as
"I am that I am,"[36] and, on the other hand, the *cogito* of Descartes, the I-think
of Kant, and the statements about the I that have been cited earlier from Hegel,
to name only these later philosophical thinkers. And Jung, too, took notice of
this form change in formulating what he called his "psychology 'with soul'."[37]
Indeed, by his lights, modern psychology in general is to be conceived of as
having arisen negatively, if I may put it this way, as the precipitate remainder
of the religion that preceded it. "All ages before us," he declared, "believed in
gods in some form or other. Only an unparalleled impoverishment of symbolism could enable us to rediscover the gods as psychic factors, that is, as archetypes of the unconscious."[38]

Although Jung speaks here of "rediscover[ing] the gods," it is really a matter of a change from the soul having the form of gods to it having the form
of subjectivity. Earlier I cited Jung as saying that psychology is not an explanation of the psychic process, but an expression of the coming to consciousness of this. Returning to this point in the present context, it is important to
realize that despite what I just said concerning its provenance, psychology is
not the *explanation* of the religion that proceeded it. Having arisen in the
wake of that earlier form of the soul, it is rather to be regarded as the *phenomenological expression* and *speculative result* of the soul's having obtained
the form of subject.

Expressing this in Hegelian terms, we could say that the verticality of the relationship that had formerly been conceived in pictorial terms as God above and Man below has in the modern situation gone under and across to become the infinitely negative I,[39] and this, moreover, in a manner that preserves the vertically of the former relation, which is also to say, the gradient of that former difference, if only by being what may variously be described as the seriousness, rectitude, universality and integrity that I as me am capable of when, cognizant of what is and mindful of others, I am up to the situation in which I find myself, true to myself therein.[40]

But here it may be objected, is this not asking too much? It is no small feat to be up to the situations we find ourselves in, let alone to "be a man in the place where no men are," as a saying from the Talmud admonishes.[41] Not even for those who have gone in for meditation, mindfulness, and techniques of the like. For they, too, may find, despite the mastery they have achieved with respect to regulating their thoughts and emotions, that they are just as daunted as anyone else when it comes to that "larger part of the soul that is outside the body."[42] A go-between may therefore be needed if there is to be any coming to terms with what Jung, updating this line from the alchemists, called the objective psyche. A mediator between the personalistic subjectivity of the individual and the objective subjectivity of the soul. Which is why Giegerich in one of his essays coins the term *"vicarius animae"* to designate the role of the psychotherapist.

Presenting Problems in the Light of the Psychological Difference

Giegerich's introduction of the term *vicarius animae* into our discourse has as its context a discussion of what the stance of the analyst must be with respect to symptomatic suffering and presenting complaints. The analyst, he insists, must have acquired, both for himself and for his patient's sake, a steadfastness in the face of disturbing psychic material and distressing symptoms. He cannot, as would those who indulge in the prissy spirituality of what Goethe, Hegel, and others of their period critiqued under the heading of "the beautiful soul," eschew the horrible and the bizarre, the sick and the wrong, declaring these to be inhuman or unsoulful. On the contrary, he must endeavor "to become the unshaken, unperturbed holding vessel for the patient's pathology."[43]

My patient is entitled to expect from me a genuine composure vis-à-vis the horrid aspects of his story…. I must be able to honestly *allow* his story *to be* the way it is … Despite its possibly horrid and inhuman appearance, … as therapist, as 'the *vicarius animae* on earth' (the representative of the soul standpoint in real life), I must accept it as *not*-alien and thus, with methodological awareness, give it its own place within the sphere of what is *humanum* and soulful. Each new pathology is a challenge and an invitation to me to conquer for myself the soul standpoint once again by overcoming myself as the "ego," the habitual everyday or man-on-the-street point of view, and so also my fear of or disgust for the abnormal.[44]

It will be noticed that the unflinching steadfastness that is central to Giegerich's characterization of the therapist as "the *vicarius animae* on earth" is conceived by him in terms of the psychological difference. Presented in this passage as the difference between the everyday viewpoint of the ego, on the one hand, and the analyst-mediated viewpoint of the soul, on the other, the psychological difference may also be figured as the difference between the horizontal and the vertical, as was discussed in the previous section. It must immediately be added, however, that ego and soul, horizontal and vertical, are not in our day the symbolically hypostasized, already distinct substantial opposites that they were for our religious forebears. They are not, that is to say, for us two already existing entities or domains that we subsequently bring together. In modern times, it is rather a matter of our starting from the everyday level of the ego, from the horizontal and earthly, and producing the verticality of the soul's view of things via an act of interpretive insight and seeing-through. Just as Menelaus in *The Iliad* holds the shapeshifting Proteus in an all-encompassing grip until a prophecy is wrung from him, and just as the alchemists placed the substances they were endeavouring to transform in a hermetically sealed vessel, so it is that via the therapist's steadfastness in the face of the patient's material, no matter how distressing and disturbing that material may be, that the psychological difference is opened up and the standpoint of the soul achieved.

It is a matter of feeling, or as Giegerich further points out, of the therapist's access to and use of a special kind of feeling which is not emotional, in the sense of having feelings, but rational, in the sense of exercising judgment.[45] Identified by Jung as "the feeling function,"[46] it is the therapist's capacity to discern what is truly of psychological significance from what is not by means of this rational kind of feeling that is important in our context. "Without feeling," writes Giegerich, "the soul cannot be apperceived. Feeling in this [rational] sense is what has the power to connect modern consciousness with the soul-in-the-real across the gap of our fundamental alienation from it. The capacity to feel is the bridge across the psychological difference, the bridge also across and beyond our subjective positive or negative feelings, so that we may become open to the heart of what *is*."[47]

But what has the feeling described got to do with that more objective level of subjectivity which (like some voice crying in the wilderness) the analyst hears in the patient's situation even as at the same time he enunciates it on his behalf?[48] In a statement subsequent to those I have already cited, Giegerich explicitly connects this mediating, psychological difference-establishing proclivity of the feeling function with the vicariusly mediated, more-than-egoic I. "Feeling," he writes, "is that mode *in* the empirical I in which the I with its initial egoic survival interests has gone under, has learned to be silent—has *died* as 'the ego.' Feeling is the soul's ambassador, ally, advocate, 'fifth column' in the empirical person, ... the *vicarius animae*. And as such it is the *copula*, the *ligamentum* or *vinculum* in the sense of alchemy, between empirical man ('I') and the soul ... as well as between positive-factual reality and the Mercurial spirit 'imprisoned' in that reality."[49]

So much, then, for the mediation that the analyst as *vicarius animae* provides. It only remains to be discussed how presenting problems, distressing symptoms, and the like can be insightfully grasped in their verticality and truth.

Giegerich has written about interpretive occasions wherein it becomes evident that *"What first appears as a content of consciousness is in truth the seed of what wants to become a radically new form of consciousness at large."*[50] Adapting this adage to the terms of our present discussion, we could also say that what is at first apperceived *horizontally* via the ordinarily prevailing subject here/object there difference of consciousness is the pivot point of what wants to be known *vertically*, speculatively, overarchingly and conceptually as the sublation of that flat external difference. Only think in this connection of those by no means uncommon dreams in which the figure of the dreamer desperately tries to evade what seems to be an imminent calamity; the threat, for example, posed by a menacing pursuer. Usually, it takes the steadfastness of the analyst in the face of such fraught situations to mediate for the dreamer the realization that the seemingly external other that the dream-I is intent on escaping *is its own other* and that what is happening on the ground, so to speak, has rather and more vertically to do with a transformation of consciousness, a changing of the mind. Beset by doubts, vexed by troubling anomalies, prey to second thoughts, the concept that the dreamer exists as (a.k.a. "the soul") is going through a self-negation. It is having to realize, as Giegerich puts it, "that the matter has all along *not* been what it had seemed to be,"[51] which, at the same time, is already its being exposed to the new form of the matter, the new apperception of its objective situation, the new form of truth.

So there we have it. The point is made. In the psychotherapeutic context the epithet "vicarius" is only fitting for the mediation of what is vertical. It only remains to be added that in its first immediacy the vertical corresponds, on the one hand, to the steadfastness of the analyst in the face of negations, and on the other, to those phenomena that are implicitly vertical in that they stick out like a sore thumb from the horizontal dimension, or as a stumbling block along the path of the ordinarily prevailing difference of consciousness. Hearing of such phenomena as he listens to the patient's account of his presenting problem, the analyst feels their surplus value, the import for the mind of what is suffered in the flesh, and "interpret[ing] from above downwards,"[52] as Jung once put it, speaks accordingly. And so it is—as the comeuppance of a truth hurts dialectic—that the verticality of the soul is produced, the soul side of the psychological difference insighted.[53] Changed-up by what it wants to but is unable to keep at bay, consciousness becomes self-consciousness. And this it achieves, in no small part, due to the analyst's vicariusly bringing forth from the patient's situation some version of that question, so productive of speculative insight, that Jung had raised on his dreamer's behalf, "Who am I that all this should happen to me?"

Notes

1 C. G. Jung, *CW* 8 § 429.
2 G. W. F. Hegel, *Phenomenology of Spirit*, A. V. Miller, trans. (Oxford: Oxford University Press, 1977), original work published 1807, § 17, 10.
3 William Shakespeare, *As You Like It*, Act II, Scene VII, line 138.
4 Jung, *CW* 8 § 429. It is interesting to reflect Jung's denouncement of the naïve, straightforward idea of explanation in favour of an emphasis upon "the coming to consciousness of the psychic process" in the following line from Hegel. Addressing what might be called the negation of explanation, Hegel writes, "The reason why 'explaining' affords so much self-satisfaction is just because in it consciousness is, so to speak, communing directly with itself, enjoying only itself; although it seems to be busy with something else, it is in fact occupied only with itself." Hegel, *Phenomenology of Spirit*, § 163, 101.
5 Of course, below the niveau of a truly *psychological* psychology, many psychologists do adapt a stance of external reflection and give explanations. For a discussion of how such clinical literalism may tend to hystericize the analytic process see my *The Dove in the Consulting Room: Hysteria and Anima in Bollas and Jung* (Hove and New York: Brunner-Routledge, 2003), 96–118.
6 I say "one for all" here to expand the sphere of reference of the more usual analytic term, "the third of the two."
7 Cf., Jung's reference to behaviours and happenings that are "merely staged, but staged in the peculiar way characteristic of hysteria, so that a *mise en scène* appears almost exactly like a reality." *CW* 4 § 364.
8 The reference here is to occasions when an actor in a play breaks out of the scene he is in by speaking directly to the audience.
9 "As I see it, the psyche is a world in which the ego is contained," Jung, *CW* 13 § 75. "You rightly emphasize that man in my view is enclosed in *the* psyche (not in *his* psyche)." Jung, 14 May 1950, Letter to Joseph Goldbrunner.
10 Note here in this phrase the word "vicarious" and its difference from my references in this chapter to "vicarius." Kohut, for whom empathy was of paramount important, avers that the "idea of an inner life of man, and thus of a psychology of complex mental states, is unthinkable, without our ability to know via vicarious introspection—my definition of empathy." Heinz Kohut, *The Restoration of the Self* (New York: International Universities Press, 1977), 306. "Vicarius," by contrast, is a Latin word meaning substitute or deputy, as will be discussed later in this essay.
11 Cited by John Haule, "Analyzing from the Self: An empirical phenomenology of the 'third' in analysis" in Roger Brooke, ed, *Pathways into the Jungian World: Phenomenology and Jungian Psychology* (London, New York: Routledge, 2000), 257.
12 Haule, "Analyzing from the Self," 258.
13 On this point compare Hegel's statement: "When I think, I give up my subjective particularity, sink myself in the matter, let thought follow its own course; and I think badly whenever I add something of my own." G. W. F. Hegel, *The Encyclopaedia Logic. Part 1 of the encyclopaedia of philosophical sciences with zusätze*, trans. T. F. Geraets, W. A. Suchting, H.S. Harris (Indianapolis/Cambridge: Hackett Publishing Company, 1991), § 24, 58.

14 C. G. Jung, *CW* 12, 39–223.
15 Jung, *CW* 12 § 45.
16 Jung, *CW* 12 § 49.
17 Jung, *CW* 12 § 151.
18 Jung, *CW* 12 § 152.
19 Jung, *CW* 12 § 152.
20 Cf. "In the Logic, thoughts are grasped in such a way that they have no content other than one that belongs to thinking itself, and is brought forth by thinking. So these thoughts are *pure* thoughts. Spirit is here purely at home with itself, and thereby free, for that is what freedom is: being at home with oneself in one's other, depending upon oneself, and being one's own determinant." Hegel, *The Encyclopaedia Logic. Part 1 of the encyclopaedia of philosophical sciences with zusätze*, § 24, 58.
21 G. W. F. Hegel, Hegel's *Philosophy of Right*, T. M. Knox, trans. (London, Oxford, New York: Oxford University Press, 1976), 226.
22 Genesis 2: 23.
23 Wolfgang Giegerich, *The Soul's Logical Life: Towards a Rigorous Notion of Psychology* (Frankfurt am Main: Peter Lang, 1998), 204.
24 The allusion is to the rib of Adam from which Eve was made.
25 Hegel, *Phenomenology of spirit*, § 177, 110.
26 C. G. Jung, *C. G. Jung Speaking: Interviews and Encounters*, William McGuire and R. F. C. Hull, editors (Princeton: Princeton University Press, 1977), 360.
27 Jung, *Jung Speaking*, 360. Although in this passage Jung refers to God and to "the unconscious" in substantializing terms, the reader will understand that what is important in our context is the dialectical character of the thinking which interpretation involves. If the analyst can interpret boldly, it is because he is open to his interpretation going under and across into a better, truer one.
28 Wolfgang Giegerich, "Is the Soul 'Deep'?—Entering and Following the Logical Movement of Heraclitus' 'Fragment 45'," in *The Soul Always Thinks* (*Collected English Papers, Vol. IV*) (New Orleans, LA: Spring Journal Books, Inc., 2010)161–162.
29 Leston Havens, *Making Contact: Uses of Language in Psychotherapy* (Cambridge, Massachusetts: Harvard University Press, 1986), 27.
30 Havens, *Making Contact*, 29.
31 "The most tactful question in the world," writes Havens, "is still inquisitive and requests an answer. To some measure, it carries the memories of all questions that could not be answered or were shaming or damning to acknowledge." *Making Contact*, 107.
32 Havens, *Making Contact*, 32.
33 Havens, *Making Contact*, 37.
34 It might be wondered if, when using imitative statements, the wires sometimes get crossed. Havens closes his chapter on imitative statements with an example in which this is the case. To a patient feeling badly that the treatment was taking so long, Havens said very earnestly, "I am responsible." Though Havens was here talking as himself, the patient at first took it as an imitative statement, something Havens was saying as him, for him, with respect to how he felt. But when it become apparent that this was not the case, and that Havens was indeed taking the responsibility, this was also helpful. As Haven puts it, "Only gradually did it become apparent that the *I* was really *me*, that the treatment was *my* responsibility, and that at least here, in this space, he might be given something of his own." Havens, *Making Contact*, 39.
35 See note 9 above.
36 Exodus 3:13.
37 Jung, *CW* 8 § 661, "... we can perhaps summon up courage to consider the possibility of a 'psychology *with* soul,' that is [with] a psychology [*Seelenlehre*] based on the hypothesis of an autonomous mind [*Geist*]" (trans. modified).

38 Jung, *CW* 9, i § 50. With respect to this account of psychology's provenance, the following statement of Jung's is also pertinent: "Whenever there exists some external form, be it an ideal or a ritual, by which all the yearnings and hopes of the soul are adequately expressed—as for instance in a living religion—then we may say the psyche is outside and there is no psychic problem, just as there is then no unconscious in our sense of the word. In consonance with this truth, the discovery of psychology falls entirely within the last decades, although long before that man was introspective and intelligent enough to recognize the facts that are the subject-matter of psychology." *CW* 10 § 159.

39 The infinitely negative I is the I that is no longer merely the self-identical me, but rather, is just as much constituted by or as the return from the otherness of all that I am not. Against the foil of all that I am not, I am thrown into relief on the soul side of the psychological difference as (infinitely negative) I.

40 It may be added here, by way of an aside, that reflective of the verticality that is imparted by our being true to ourselves and our situation is the fitness of the names that we assign to the things of our lives and world. Just as Rilke famously asked if we are here just for saying House, Bridge, Jug, Fountain, Gate, etc., so, answering in the affirmative, must that verticality that no longer holds God and man together and apart in their difference continue via the names we think with to weigh whatever phenomenon is of compelling interest to us against itself as against a feather as to the question of whether, having been taken up in this wise into the form of subject, it is truly in accord with its concept, truly worthy of its name.

41 "… in a place where there are no men, strive to be a man." Ben Zion Bokser, trans., *The Talmud: A Selection* (Mahwah, New Jersey: Paulist Press, 1989), 222.

42 "maior autem animae [pars] extra corpus est." Sendivogius, "De Sulphere," *Musaeum Hermeticum* (1678). Cited by C.G. Jung in his 12 July, 1951 letter to Karl Kerényi, *Letters*, vol. 2, 19. See also Jung, *CW* 12 § 396, 399.

43 Wolfgang Giegerich, "Psychologie Larmoyante" in *The Soul Always Thinks* (*Collected English Papers, Vol. IV*) (New Orleans: Spring Journal Books, Inc., 2010), 503.

44 Giegerich, "Psychologie Larmoyante," 503–504.

45 Of course, by "exercising judgment," I do not mean "being judgmental" in the pejorative sense of that phrase. It is rather a matter of assessing whether, by its own standards, a particular phenomenon is in accord with its concept (this friend a true friend, for example).

46 Jung, *CW* 6 § 723–729.

47 Giegerich, *Psychologie Larmoyante*, 510.

48 I speak of the objective subjectivity of the patient's situation being heard by the analyst *even as and at the same time* he enunciates it. The italicized words indicate that it is not a matter of the analyst's first hearing and then articulating what is heard. Between the analyst's hearing and speaking there is rather a dialectical relation. The analyst dares to speak, i.e., to think out-loud (at times, to be sure, only inwardly and to himself), in order to hear what is to be heard in the first place. There is nothing to hear until he speaks. This is what it means to have left the ordinary prevailing subject here, object there difference of consciousness behind, or better said, to have sublated this ordinary difference.

49 Giegerich, "Psychologie Larmoyante," L511.

50 Giegerich, "Is the Soul "Deep"? 149. Cf., Giegerich, *The Soul's Logical Life*, 147–148.

51 Giegerich, "'The Unassimilable Remnant': What is at Stake" in *The Soul Always Thinks* (*Collected English Papers, Vol. IV*) (New Orleans: Spring Journal Books, 2010), 472.

52   Jung, *CW* 14 § 205.

53   Pertinent to the seeing through of suffering that is experienced on an ego level to the suffering on the logical level that consciousness in the larger sense experiences in the course of its dialectical unfolding is a passage from the Christian Apocrypha's *Acts of John* in which Jesus declares: "You hear that I suffered, yet I suffered not; and that I suffered not, yet I did suffer; and that I was pierced, yet I was not wounded; that I was hanged, yet I was not hanged; that blood flowed from me, yet it did not flow, and, in a word, that what they say of me, I did not endure, but what they do not say, those things I did suffer. Now what these are, I secretly show you ..... You must know me, then, as the torment of the logos, the piercing of the logos, the blood of the logos, the wounding of the logos, the fastening of the logos." Willis Barnstone, ed., *The Other Bible* (New York: Harper & Row, 1984), 420.

Chapter 9

Consciousness, Reflexivity and Evolution

Philip Kime

Introduction

In 1849, Kierkegaard wrote the following: "But what is the self? The self is a relation that relates itself to itself or is the relation's relating itself to itself in the relation; the self is not the relation but is the relation's relating itself to itself."[1] With this dense, almost impenetrable and psychologically acute sentence, Kierkegaard opened one of the most beautiful works in the Western canon, *The Sickness unto Death*. It demonstrates the kernel with which much of his middle-to late-period works were occupied. The sophistication of this view of selfhood was far ahead of its time, and we still trail behind this insight in a morass of reifications and clumsy, excitable information-processing metaphors. Notice the redoubled abstraction; it is not enough to move to a merely more sophisticated ontology of relations. Immediately we are told, when selfhood seems to be settled as existing as a relation, that rather the essence of selfhood is not the relation but the relation relating itself to itself. It is not reflexivity but the performance of the act of reflexivity. The difficulty in thinking in these terms is, in my view, quite significant. It is not that a "process" view is anything particularly difficult in itself, but the temptations, distortions, and infiltration of our habitual nominal view of nouns is a habit with a vast history that confounds us every time we try to keep such a view as Kierkegaard's in focus.

My contention will be that we must keep such an idea in focus since, being structural and not contentful, it is at the essence of what Giegerich calls "the psychological difference"; without this, psychology, as it is conceived of by mainstream culture and academic thought, will and should be subsumed into empirical science, specifically into modern evolutionary theory. I would like, therefore, to suggest a fundamental structure that lies at the core of Kierkegaard's view of self and Giegerich's notion of psychology, which can be used to avoid the pending subsumption of psychology under evolutionary theory explicitly. The concept I would like to discuss is reflexivity. Simply, the relating of something to itself. Our topic is not, as Kierkegaard rightly says, the reflexive relation but the reflexive relating. The numerical relation "is equal to" is a reflexive relation (that is, "$x = x$" is a meaningful formula) but this is not

DOI: 10.4324/9781003381150-10

something that the variables do; it is misleading to say the variables are relating as they are simply there a necessary part of the demonstration that the relation "is equal to" is reflexive.

Many transitive relations with an individual person as subject can be reflexive – "John likes himself," "John thinks about himself," "John is appalled at himself." One might be tempted to say that it is intensional relations that have this reflexive characteristic, but this is not quite right as we also have the perfectly legitimate extensional reflexive relations "John hits himself," "John points at himself." However, it is important to note that even these seemingly extensional relations require a recognisable level of consciousness for them to be meaningful in anything but an accidental way. An animal can "point" at itself or "hit" itself if we extend the definition of these terms to encompass acts that could be interpreted as "pointing" or "hitting," but of course, this is merely to reinforce the notion that interpretation of the merely physical movements is required in order to make the acts reflexive in any real sense. This introduces the idea that consciousness is required for reflexive acts, irrespective of whether the consciousness is that of the performer or the observer. This idea has a long history in continental philosophy from Husserl through Sartre, who is perhaps the most famous proponent of a variant of this view.[2] To hit oneself, there needs to be a consciousness of oneself, that is, a reflexive consciousness. To point to oneself, one needs to be reflexively conscious. The requirement of consciousness is more pronounced in the case of intensional relations. To think about or to be interested in oneself, there needs to be a very developed self-consciousness which can persist for some duration since thinking is a temporally extended process; compare hitting and pointing, which are comparatively point-like in duration, which is why they require less consciousness and why presumably a case can be made that animals can perhaps manifest limited reflexivity in extensional relations.

It is fashionable in some circles to imbue consciousness with qualities that are intended to somehow place it outside of a broadly evolutionary viewpoint. I contend that this usually fails due to romantic and vague notions of consciousness and no less of an element of ignorance regarding the sophistication of modern evolutionary theory, which can credibly account for a great deal of behaviour that is often seen, at least in the mainstream, as being "psychological." With Giegerich,[3] I hold that any philosophically credible notion of what properly constitutes psychology lies outside the mainstream definition. One should give over the mainstream notion of psychology to modern evolutionary theory as it is a far more credible account of the matter than the often arbitrary and desperate theoretical machinations motivated more by desires to protect status and profession than by desires to account for the evidence. However, how then to operationalise the defence of a properly psychological element that relies on the notion of the role of consciousness? In the following, I try to do this by concentrating specifically on intensional reflexivity and the structure which this instigates. Broadly speaking, I will argue that as soon as intensional reflexivity is extant, despite its genesis being accountable in terms of evolutionary theory, its operation and productions generally cannot be; it is here that the domain of the properly psychological draws its boundary.

Evolutionary Psychology

I am of the opinion that "evolutionary psychology" is somewhat of an oxymoron. However, one should be clear about what this means – it means that I do not believe that what modern evolutionary and genetic approaches consider as psychology are really deserving of the name, without intending to deny that such approaches have any legitimate subject matter. To deny such approaches any worth would be a mistake, as the enormous advances and the furious pace of research into broadly evolutionary models in recent years cannot be denied. The improving public availability of data, the increasing sophistication of statistical tools and the convergence of genetic and evolutionary models has resulted in an explosion of high-quality research in this area of which many people are unaware.[4] The mainstream status of an idea is quite well indicated by there being dedicated and revised university textbooks available.[5] Depth psychology in general might find this threatening, as evolutionary models do indeed suppose to explain things like male-female interaction, hierarchy dynamics, positive effects of religion on individuals and groups, familiar Freudian intra-family structures and long-term cultural patterns.[6] It is impossible, having sufficient familiarity with the literature, to dismiss this work in a hand-waving manner as "reductionist" or "materialist"; this would be to underappreciate the sophistication and coherence of this body of work which makes the depth psychological attempts at empirical research look clumsy and naïve at best.

Famously, since Hamilton's work on inclusive fitness[7] and the subsequent rehabilitation of group and multi-level selection after,[8] it has been clear that evolutionary theory has something quite significant to say about social phenomena and behaviours quite beyond the narrower confines which were accorded to earlier post-Darwinian models. Group and multi-level selection theories have pushed far into territory once considered immune from the individualistic ground of early evolutionary theory, despite resistance from more traditional theorists such as Dawkins. In recent decades, models are able, using standard evolutionary concepts, to account for the rise to ascendance of inter-individual dynamics and preferences which previously were accounted for by "social" or "familial" feeling, explained largely by psycho-socialisation and purely environmental factors. This was the beginning of the expansion of the notion of "selection" to encompass that performed by units larger than individuals – by groups of various sizes and by environmental forces larger than those having impacts only at the level of individuals.

Suddenly, theoretically recalcitrant phenomena such as homosexuality, suicide, and celibacy found potential explanations within an expanded evolutionary theory.[9] Now, this clearly begins to step on the toes of many depth psychologists who conceive of such phenomena in very different explanatory terms. However, given the state of current research, there is simply no way to dismiss wholesale evolutionary models of moderately complex human behaviours unless one has some way of isolating behaviours from such explanation by some credibly motivated criteria. The most obvious attempt is to draw the line at some arbitrary point of behavioural complexity beyond which evolutionary or genetic explanations are no longer applicable. Unfortunately, the empirical world is replete with famous examples of complex behaviours which refute attempts to draw this line.[10]

Depth psychology should give up trying to play the empirical game because it has been dramatically outplayed and will not catch up. Even this makes this situation sound too optimistic as such talk sounds as if the difference is merely quantitative, a result of disparity of effort, but it is not so. The difference is fundamental and is to do with the enormous variation in what schools and theoretical frameworks mean when they talk about what is "psychological". I am perfectly prepared to give up to evolutionary theory a great deal, not because it is a better psychological theory but because it is not properly psychological at all, and the topics it covers were never psychological in the first place. The topics which "evolutionary psychology" covers are far-reaching and interesting but they are not, in any sense that captures the essence of what makes humans a unique phenomenon, psychological topics.

This means that if depth psychology as a whole tries to make itself empirically relevant to mainstream psychology, it will in fact be forcibly orienting itself by an un-psychological and irrelevant discipline, perhaps attracted by its undeniable success. However, its success is not success in understanding psychology but rather a unified and important victory of sophisticated animal behavioural pattern analysis. This is interesting, but it is not psychology and is nothing to chase after if one is concerned with psychology proper. Naturally, then, the question as to what constitutes psychology proper is paramount and Giegerich has provided the best modern attempt to address this (and is one of the few attempts at even raising the question). My intention is to elucidate as best I can the elements of psychology proper which constitute a domain outside of the evolutionary model. If we do not think that there is such a domain and try instead to fit into the empirical models which dominate what is thought to be psychology, then we are lost and will discover that in fact such a desire was doomed long before depth psychology was even conceived of.

It is common in so-called New Age literature to resist a perceived advance of materialism by a retreat to clumsily reified domains of spirit or energies that are somehow immune to the incursions of theories which successfully regiment matter. This is not a winning strategy for many reasons, the most obvious of which is the repetitive philosophical ignorance that suffocates the successive waves of such material. The solutions are always in some manner naïvely ontological, trying to find in the final reckoning a safe, more or less literal place that is exempt from the regularities which circumscribe the empirical. This is not a possible psychological approach, which must, if it believes in an exceptionalism at the heart of psychology, find the exception in the structural rather than the contentful. The essence of a psychology which exempts it from an evolutionary reduction must have to do with the geometry of the psychological as opposed to its contents or some barely coherent notion of the "location" of psyche or "spirit".

The reason that we must have a structural approach is that the battle over content and origins has already been lost. It would be a brave, perhaps simply foolish man who would challenge the evolutionary model on its home territory. To perhaps try to tell a story of the genesis of the psychological which progresses entirely outside of modern evolutionary theory is a hopeless task. There is simply too much evidence that much of what we call psychological (even properly psychological in the Giegerich sense) is intimately related by successive stages to phenomena which have credible, well-researched, and often genetically supported models. Evolutionary theory has a monopoly – a rapidly growing monopoly – on genesis stories of all aspects of human life; and I really do mean all aspects. It is a mistake, in my opinion, to try to reserve in principle a space for genesis stories of aspects of human life which one would like to protect from evolutionary explanation for perhaps sentimental or half-formed theoretical reasons. Give it all up, the genesis stories are a lost cause, they were always already won by empirical, data-driven science since its inception and it has simply been just a matter of the calculations catching up with the idea, since at least the time of Leibniz and Newton. The modern age and the regressive, often anti-scientific longings of the post-modern have been a process of coming to terms with the brutal fact that genesis stories of empirical phenomena are scientific stories and have been for as long as the idea of empirical science has existed in an identifiable form. The extreme submission of modernism and the extreme resistance of post-modernism to the establishment of empirical science as the de facto conceptual framework provide two poles of orientation, neither of which are adequate. Modernism is a wholesale surrender which, in its total capitulation, collapses distinctions which properly serve to delimit the reach of empirical science. Post-modernism is an hysterical regression back to a pre-scientific view, disguised in verbiage designed, only partly consciously, to prevent both readers (and often its writers) from feeling the embarrassment of the regressive longing that it embodies.

The model of the origins and genesis of human psychology should be handed over to evolutionary and genetic theory wholesale without regret because this model is not relevant to the explanatory status of the psychological, once extant. The temporal genesis of psychology and its status in the face of empirical theory, once human psychology exists, are two entirely different things and this is merely a restatement of Hegel's great idea concerning the fundamental difference between the temporal and logical orders. Empirical science is supreme in explanations of the temporal order, of genesis, of the history of phenomena, but it has its limit where the geometry of the results of temporal progression reset the temporal order and assert themselves as, in Hegel's term, the prius.[11] When a child learns to walk, the world is forever different, conceived of in terms of distances in a new way which is so fundamental that it asserts itself as a very beginning of thinking about the world in a certain manner. Such changes are so fundamental, the time that preceded them is as nothing, is irrelevant, the logical change overriding the temporal history completely. One could multiply such examples but there is a more fundamental change, a most fundamental change that eclipses all others and this is the "advent" of psychology which, let us say, did occur in time or over time. However, this change is so essential that it asserts itself as prius in such a way that the very notion of the "advent" of psychology is now inconceivable. As O'Hear says, "What is crucially at issue here is not how human self-consciousness might have come about, but what its significance for its possessor is once it has come about".[12]

It is all very well to speak like this in philosophical gestures but we must try to be more specific and delve into the particular geometrical features of psychology which perform the seeming miracle of putting it, as soon as it exists, outside of the temporal and empirical order and therefore outside of the explanatory framework of evolutionary models, despite being within the remit of their framework of temporal genesis. Simply put, evolutionary theory has a good and credible story to tell about the origins of human psychology but once psychology exists, this story is, in an important sense, irrelevant, since psychology asserts itself as the prius and its own structure is thereafter the only explanatory framework that matters from this point onward. As an aside, it is also true to say that from this point onward, psychology asserts itself as always having been the only relevant consideration. As soon as it exists, its very geometry establishes that it cannot be conceived of as not existing and therefore must be and therefore have been the only explanation of itself. One cannot conceive of a time before conceptions because as soon as conceptions are, they are not simply a new content but are the very form which defines the notion of "content". I do not claim to be able to make this idea more clear than Hegel did and pass on to the less ambitious current project which is: what can we say about the geometry of psychology proper and how does it assert itself in a way that makes its temporal origin and therefore its evolutionary account irrelevant?

Jung, Freud, Mind, and Matter

It is useful to briefly explore how conscious and unconscious are demarcated by the two psychologists who largely introduced and developed this distinction. We see, I believe, some insights, though largely undeveloped, pointing in the direction I wish to take.

Freud, in his seminal work on dreams, made some astoundingly perceptive observations about how, in unconscious material, complex logical structures collapse and make conscious interpretations difficult or impossible. These rarely discussed insights indicate an essential difference between conscious and unconscious phenomena in terms of logical structure. The central idea is that dreams and by extension unconsciousness in general, "... reproduce *logical connection* by *simultaneity in time.*"[13] (emphasis in original). This is a fundamental loss of structure in unconscious material and therefore consciousness represents a structural sophistication. Freud clearly saw this as a fundamental sophistication, relating it to differences between primitive and modern languages[14] and going on later to say that "The language of symbolism ... knows no grammar"[15]–a remarkable insight into the structural nature of the difference between conscious and unconscious. Freud's attempts at logical reconstruction of dreams are extremely informative in this respect and show how well he understood the nature of the difference, contrary to popular accounts which misunderstand psychoanalysis as a form of conscious storytelling projected onto unconscious material. Jung inherited this idea of a structural, formal difference and although not keeping it as clear as Freud had, due to his somewhat over-enthusiastic penchant for particular images of structure, he nevertheless intuited the central and most important structural feature of consciousness on which my argument turns.

The theme of the limits of natural phenomena is explicit in Jung and we can see the seeds of a vision of the geometry mentioned earlier in his comments on consciousness. He speaks of the "impropriety" resulting from consciousness: "This impropriety is the exclusive prerogative of man, whose consciousness and free will can occasionally loose themselves *contra naturam* from their roots in animal nature."[16] This notion of contra naturam played a central role in Jung's model of the conscious man but there was ever a regressive pull back towards bare nature in Jung which resulted in a subtle deprecation of consciousness as something inchoate and arrogant, destined to collapse due to the overweening pride of rationality: "It is the assertion of mind over matter, the opus *contra naturam*, a symptom of the youthfulness of man, still delighting in the use of the most powerful weapon ever devised by nature: the conscious mind."[17] In a telling end to this paragraph, Jung suggests that mankind might cease to delight in this weapon, thereby implying that it does not represent something "higher" than nature. This latter was certainly Jung's view, that the contents of consciousness were not in any final sense a positive development above unconscious nature. If one is comparing contents: images, dreams, thoughts even, then I would largely agree with this because consciousness does not replace unconsciousness – it merely adds a new aspect, invoked sporadically, that adds to the picture of the human psyche and which institutes a different and parallel set of concerns. However, consciousness is not merely a bag of new concerns or themes; it is a structural change of enormous moment as it is the appearance of a stable subject/object distinction, something radically different from the ontologically unitary, merged unconscious.

Therefore I do not really agree with the idea that consciousness should be spoken of in terms of a "symptom of youthfulness"; rather it is a marker of psychological adulthood, the mark of a transition into a realm of a completely different structure to the unconscious, merged state of bare nature. A structurally essential aspect of consciousness is the subject/object distinction and the reflexive nature of this when the subject can also be the object, that is, the phenomenon of self-consciousness is paramount. Further, this essential reflexivity is not transitory, not ultimately inessential as Jung often hints, but something fundamentally and forever new, *contra naturam* in a real sense in that it cannot be reabsorbed by nature as it constitutes, once it exists, a realm utterly different from it, despite having been generated by it. Jung's view of consciousness was in my view too narrowly related to his idea of rationality, too much defined by rational discrimination:

> The essence of the conscious mind is discrimination; it must, if it is to be aware of things, separate the opposites, and it does this *contra naturam*. In nature the opposites seek one another – *les extrêmes se touchent* – and so it is in the unconscious, and particularly in the archetype of unity, the self.[18]

Discrimination is certainly an aspect of consciousness but, I would argue, not the essential one. Making distinctions is not particularly fundamental as it is not as if there are no distinctions in unconscious material – it is merely that they are not stable because there is no fundamental subject/object distinction to fix them by.

Jung did seem to have an intuition about the essential fundamental, structural aspect of reflexivity but things are confused because of his general tendency to think in specific images which constantly push contents in the way of a clearer vision of the underlying form. One sees this in the discussion of Dorn's tenebris contra naturam[19] and Origen's comments on the micro and macrocosm.[20] The general intuition, again clothed in obscuring imagery, is present in Jung's approach to the concept of incest, particularly in the later casting of this in terms of alchemical symbolism.[21]

It is not the sorts of themes, topics, or contents which give the essence of consciousness, nor is it the granularity or catalogue of relations between contents. The essence of consciousness, particularly in distinction from Jung's idea of unconsciousness, turns on formal, structural features and none more so than reflexivity.

Reflexivity

There is a fundamental duality in an evolutionary model between an organism and the environment of the organism. This is a structural, logical duality and not necessarily a material one since the chemical and physical line between amorphous organisms and their environment may be blurred and complex, but selection in an evolutionary model, whether natural, sexual, or group is attunement to something essentially "other" than the organism. The "other" is what selects attributes in the organism as being fit or unfit for a particular purpose relevant to differential reproduction. This, logically, is a relatively simple model which has extremely complex results due to the large number of attempted solutions to the selection problem, coupled with the huge number of simultaneous times that the problem is posed, plus random elements which ensure that equilibrium is never reached. The complexity in evolution comes not from its internal logic but from the sheer scale of the process. However, what happens to the logic of the theory when the adaptor and adapted-to are the same? Does it even mean anything to pose such a question? I believe that it does and this is the situation we have with conscious organisms.

Consciousness is essentially reflexive, that is, *it can be its own object*. Consciousness can ask questions about consciousness, not in the abstract (for that is merely a special case of asking questions about an "other", albeit a special and related type of "other") but about itself in the most intimate sense. As a conscious being, one is able to reflect on one's current attempt at reflection in real time, real reflection. The ability to do this is reflexivity; reflexivity is a special type of possibility, always, so to speak, "in the air" which can at any time manifest and it is this tone, this permanent possibility which is the essence of reflexivity; this chord sounding in the background effects everything, forms the structural, logical ground of everything that a conscious being can possibly manifest.

As soon as the ability to reflect upon the structure of reflection arises – to be able to shift position between subject/object – we are outside of the physical historical line of natural evolution. This is because the environmental pressures which govern the changes, and the changes themselves, are no longer clearly "environmental" in any sense that has relevance to evolutionary advantage. The environment for a reflexive capacity is *itself*, and this is a fundamental break from the logic of empirical adaptation to an environment which is definitively not identical with oneself. This should not be taken as a claim that conscious beings are outside of evolutionary models. This cannot be the case because conscious beings are not pure consciousness and are also physical creatures governed to a greater degree than most like or realise by biology. However, consciousness, due to its reflexive nature, constitutes something outside of this due to its logical structure because it is capable of being its own object.

Let us look at this in the typical language of evolutionary theory. The act of reflexion, of consciousness being its own object (as opposed to "reflection", which has misleading connotations because one can be "reflective" without being reflexive) constitutes an "environment" which only one individual occupies. One can react to oneself, attune to oneself, selecting for "traits" which are simply oneself as object. Without consciousness, one is relating to something else which exerts selection pressure. With consciousness, there is a possibility to relate to oneself. The "selection pressure" from oneself is a closed loop; it is not a shared "environment" which could exert differential selection pressure between individuals because for each individual, such reflexive loops are closed to all others because their object is the individual subject. Evolutionary advantage and differential responses to selection pressure no longer apply to phenomena which are logically isolated in this way – these logical islands of reflexive consciousness are outside of the influence of evolution. Consciousness leads to reflexivity and reflexivity leads to unitary environments in which development can occur but which are logically isolated from evolutionary pressure. Evolution leads to consciousness which leads to reflexivity, which leads to an area logically (but not temporally) outside of evolution. This "area" is not the omnipotent "environment" of the anti-geneticists, it is a logical environment created by reflexivity, purely and solely internal and inhabited by or rather constituent of, one individual. This is, I think, the individualism which Jung strove to justify, but he could not decouple it from an actual, external sense of individualism which is too intimately connected to the social and public world.

Let us take an example: a win on the lottery may be a solution to a real, concrete problem that I have and the lack of such a win might decide my fate one way or another. In such a case, the obtaining of the win is something I cannot control and which has real consequences for me. The *idea* of winning the lottery is something I can control. I can imagine it, comfort myself with it, explore it in order to reveal what my priorities would be under conditions of a win (and so perhaps reveal my priorities in general). The idea of not winning can also be controlled and used in many ways not so cleanly related to the natural consequences of not winning in reality. This shows the insulated nature of consciousness which can think about thinking, can reflect on a fantasising reflection and therefore effectively neutralise, change, or manipulate any effects which the unreflected upon reflection might immediately have. This is something that cannot be done with a neutral empirical reality. One cannot change the fundamental nature of what happens in order to change the differential adaptation that must occur in the face of reality. One might adapt to what happens but this is to, in a very deep way, accept what happens as external and "other". With consciousness, with ideas, one does not have to accept or adapt, one can *redefine* – and this is a weapon which proves that there may be no determining empirical "environment" or "other" for it, demonstrating a completely different structure of relation and one which is simply not commensurate with an empirical theory like evolution.

Naturally, evolutionary theory has tried to account for consciousness, and as I mentioned, there is no particular problem in allowing the temporal genesis of consciousness a place in evolutionary history as long as one is careful to distinguish this from the logical structure which exempts it. Now, one could argue – and there are those who have tried to so argue – that the "competition" between ideas within an individual is a form of selection and one might therefore deign to speak of the "individual evolution" of perhaps the ideas thought to constitute the individual. It is not clear to me what sense can be made of this since the artifices of rhetoric might be employed to circumvent any particular rule of selection between ideas which one might care to propose. The competition in evolutionary theory is real, empirical, physical, demonstrable as competition rather than definable as a species of competition. You cannot have evolution as a hallmark of empirical science and then have it appear wherever you please by excusing it from any empirical basis. All you are left with then is a hollow definitional jingoism that says, "since one could broadly say that one idea 'beat' another, there must have been evolutionary competition". The history of competition of ideas is not a history of competition of ideas at all but a messy history of more banal and concrete competition of people and politics and so on. The phenomenon of the textbook in the hard sciences, which is where all students start, is responsible for a great deal of mistaking a reconstructive logical history for temporal history. Science and history of science are radically different fields which can be practised in total isolation from one another since they are concerned with entirely different modes of connection. The fact that one idea became dominant and other ideas faded into obscurity does not mean that they "competed" in any sense usable by evolutionary theory.

Another attempt to naturalise consciousness is with the idea that people compete with ideas for dominance in, say, academia and that this can be given an evolutionary explanation. This is of course true but not really relevant. The reduction of progression of ideas to competition between people must relentlessly undermine any idea that logic or internal, essential differences exist between theories or statements. Holding such a naturalised view is essentially impossible because any such naturalism can only be derived from the independence of the very things naturalised. The mapping of anything onto the models required by evolutionary theory requires that the mapping not be naturalised; otherwise the very bringing of a phenomenon under an evolutionary interpretation is itself undermined because the mapping is nothing other than an evolutionary byproduct too, which is the very argument used to prove that justification is impossible. At its heart, this is merely a variant of the liar paradox which establishes that evolutionary theory, if it accounts for everything, must account also for itself. This undermines any pretensions it has to being anything other than the most contingently (and temporarily) successful theory in the current academic "environment". Not a conclusion any theorist of any slant is likely to embrace or really, believe, postmodern protestations notwithstanding.

However, leaving aside the logic of such "selection", let us allow it to stand, for if we at least say that such a process does not follow selection by a shared, interpersonal environment, we have already separated it fundamentally from whatever is meant by "selection" in evolutionary theory as it manifests as a putative general explanation of psychology. Consciousness then, with its reflexive self-enclosure, becomes a black box for evolution and we can only legitimately discuss in biology its non-reflexive shared features, holding, for example, that it as a whole has certain evolutionary advantages (deferred gratification, forward planning, positing of hypotheticals, etc.) and disadvantages (depression, anxiety over hypotheticals, etc.). The changes in phenomena which are essential consequences of reflexive consciousness, for example the logical as opposed to the temporal and pragmatic progress of theoretical science or mathematics, is not addressable by evolutionary theory, especially where there is no space for an idea which could empower it to become a driver for differential selection.

Possibility

As fundamental as I believe the phenomena of reflexivity to be for the eventual empirical status of psychology, it is rendered more remarkable by the fact that the work done by reflexivity is rarefied by only its *possibility* being necessary to mark out an area of truly psychological relevance. The possibility of the actualisation of a capacity is, psychologically, a tremendously important category. For example, the ability to protect oneself due to some training in martial arts or perhaps due to carrying a firearm can radically change one's relation to the world and one's psychological orientation, even if this ability is never actualised. Therefore, the active ingredient in such an ability is not an individual empirical matter in any straightforward way; one may have no empirical evidence that the ability would suffice for any particular task or situation, but this lack of empirical evidence does not detract from the very real effects that the possibility brings. The fact that we, as conscious, may possibly at any time relate reflexively to our own conscious process is in itself an omnipresent and tremendous structural feature. This possibility is not an extrapolation, an inference or perhaps induction from actions, but is an experience which saturates all empirical experience. This is an essential element which allowed Husserl to hope for a phenomenological basis for philosophy. Whatever one might think of that project as a whole, the insight of his that the possibility of an action is just as much a ground of consciousness and a part of the world as is an action, is an acknowledgement of what we are here considering:

> We must not fail to note that the transfer of an actually experienced "I can and I effect" to a new case is not simply an inductive ontological belief, related to my ability as a fact, but that I experience in practical consciousness itself a possible ability.[22]
>
> This possibility, as hypothetically ideal potentiality, is an essential component of the sense of the surrounding world.[23]

It is more correct to say not that the reflexivity involved in consciousness is the essential ingredient in a properly psychological model but rather that the permanent, omnipresent possibility of reflexivity is the constitutive factor.

We must move to this position because actual reflexivity is in fact comparatively rare, as evidenced by its more obvious manifestations such as self-consciousness and self-awareness being comparatively rare. There is nothing permanent or omnipresent about reflexive consciousness (otherwise there would presumably be a radically reduced need for psychotherapy) but one cannot say this of its possibility, which results in a subtle and fundamentally transformative tone or emphasis, whether or not the instantiations of reflexivity are regular, few, or even entirely absent.

Reflexivity is the permanent possibility of turning subject into object, and even when this is not done, the fact that it is omnipresent possibility *is* the defining element of consciousness. However, it is more subtle than this. Reflexivity also entails the possibility of making its own possibilities into the object. That is, just as one can reflect on oneself, the contents of one's thoughts perhaps, it is also possible to reflect on the structure of the reflection and thereby be conscious of the act of reflection; to make into object the way in which one makes subjects into objects. This is true reflexivity, where reflexivity itself is the object of reflection. The reason that I have dwelt on these somewhat abstruse geometries of consciousness is that they make a qualitative difference to evolutionary theory as the simple organism/environment duality is undermined. Reflexive phenomena change the definition of or *produce* their environment, and this disturbs the logical split which evolutionary explanation requires, between the adapter and the adapted-to. This is because "adaptation" to an environment consisting of oneself is indistinguishable from producing the environment.

One sees this producing aspect of reflexivity clearly in Hegel's lectures on the history of philosophy where it is the root of his avoidance of philosophical relativism. In the same vein, reflexivity is the root of psychology proper which avoids a species of relativism which would render all of psychology as mere evolutionary adaptation. The psychological difference is a structural difference, intimately related to the reflexivity of consciousness, and it is this astounding phenomenon which breaks apart the temporal genesis and logical status of human psychology, leaving the former to empirical science and the latter to psychology proper.

Notes

1 Søren Kierkegaard, *The Sickness unto Death*, vol. KW XIX of Kierkegaard's Writings (Princeton, NJ: Princeton University Press, 1980), 13.
2 Jean-Paul Sartre, *Being and Nothingness* (1943; New York: Washington Square Press, 1956), 214–215.
3 Wolfgang Giegerich, *The Soul's Logical Life: Towards a Rigorous Notion of Psychology* (Frankfurt am Main: Peter Lang, 1998) is the seminal statement of his view, expanded and developed a great deal over the succeeding decades.
4 Good academic accounts of a broad cross-section of modern research are provided in, for example, Alexy S. Kondrashov, *Crumbling Genome: The Impact of Deleterious Mutations on Humans* (New Jersey: Wiley Blackwell, 2017); Marco Del

Guidice, *Evolutionary Psychopathology: A Unified Approach* (Oxford: Oxford University Press, 2018); Matthew Alexander Sarraf, *Michael Anthony Woodley of Menie, and Colin Feltham, Modernity and Cultural Decline: A Biobehavioral Perspective* (Cham, Switzerland: Palgrave Macmillan, 2019).

5   See David M. Buss, *Evolutionary Psychology: The New Science of the Mind*, 5th ed. (New York: Routledge, 2016).

6   David Sloan Wilson, *Darwin's Cathedral: Evolutionary Religion and the Nature of Society* (Chicago: University of Chicago Press, 2002) is the central text in this area.

7   William D. Hamilton, "The Evolution of Altruistic Behavior," *American Naturalist 97 (1963)*: 354–356; William D. Hamilton, "The Genetical Evolution of Social Behaviour I and II," *Journal of Theoretical Biology 7* (1964): 1–52.

8   David Sloan Wilson and Elliott Sober, "Reintroducing Group Selection to the Human Behavioral Sciences," *Behavioural and Brain Sciences 17*, no. 4 (1994): 585–608.

9   Wilson, *Darwin's Cathedral.*

10 The most famous cases are those of the many parasites which modify the behaviours of their host insects in astoundingly complex ways in order to benefit the parasite life cycle (Libersat, Frederic, Maayan Kaiser, and Stav Emanuel. "Mind Control: How Parasites Manipulate Cognitive Functions in Their Insect Hosts," *Frontiers in Psychology 9* (2018). https://doi.org/10.3389/fpsyg.2018.00572.)

11 Georg Wilhelm Friedrich Hegel, *Philosophy of Mind*, trans. William Wallace and A. V. Miller (1894; Oxford: Oxford University Press, 1971), 417.

12 Anthony O'Hear, *Beyond Evolution: Human Nature and the Limits of Evolutionary Explanation* (Oxford: Oxford University Press, 1997), 22.

13 Sigmund Freud, *The Interpretation of Dreams I, vol. IV of The Standard Edition of the Complete Psychological Works of Sigmund Freud*, trans. James Strachey (London: Vintage, 2001), 314 (hereafter cited as SE IV).

14 318 SE IV, footnote from 1911.

15 Sigmund Freud, *Beyond the Pleasure Principle, Group Psychology and Other Works, vol. XVIII of The Standard Edition of the Complete Psychological Works of Sigmund Freud*, trans. James Strachey (London: Vintage, 2001), 212 (hereafter cited as SE XVIII).

16 C. G. Jung, *Two Essays on Analytical Psychology, vol. VII of The Collected Works, 2nd ed.*, ed. Herbert Read et al., trans. R. F. C. Hull (Princeton, NJ: Princeton University Press, 1953), ¶ 41 (hereafter cited as CW VII).

17 C. G. Jung, *Psychology and Religion: West and East, vol. XI of The Collected Works, 2nd ed.*, ed. Herbert Read et al., trans. R. F. C. Hull (Princeton, NJ: Princeton University Press, 1958), ¶ 787 (hereafter cited as CW XI).

18 C. G. Jung, *Psychology and Alchemy, vol. XII of The Collected Works, 2nd ed.*, ed. Herbert Read et al., trans. R. F. C. Hull (Princeton, NJ: Princeton University Press, 1953), 30 (hereafter cited as CW XII).

19 C. G. Jung, *Mysterium Coniunctionis, vol. XIV of The Collected Works*, 2nd ed., ed. Herbert Read et al., trans. R. F. C. Hull (Princeton, NJ: Princeton University Press, 1963), ¶ 137 (hereafter cited as CW XIV).

20 CW XIV, 6.

21 C. G. Jung, *The Practice of Psychotherapy, vol. XVI of The Collected Works*, 2nd ed., ed. Herbert Read et al., trans. R. F. C. Hull (Princeton, NJ: Princeton University Press, 1954), 469 (hereafter cited as CW XVI).

22 Edmund Husserl, *Ideas Pertaining to a Pure Phenomenology and to a Phenomenological Philosophy: Second Book: Studies in the Phenomenology of Constitution* (Dordrecht, The Netherlands: Kluwer Academic Publishers, 1989), 342.

23 Husserl, *Ideas*, 206.

Chapter 10

A Temporal Dance with the Psychological Difference

Lessons from Lesson of the Mask

Colleen EL-Bejjani

More than twenty years ago, seeped in Jung and deep in Kibola, a village in Guinea, West Africa, I took part in a cleansing ritual by a village elder. A tall, stoic, silent woman performed the event, which was equally stoic and silent – without any pomp or ceremony. After weeks of busy city life in Conakry, I couldn't sleep that first night in the village as I wondered what to expect from the next morning's event. I suppose I imagined a sort of sensational experience, maybe even otherworldly. The day before had been filled with long walks in rice patties that appeared to reach toward the ends of the earth. Women bent over reeds, singing in Susu – high notes and sounds familiar to me, though always foreign. That night, absent of artificial light, was so dark one couldn't see more than a foot ahead. I couldn't sleep, imagining large spiders and bats just outside my mosquito net, and I ventured out of my hut, groping in the dark to find a place to sit and wait for sunrise, an event which happened suddenly – not a slow shift from dawn to day, but an instantaneous shift from night to day. As I sat, somewhat mesmerized by the turn of light, a dozen goats calmly walking unattended surrounded me; a man on a bicycle with a basketful of baguettes slowly made his way deeper into the village – much activity for a village where no cars, electric lights, toilets, refrigerators, the taken for granted conveniences of modernity, could be found for miles and miles. Later that morning, I met the elder woman known as the doctor for the village – a sort of soul doctor.

It was this trip to Africa where a substantial part of my study of Guinean culture occurred. I had spent decades working with dozens of Guinean-born artists and *jellis* (oral historians), studying, teaching, and performing traditional drum and dance from the region. My interest in this work began alongside my interest in Jungian psychology. As my interest in psychology as the discipline of interiority expanded, both my work with traditional drum and dance and traditional Jungian psychology began to crumble. Needless to say, Giegerich's essay, "Lesson of the Mask"[1] had come to hold a particular relevance for me.

Now, of course, learning any lesson, whether it be dance or psychology, depends much on the discipline that we apply to that learning endeavor. At this point it might serve us well to be reminded of the level of discipline required

DOI: 10.4324/9781003381150-11

for our work, by Giegerich's observation that "… psychology begins where any phenomenon (whether physical or mental, 'real' or fantasy image) is interiorized absolute-negatively into itself, and I find myself in its internal infinity. This is what it takes; psychology cannot be had for less."[2] Allowing this insight to serve as our North Star, we begin the journey into the phenomena of the masked dance and thereupon discover a multiplicity of lessons.

Psychology begins with its relentlessly giving itself over to each topic and subject matter – to in essence its putting on the mask of their eachness – and dancing with itself in what it has apperceived as its own other. Giegerich's brief essay interiorizes the phenomenon of the mask dance into itself, allowing us to see how this hollow, lifeless object, when met with the dancer, sets the performance of the psychological difference into motion. Might it be that every topic and subject matter for psychology has this mask-character, that implicit in this "lesson of the mask" is the "lesson" of our need to put on the mask of whatever phenomena lay claim to our attention? At this moment of thinking these thoughts of the lesson and the mask, I am reminded of the masked dances that I have seen first-hand, and these lines from Giegerich, both which have served to inspire this essay of mine:

> The *dancer* who in everyday civil life is an ordinary member of the community familiar to everyone, first of all puts on a mask of some *spirit, demon, or god*. He thus shows himself as being different from himself. The need to wear the mask expresses the implicit notion that he is not exclusively himself, is not confined to and within his own empirical reality and personal identity. He is more. He is also what he is definitely **not**. Thus, by putting on the mask, the dancer sets himself up as, enacts, and thereby becomes, the "psychological difference," the difference between himself as an individual of the species homo sapiens and himself as *soul, spirit, or divinity*. He is both at once; in other words, he is the unity of his identity with himself and his difference from himself.[3] [emphasis mine]

Let's look at that same paragraph substituting the word psychologist for dancer in the first sentence, and some of the other words to make my point.

> The *psychologist*, who in everyday civil life is an ordinary member of the community familiar to everyone, first of all puts on a mask of *some subject or phenomenon*. He thus shows himself as being different from himself. The need to *enter the phenomenon* expresses the implicit notion that he is not exclusively himself, is not confined to and within his own empirical reality and personal identity. He is more. He is also what he is definitely not. Thus, by putting on the *subject he wishes to interiorize, the psychologist* sets himself up as, enacts, and thereby becomes, the "psychological difference," the difference between himself as an individual of the species homo sapiens and *himself as soul*. He is both at once; in other words, he is the unity of his identity with himself and his difference from himself.

The obvious lesson of Giegerich's essay is the example of how the psychological difference is made explicit by the masked dancer, and how ritual enactment served to articulate the logical life (the logic of their embeddedness in their ritualistic mode of being in the world) of pre-modern culture. The implicit lessons of the essay are extensive, such as the need for not only the empirical dancer to give himself over to the *concept* of the mask – which on its own is "a dead and man-made object," and, psychology's artful act of giving over of itself to the hollow, thin and always ever-thinning absolute negativity of all phenomena studied psychologically, or more so, for each performance of psychology to be a masked dance in and of itself. And what a contradistinction this is to Jung's idea of the mask as persona! For Jung the mask stood in front of the soul as though it (soul) were a possession of subjectivity, a reified and resuscitated presence of the mythological world held in the interior of our true selves. The PDI lesson is that when psychology, through psychological thinking, relentlessly dances with the soul side of the psychological difference, "the real human being is reduced to the status of an instrument, a mere support for the 'unreal' image shown by the mask that is unable to stand on its own."[4] Again, the mask in our modern context is only the interiorized subject matter – not the material object used in the pre-modern ritual of the masked dancer.

Temporality and Disappearance

Giegerich writes:

> It [the concept of the mask implicit within the object of mask] is not simply there as a given, natural reality. And as spirit or god it is also not an eternal being that demands human devotion. No, it is in itself temporal, a momentary event. It ... has to be brought forth ... through the act of the empirical person's disappearing behind the mask [as object]. ... To the extent that the human person disappears the (to begin with unreal) true self, i.e. the spirit or god, can manifest and become real...[5]

I want to address two very significant characteristics of the psychological difference that are brought forward within this paragraph: first, the significance of temporal event, and second, the significance of disappearance.

In another essay, "The Soul as the Axis of the World," Giegerich notes that ritualistic culture's performance of ritual created within the moment of the performance itself is the very axis of the world *for that moment*. In other words, each event of dancing the masked dance of psychology is within that moment an event that temporally establishes itself – and its own destruction. The life of the soul is a temporary moment of being, becoming, and ceasing to be, as opposed to an entity existing in a location, or due to a performative repetition. As Giegerich writes,

[T]he performance of the ritual that you (ritualistic culture) performed originally *established* the center *ad hoc*. The spot where the ritual was performed
turned, for the duration of the ritual and by virtue of its power, into the spot
where the *axis mundi* both penetrated the ground below and rose to heaven. ...
'Soul' is merely a name we give to this real movement and event.[6]

And, "as such the dance could also be said to be the 'psychological difference'
comprehended dynamically, as logical *life* or dialectical *movement*"[7] Thus, the
psychological thinker's lesson is to approach each new 'dance' with the psychological difference not only relentlessly giving way to the soul side of the equation, but in so doing to comprehend each event of soul-making as an end
within itself. The "logical infrastructure created by ritual society was a sensuous, temporal event, whereas for us it becomes an event of consciousness – a
performative act of thinking *thinkingly* the logic of our subject matter; an act
of dialectical movement within thought."

Now let me move on to the second significant aspect of the Giegerich paragraph where he speaks to the necessity of disappearance. The word disappearance appears eight times on page 260, and many more times in "Lesson of the
Mask." This leaped out at me and I began looking for it in other essays and
thinking about the logical act of disappearance as it relates to the psychological difference. I would like to add here that in Guinea, as in many West African
countries, there are masked dances that employ a dancer able to perform feats
with the intention of confronting the observers' reality. The dancer is able to
appear out of nowhere and disappear into nowhere in unexpected ways. This
no-where, no-time quality allows for the possibility that he is always there,
somewhere. In Guinea this is magic, a fetish dance. I will come back to this idea
in a moment. First I want to spend time considering the logical disappearance
of empirical man as it relates to the performance of the psychological
difference.

It is easy for us all to utter the words that we must disappear as ego in order
to approach the phenomena at hand from its interiority, or, in order for the
masked dancer to enact the psychological difference he must give himself over
relentlessly to the negative concept of the mask that is dancing him; that he as
empirical man must disappear. We are also all aware of the so-called dangers
of giving our ego selves over to the archetypal – the dangers of inflation. So
how might we approach this idea of disappearance in a manner that does not
involve inflation or the paradoxically ego-driven claim of allowing the subject
matter to occlude us as empirical human beings?

Referring to the psychological difference, Giegerich writes, "[I]t is all movement, all given over to the flow of time and thus also to its coming-to-be and
passing-away."[8] Or, in Hegel's words, "[w]hat is thus found only *comes to be*
through being *left behind* ... the reflective movement is to be taken as *absolute
recoil* upon itself."[9] Giegerich's notion of historical time is akin to Hegel's in

that it is a movement of the logical life toward its becoming the truth of its essence (from substantiated, sensual, and externalized toward absolute negativity, thought, consciousness); in other words, "the soul *is* historicity."[10] Historical time is always pregnant with the next stage of itself, always a becoming, always both the past and the future and not either. Even the present moment is a becoming of another moment and the release of a past moment. In such, the psychological difference as a methodological interpretation of soul display has in its very nature the temporal.

With these thoughts in mind, disappearance as a significant aspect of the psychological difference concerns itself with what *remains* in disappearance, the negative aspects of the equation and our conscious reflection which can only go under, interiorize, when we have faced the "rock of impenetrability."[11] For the masked dance of ritual culture this meant that the unseen soul's appearance could only be had by the disappearance of empirical dancer behind the negative object – for modern psychological thinking it means that the unseen soul's appearance can only be had by the disappearance of the empirical psychologist behind the negativity of recursive reflection. "So it is only in the return itself that what we return to emerges at all."[12] It is only by our performance of reflection that what we reflect upon comes into being – mask up front. "Take away the illusion and you lose the truth itself. A truth needs time to make a journey through illusions to form itself."[13] Mine began as a journey through the illusion that I could somehow be cleansed of my crumbling commitment to a world animated by first immediacy and ended in recursive reflection.

Our reflecting on the psychological difference results in our having danced with the temporal event of soul-making. Our dance partner remains in disappearance, never to hold us, or to be held by us, for it is the unseen that engages us in this performative act.

Notes

1 Wolfgang Giegerich, "The Lesson of the Mask," *The Neurosis of Psychology: Primary Papers Towards a Critical Psychology*, ed. Greg Mogenson (New Orleans, Louisiana: Spring Journals, Inc., 2005).
2 Wolfgang Giegerich, *The Soul Always Thinks* (New Orleans, Louisiana: Spring Journals, Inc., 2010), 161–162.
3 Wolfgang Giegerich, *The Neurosis of Psychology: Primary Papers towards a Critical Psychology*, (New Orleans, Louisiana: Spring Journals, Inc., 2005), 258.
4 Giegerich, *Neurosis of Psychology*, 259.
5 Giegerich, *Neurosis of Psychology*, 260.
6 Giegerich, *Neurosis of Psychology*, 297.
7 Giegerich, *Neurosis of Psychology*, 261
8 Giegerich, *Neurosis of Psychology*, 261.
9 Georg Hegel, *Science of Logic Muirhead Library of Philosophy* (London: Routledge, 2014), 402.

10 Wolfgang Giegerich, *What is Soul?* (New Orleans, Louisiana: Spring Journals, Inc., 2012), 73.
11 Wolfgang Giegerich, *The Collected English Papers, The Soul Always Thinks*, Vol. Volume IV (New Orleans, Louisiana, Spring Journal. 2010), 166.
12 Slavoj Zizek, *Event: Philosophy in Transit.* (London: The Penguin Group, 2015), 43.
13 Slavoj Zizek, *Event: Philosophy in Transit*, 94.

Chapter 11

Deconstruction and the Modern Self

Daniel Anderson

All that is solid melts into air, all that is holy is profaned, and man is at last compelled to face with sober senses his real conditions of life, and his relations with his kind.

Marx, *The Communist Manifesto*

Introduction

Psychoanalysis, as inaugurated by Freud, is a psychology of the unconscious. However, this unconscious is a formation determined in significant part by the nature of the "I." Since this chapter focuses on the modern configuration of the "I" the terms "I" and "ego" will be used interchangeably.[1] The ego is shaped by genetics, parenting, personal experiences (especially in childhood), the *immediate* socio-economic environment and the broader cultural environment. There is an intimate, even reciprocal, relationship between the ego and the unconscious. While the *instinctual* dimension of the unconscious (sexual and aggressive or survival instincts) may be an anthropological constant, much of the unconscious is determined by the nature of the ego. A direct line can be traced from culture (narrowly and broadly conceived) to the unconscious insofar as the former shapes the ego, which then shapes the unconscious.

Breuer's seminal case of "Anna O"[2] shows how culture, narrowly conceived as a socio-economic group, determines which thoughts and feelings must be made unconscious, and the symptoms that result. One of the many symptoms that "Anna O" suffered was a weeks-long inability to drink water after seeing her lady-companion's dog drink from a glass of water. Breuer notes that Anna "did not care for" her lady-companion or her dog ("horrid creature!"); when she saw the dog drink from the glass she said nothing "as she had wanted to be polite."[3] Apparently, repression of intense anger contributed to the symptom's formation because when she gave "energetic expression to the anger" her symptom disappeared and she immediately could again drink water.[4] This impressive conversion symptom originated not in violent trauma—a bomb exploding nearby or a vehicular accident—but in *a dog drinking from a water glass.*

DOI: 10.4324/9781003381150-12

Viennese upper-class etiquette dictated that "Anna O" could not express the intense anger she felt in that moment. She had to repress her anger, render it unconscious. The cultural relativity of the unconscious could hardly be more clearly demonstrated.

We may conclude that culture imprints the ego's norms, ideals, and mores, which determines what must be made unconscious. Ego and unconscious shape each other, similar to the principle of physics that for every action there is an equal and opposite reaction. A psychology of the unconscious therefore is a psychology of the unconscious *and* the I as a mutually constituting pair. The case of Anna O shows how the immediate cultural environment (wealthy Victorian Viennese society) shapes the nature of the ego. But in the 20th century a widespread form of the ego emerged which cuts across socio-economic groups. Jungian analyst Wolfgang Giegerich argues that the 20th-century ego yields a form of consciousness in which subjectivity is separated from a world of "dead" objects that results in the reign of objectivity, empiricism, and "positivity."[5] This ubiquitous form of the ego generates a configuration of the unconscious which produces a uniquely modern form of pathology, neurosis.[6]

The unconscious is always on two sides of the individual; on the one side is the *personal unconscious* (the unconscious which is instinctual and a repository of experiences) and on the other that which Giegerich calls the *objective psyche,*[7] the sum effect of cultural structures, beliefs, and practices that yields a particular configuration of the I in the first place. In all times and places, there are two faces of the unconscious: the unconscious that is personal and the unconscious that is cultural, the objective psyche. The objective psyche shapes the personal unconscious via the ego which is itself shaped by the objective psyche.

It may be helpful to understand the term "objective psyche" with reference to familiar terms such as the Renaissance, the Enlightenment, the Industrial era, the modern era, and the information age. These terms refer to cultural constellations that include predominant values, family structures, religious structures, technologies, art, and political systems, which together assume a certain character and exert a tremendous force. Giegerich calls this force "the objective psyche."[8] An exemplar of the objective psyche is language: each of us is born into a specific language—*thrown* into it—such that our entire being-in-the-world is unthinkable apart from the language used to understand the world. The same can be said about all aspects of the objective psyche. It would be every bit as unthinkable for the Hebrews of the biblical era to conceive of the world apart from Yahweh as it would be for any person to conceive the world apart from language. The objective psyche is that force field that collectively shapes the minds of persons in any given culture, as inescapable as the force of gravity itself.

Our discussion will begin with the modern structure of the ego, which has been called the "atomic self," then move to the post-modern structure of the ego, influenced by the Internet, social media, and contemporary modes of communication such as texting, and which has been called a "smeared-out self."[9] The foundation for the latter, I will argue, is nothing less than the "death of God" and the consequent proliferation of competing discourses. It will be my contention that psychoanalysis is founded on the atomic self, a particular configuration of the self that no longer prevails. For psychoanalysis to remain relevant, not to mention effective, it must examine the full implications of the smeared-out self, and what this means for a psychology of the unconscious.

The Atomic Self and the Smeared-Out Self

Charles Ess characterizes a modern self that he calls the "atomic self" and a post-modern self that he variously calls the "smeared-out self," "the networked individual" or the "relational self."[10] Concerning the "atomic self" Ess observes that,

> the modern (Western) sense of the self [is] as an "atomic" individual–e.g., a Cartesian rationality radically separate from its own body, much less from any other entities and its environment. ... [This] atomic sense of self, especially as it becomes defined in terms of its essential freedom—in Kantian terms, its *autonomy* as its ability to give itself its own law—thereby becomes foundational for the modern liberal and democratic state.[11]

Ess highlights how the nature of reflective thought, and even political structures, change with the emergence of writing and literacy in cultures that previously transmitted knowledge orally. He references research that shows

> strong correlations between the skills and communication technologies affiliated with literacy (in contrast with the earlier stage of orality) and the emergence of critical thinking and logic (with the ancient Greeks) and then between those affiliated with print and the rise of modern science and democratic governance. ... This virtue of self-development, finally, seems to depend crucially on the sorts of reflection and self-representation—if not self-construction—that writing makes possible.[12]

A culture of *reading* and *writing* leads simultaneously to the modern "atomic self" and its associated reflective capacities, which serve as the foundation for liberal democracies.

Ess moreover argues that the Internet, which privileges the visual and oral (YouTube) and acutely abbreviated written communication (Twitter), leads to "secondary orality," a kind of regression with implications for the character of the self and political systems.

> [Our] immersion in the internet and affiliated contemporary communication technologies ... incline us away from the sort of critical rationality affiliated with literacy and print and towards a relational self affiliated with the visual and the secondary orality of cyberspace. ... Especially in light of

increasing evidence that our immersion in the internet, along with affiliated contemporary communication technologies, thereby inclines us in the direction of a secondary orality—and with it, a smeared-out self characterized by shorter attention spans and less capacity to engage with critical argument—it may not be an exaggeration to worry, following Postman, that the communication media of secondary orality indeed threaten to undo our capacity to think in the ways required for the autonomous self and liberal democracies.[13]

The smeared-out self is not only dispersed into the media of the Internet, social media, and relationships mediated by texting, but is less capable of critical thought—in other words, it is a self subject to "influencers" of all sorts, including political ones.

The Modern Era and the Death of God

Ess and Giegerich[14] link the demise of the atomic self and the rise of the smeared-out self to modern communication technologies. It could be argued that this outcome is less a product of any trends in a so-called objective psyche than a natural progression and advancement of technology. But this argument is too facile. It overlooks how cultural priorities focus the minds of their age. In the Middle Ages, for example, the Church absorbed great minds in the service of God and theology. Other disciplines and avenues of thought, such as science, were not supported, or were discouraged or suppressed. The spirit of the times frames, even dictates, the parameters of permissible intellectual inquiry. Perhaps more importantly, the smeared self is the outcome not only of the *character and pace* of communication—rapid-fire, via the Internet, social media, 24-hour news channels, and text—but also of the *content* of what is communicated. The latter is clearly shaped by the objective psyche. It therefore becomes necessary to examine the nature of post-modern thought and its historical antecedents.

A basic antecedent of post-modern thought is nothing less than what Nietzsche called the death of God. "God is dead. God remains dead. And we have killed him. How shall we comfort ourselves, the murderers of all murderers?"[15] Nietzsche's classic formulation is, of course, not his personal preference or belief. It is merely his *recognition* of a prevailing cultural reality that affects us all: "Jung, too, had viewed Nietzsche's dictum about the death of God as something that was 'a truth which is valid for the greater part of Europe' 'because it stated a widespread psychological fact' (*CW* 11 § 145)."[16] Regardless of individual belief, the *objective psyche* has rendered its verdict: God is dead.

Derrida and the Death of God

Giegerich, while noting the profound consequences for the individual of the modern age, does not explicitly link this development to the death of God.[17]

However, Derrida arguably does in his landmark, "Structure, Sign, and Play in the Discourse of the Human Sciences."[18] Derrida presented this paper at a conference dedicated to exploring the intellectual movement known as structuralism. Derrida notes that a structure necessarily implies a *center* and it is this center that Derrida interrogates. Ultimately, Derrida argues that all structures—in the *human (not natural) sciences*—are dependent on language. Since structures in the human sciences are dependent on language, which itself is without center and without a point of external reference (one can only levy a critique of a theory expressed in language with more language) the concept of structure itself is undermined. Derrida explores the notion of "center" and structure itself.

> [The] whole history of the concept of structure, before the rupture I spoke of, must be thought of as a series of substitutions of center for center, as a linked chain of determinations of the center. Successively, and in a regulated fashion, the center receives different forms or names. The history of metaphysics, like the history of the West, is the history of these metaphors and metonymies. Its matrix ... is the determination of being as *presence* in all senses of this word. It would be possible to show that all the names related to fundamentals, to principles, or to the I center have always designated the constant of a presence—*eidos, arche, telos, energia, ousia* (essence, existence, substance, subject) *aletheia* [truth], transcendentality, consciousness, or conscience, God, man, and so forth.[19]

From here we can trace a line to Giegerich's observation that the death of God results in a "fundamental historical change precisely on the level of the syntax of the world."[20] God is not merely a divine figure worshiped by religions. God, as a living reality in the objective psyche, serves as an *organizing center* for the culture as a whole. God was the hub of the cultural wheel. When this hub is removed so too are all its analogs—as Derrida indicates *all forms and manifestations of "center" necessarily collapse with the archetypal center*. It is this center that gives so many cultural forms their stability. Centers, by their nature, create stability, solidity, *structure*. Small surprise then with the wholesale loss of centers, "all that is solid melts into air, all that is holy is profaned."[21]

But centers do not collapse just like that—nor do they collapse entirely. The process occurs more subtly. Derrida provides some helpful indications. Conceptual systems and theories are necessarily organized according to centers. As Derrida observes, "one cannot in fact conceive of an unorganized structure" and "even today the notion of a structure lacking any center represents the unthinkable itself."[22] The change in the *nature* of centers in the modern age came about when *structurality itself* came under scrutiny. When the relation of structure and its center came to be *thought*, all structural centers came to be seen as *relative to culture, perspective, and "discourse."* Analysis of structure itself led to the realization that any center is not *absolute* (like God is Absolute) but rather a feature necessary to create *this structure at this time* but which can be easily substituted by another structure. "From then on it was probably necessary to begin to think that there was no center."[23]

A genuinely transcendent cultural center functions analogously to how our eyes function. Our eyes are the *means of* our seeing: no eyes and we see nothing. We are blind. Similarly, for the biblical Hebrews, God served as the condition precedent for all knowledge and cultural structures. Reality was (literally) unthinkable apart from God. More than the hub of the Hebrew cultural wheel, God constituted the spokes and the entire wheel itself. "Center" means simultaneously center and "spiritual substance."

Why does Derrida say that *thinking about*, or reflecting on, structure and its center constitute a "rupture?" Precisely because in the pre-modern era, thinking about the center *qua* center was impossible. To return to our analogy: it is impossible to see our own eyes *because our eyes are the means of our sight*. We cannot see that which permits seeing in the first place. For biblical Hebrews, God could not be an *object of thought* because God served as *the means by which all thought occurred*. And this is true not only of the center named God for the biblical Hebrews; it is inherent in any transcendent center. As a means of seeing (or knowing) the center cannot itself become an object of scrutiny.

This is why Derrida rightly calls the modern turn to examining structures and their centers themselves a "disruption" and a "rupture." From an intellectual and cultural standpoint, such a change is no less radical or shocking than human eyes suddenly developing the capacity to *see themselves seeing*: that is, simultaneously seeing and being caught (or seen) in the act of seeing. "Rupture," if anything, is an overly modest characterization of this stunning development. Moreover, the death of God is its condition precedent. Only with the death of God does the captivating grip of God on the cultural mind as its very means of thought loosen to the extent that then God himself can be examined. Indeed, the examination *of* God—specifically, as a *relative* cultural phenomenon—is part and parcel of God's death.

Deconstruction

A transcendent center of meaning in a culture—such as God—orders all cultural structures and their discourses into subsidiary meaning groups, such as intellectual and religious life, social and political structures, and worldview. These subsidiary meaning groups radiate outward in an organized way from the central hub of meaning. The organizing power of a transcendent center can also be visualized in terms of hierarchical structure, such as the medieval idea of the "great chain of being," which hierarchically organizes reality in terms of degrees of *being* or *essence*. God sits at the top of the chain as that which is most full of being; beneath God are the angels; beneath the angels are humans; beneath humans are the animals; beneath the animals are the plants and lowest of all is inorganic matter. Being is inseparable from spirit, ranging from the highest spiritual being, God, to matter, which is entirely without spirit. The transcendent center of God organizes all reality in terms of *value*. This hierarchical structure becomes reflected in social and political structures as well as economic structures. It also applies to the self. Selfhood in the medieval period, for example, was less a personal trait than a cultural one. One's selfhood was mediated powerfully by cultural institutions, particularly one's family or trade. One largely *received* one's identity from one's place in the cultural hierarchy. Only with the early modern period does the self emerge as a distinct, *personal* center of initiative and esteem.[24]

With the death of God, the hub of the cultural wheel gives way. What then happens with the "spokes" of this wheel, all the subsidiary meaning groups? Without a transcendent cultural meaning center ordering them, these groups— or discourses—turn on each other *and themselves*, interrogating themselves. In the case of philosophy, this is shown by the linguistic turn, in that philosophers such as Derrida expose the limitations and contradictions encountered in any critique of a language-based discipline (such as philosophy) insofar as the critiques by philosophers are dependent on concepts which belong to the very ideas being critiqued. "[We] cannot utter a single destructive proposition which has not already slipped into the form, the logic, and the implicit postulations of precisely what it seeks to contest."[25] The result is a sort of conceptual hall of mirrors. Derrida's analysis of the limits that language imposes in criticism reveals how the collapse of a transcendent meaning center (God) liberates analysis and criticism to strike out in every direction, at every structure of meaning, and even upon itself, without limit.

This passionate, unrestrained analysis of every structure, previously assumed truths, and identity inaugurated by Derrida acquires the name "deconstruction." While Derrida himself defined deconstruction variously[26] it is generally understood as, "a method of critical analysis of philosophical and literary language which emphasizes the internal workings of language and conceptual systems, the relational quality of meaning, and the assumptions implicit in forms of expression."[27] Deconstruction is the analysis of analysis or interpretation of interpretations: thought turning on itself, which means language (in which thought is formulated) turning on itself. As an analytical methodology, it explores the very limits of analyzing theories and other linguistic bodies of thought. It is also one of the most powerful trends in Western thought, expanding beyond philosophy to the humanities, law, anthropology, historiography, linguistics, sociolinguistics, psychoanalysis, LGBT studies, feminism, art, music, and literary criticism.

Deconstruction is a specific and conscious analytic methodology. A psychological approach must focus on the objective psyche and *its* autonomous action within culture. It is here worth remembering Hegel's sage observation that "philosophy is its own time comprehended in thoughts."[28] In other words, philosophy formulates in thought trends already present within the objective psyche of a culture. Philosophy's analytic methodology of deconstruction reflects an already-existing dynamic of the objective psyche. The death of God, Western culture's transcendent, organizing center, results in a sort of jailbreak of all discourses in which they turn on each other and (in deconstruction proper) themselves. It is an analytical, skeptical free-for-all. Thus, feminism, to take one example, analyzes and challenges the full range of cultural structures. But such challenges are not only *explicit*. The cacophony of attacks and arguments in all directions can be seen every day in social media, particularly Twitter, which operates according to an autonomous dynamic which no individual participant or group controls or orchestrates. Moreover, at the level of the objective psyche *all* structures come under scrutiny and attack. One such structure lies at the core of identity: the ego.

The Deconstructed Self

Giegerich and Ess observe that the nature of the ego (which Ess refers to as the self), from atomic to smeared-out, has changed with the advent of the Internet and radical changes in media and modes of communication. This accelerated the action and effect of the discourses that had already been competing and conflicting for a century and rendered unstable the identities that lie at the core of the self. To appreciate the impact of these discourses on the structure of the ego it is essential to recognize its linguistic character. The mind's profoundly linguistic nature cannot be underestimated; it has shown to be operative even *in utero*.[29] The self's linguistic nature means that the linguistic deconstruction of identity constructs actually destabilizes our sense of who we are. It strikes at the root of our very being.

Let us examine how the objective psyche's ceaseless process of deconstruction erodes identity structures. Deconstruction is a linguistic strategy of destabilizing the certainty and stability of any linguistic structure. To take one such example, let us look at the identity construct, "man" or "manhood" or "masculinity." What is a man? "Traits traditionally viewed as masculine in Western society include strength, courage, independence, leadership, and assertiveness."[30] Naturally, feminist and LGTBQ discourses have severely challenged this notion of masculine identity, generating the trope of toxic masculinity. This deconstruction of masculine identity has created deep-seated doubt and confusion in what it means to be a man. This confusion is reflected in the related—perhaps inseparable—question, "What is man in relation to woman?"

Contemporary art and music can reveal the confusion and responses given to the questions, "What is a man?" and "What is man in relation to woman?" In Rapper 50 Cent's multi-platinum album, *Get Rich or Die Tryin*,[31] the artist explores different dimensions of being a man in relation to women. The song "In Da Club"[32] forcefully projects the "gangsta" image of hyper-masculinity. 50 Cent portrays club life, in which the man plies women with drink and drugs in the pursuit of sex, not love. The song drips with masculine swagger. Its protagonist looks like a "playa" who has been shot but who doesn't walk with a limp. "Man" here is omni-potent, invulnerable emotionally and physically, a sort of macho Superman.

"21 Questions"[33] portrays a polar opposite masculine identity in relation to women. Here, 50 Cent reveals a need to be loved for himself, not for his money. The song's protagonist wants to know if his girlfriend would still love him if he was down and out and poignantly questions if his girlfriend would write back if he wrote her a love letter. This is nothing like the hyper-masculine man of "In Da Club." "21 Questions" suggests two competing identities within 50 Cent: a hyper-masculine gangsta and a sensitive male.

"P.I.M.P."[34] reveals both identities in tension. 50 Cent assumes the identity of a pimp, one who *controls* and is *superior to* women. He references visiting a strip club with greedy, vain dancers but is immune to their seduction. He's a "P-I-M-P." The first portion of the song evokes a masculine image that is pure gangsta. But as the song progresses another side of man emerges, one that wants to be in *relationship* with a woman. The song's protagonist declares to his love that he is ready to solve her problems and pick her up if she falls. Masculine identities careen back and forth between sensitivity and domineering invulnerability—even in the same line when he swears to be a friend, father, and confidant, he then adds, "bitch."

A question arises: if two discourses of male identity compete within the artist, what is the criterion for determining the reactionary or retrograde identity, the one that is out of step with the current status of the objective psyche? One indicator is that a reactive identity shows itself in the way that it needs to be propped up. An identity or discourse conforming to the objective psyche receives its support from the spirit of the times and does not need to constantly be propped up. "P.I.M.P." shows how the gangsta image of the manly "pimp" is ultimately dependent on the foil of the "hoe." 50 Cent brags to a "hoe" about his luxury cars and jewels and contrasts his expensive shoes to her cheap ones.

These lines show the "pimp's" utter dependence on the "hoe" for his image of superiority. The song's protagonist brags about his wealth and it might seem like such wealth would suffice. But, as Hegel suggests in his master-slave dialectic, the master ("pimp") is only superior to the extent he receives recognition from the slave ("hoe"). This explains why the wealthy pimp still needs to debase the "hoe." He raises himself up by pushing her down. The "pimp" needs the "hoe's" attention and recognition. The "pimp" discourse depends on the "hoe." It cannot stand on its own two feet. That, and its tragi-comic exaggeration of the traditional masculine traits of power and potency, reveal it as a reactionary buttress against the corrosive effects of contrary feminist and LGBTQ discourses. Its extreme character ironically testifies to the power of these discourses and the deconstruction they effect.

Consequences for Psychology

Psychoanalysis operates from the general assumption that the core of the personality is established in early childhood. There are significant open questions concerning the impact on this personality of communication technologies, diverse parenting discourses, and "smeared-self parenting" in general. But regardless of impacts on personality development in childhood, if we assume that *culture* dictates that post-modern factors result in a smeared self of the *adult*, what does this mean for the person? It seems that the smeared self is inherently more suggestible than the atomic self. If the smeared self lacks the critical thinking and self-reflective capacities of the atomic self, and if its stability and sense of identity are buffeted and undermined by conflicting discourses, what does this mean for conceiving and treating pathology? A full exploration of this question unfortunately is beyond the scope of this chapter. I will limit my exploration to some implications of conflicting discourses and their implications for psychotherapy.

Lacan observed that the years following World War I saw the decline of the early therapeutic successes of psychoanalysis.[35] Psychoanalytic interpretations no longer productively activated the unconscious because analysands showed up for treatment already well versed in Freud's theory and technique. As a result, the element of surprise, crucial for productively moving the unconscious, was lost. But if knowledge of Freud's theories a century ago—that is, in an era of the atomic self—could defang the potency of theory-driven interpretations, cultural developments since have made such therapeutic approaches even less tenable. The problem is not just that people are conversant with psychological theories, the problem in Freud's era. It is that in our age of deconstruction, *any* theory is preemptively neutralized, for the simple reason that *any* theory is a *coherent structure with an organizing center*, and as such is targeted like a natural-born enemy by the deconstructive objective psyche. Importantly, this is *not* a conscious impulse or activity of any person organized as a smeared-out self. Rather, in an age of constant rhetoric and attacks flying in every direction, ambient skepticism prevails. Suspicion of structures is automatic and unconscious. There is a sixth sense for ideologies, belief systems, and theoretical systems. They can be spotted a mile away and are met with an unconscious roll of the eyes. Whether it is Freud's concept of the Oedipus complex, the insistence that *all* dreams are wish fulfillments, or Jung's concept of a quasi-metaphysical Self residing at the heart of a collective unconscious, these grand psychological theories seem at best quaint, or at worst, anti-modern.

The post-modern smeared self also suggests modification of certain psychoanalytic constructs. Two such constructs are "projection" and "acting out." Both these constructs assume that an individual is ideally a contained, atomic unit that should contain or *own* its thoughts and feelings. Thus, if a person habitually lies or cheats they should (at minimum) own this fact rather than automatically attribute these qualities to another person. At this level, clearly the tendency to automatically attribute one's own qualities to another (with little or no factual basis for it) is a matter for therapeutic attention. The problem is rather with the nature of the theoretical construct itself. It assumes an insular self from which thoughts and feelings are ejected.

A case example may be illustrative. A 30-year-old male analysand, "Malcolm," presents with substance use and chronic relationship problems, both intimate and social. Relationships that apparently satisfy Malcolm's goals are maintained for a time, but then he lashes out verbally and aggressively, spoiling the relationship. He generally lacks the sort of agency and motivation that may be associated with the "atomic self." Instead, he resorts to external means to buttress his sense of self. One example of this can be seen in the importance Malcolm places on fashion. Even though he dresses in a punk style, Malcolm is punctilious about his appearance and spends a great deal of time and money on clothes. One session was derailed when he spilled a drop of coffee on his shirt. A more serious aspect of Malcolm's effort to externally supplement the self can be seen in his use of drugs, which he uses to act and realize short-term goals. He takes stimulants to work and think, sedatives and cannabis to relax and sleep, alcohol to socialize and hallucinogens to experience meaning. He tailors his life, mind, and emotions with drugs. Consistent with the post-modern "smeared self," Malcolm's selfhood and experience do not radiate outward from an internal, agentic self, but are mediated from without by the substances he consumes. Naturally, Malcolm's efforts to curate his life with substances fail. Drug use facilitates the realization of short-term goals at the cost of long-term problems. It leads to emotional instability that undermines Malcolm's relationships and career. Malcolm's drug use erodes the self he means to prop up – but he also acts out his destructiveness. A large part of his life also occurs on the Internet. He fashions himself as a leftist firebrand who spends untold hours attacking "Nazis" and "fascists" on message boards.

It seems to me helpful to conceive of a psyche such as Malcolm's as suffused by *destructiveness*, a quality that is ubiquitous and arises from the nihilism of our age[36] Because the smeared self is distributed into the world, this destructiveness is both *found* (Malcolm's online wars with "fascists" and "Nazis") and *inflicted* outwardly (his relationship-destroying lability) as well as inwardly (his drug use). This destructiveness is not only projected. There *are* fascists online. The smeared self can be likened to a cyborg: part human and part machine. The "human" part of the self corresponds to the atomic self, that part of us that is inescapably *ours*. The "machine" part of the self corresponds to that part which merges into the world—particularly media and modern communication technologies—into which we are distributed. Since part of the self really is *in* these modern spaces, such as the message boards where Malcolm spends so much of his time, one cannot speak of a projection *into* these spaces. The destructiveness that constitutes much of Malcolm's being is both inside *and* outside. Destructiveness is in both places, not merely projected.

What then is the relation of deconstruction to destruction? Deconstruction is a form of destruction specific to linguistic structures which breaks them down into components, or unveils their theoretical commitments or presumptions. Thus, feminist and LGTBQ critiques of traditional masculine identity "destroy" that identity, but in so doing create room for a new identity to emerge, a case of creative destruction. Yet, for the person whose traditional identity is being deconstructed the subjective experience is one of being attacked, pure and simple, a linguistic dismantling of a piece of load-bearing psychic infrastructure. An interesting question concerns the relation of personal self-destructiveness to deconstruction. Could such personal destructiveness arise out of a *refusal* to suffer a deconstruction, a literalistic acting out of concrete destructiveness in lieu of suffering the linguistic deconstruction of a part of the self? Another way to put it: when a deconstructive discourse is rejected in favor of a formerly dominant discourse (say, traditional masculinity), does a *literal* destructiveness result as a sort of return of the repressed discourse? Is the violence immanent in gangsta rap an expression of literal destructiveness arising from a repressed feminist discourse?

Let us return to where we began: the relationship of the smeared self, the post-modern ego, to the unconscious. Even during Freud's lifetime symptoms (and, correspondingly, the character of the unconscious) changed. Concerning the case of "Anna O," Ellenberger observes that "it radically differs from other cases of hysteria at the time, but is analogous to the great exemplary cases of magnetic illness in the first half of the nineteenth century."[37] Fink, too, recognizes that the hysterical symptoms encountered in Freud's day have dramatically declined with new symptoms taking their place.[38] The smeared self undoubtedly has yielded new forms of symptoms. These "symptoms" are now more likely to take the form of action and behavior rather than true symptoms in the traditional sense. An "Anna O" in our day, upon becoming furious at a housekeeper, might binge-watch three seasons of "Real Housewives of Vienna" instead of developing the conversion symptom of being incapable of drinking water for several weeks. This corresponds to the fact that the smeared self is dispersed in the world rather than contained within the person. We can imagine that the nature, function, and content of dreams may have changed as well. It is all happening now, rapidly, in the air and under our feet. Only by attending to the nature of this changed world can psychology hope to keep up with the changing nature of the ego and the unconscious.

Notes

1 Wolfgang Giegerich, *The Historical Emergence of the I: Essays about One Chapter in the History of the Soul* (London, Ontario, Canada: Dusk Owl Books, 2020), 99.
2 Josef Breuer and Sigmund Freud, *Studies on Hysteria*, In J. Strachey et al. (Trans.), *The Standard Edition of the Complete Psychological Works of Sigmund Freud*, Vol. II (London: Hogarth Press, 1955).
3 Breuer and Freud, 34.
4 Breuer and Freud, 34–35.

5 Wolfgang Giegerich, *The Soul's Logical Life: Towards a Rigorous Notion of Psychology* (Frankfurt am Main: Peter Lang Publishing, 2008), 117.

6 Wolfgang Giegerich, *Neurosis: The Logic of a Metaphysical Illness* (New Orleans: Spring Journal Books, 2013).

7 Giegerich, *The Historical Emergence of the I.*

8 Giegerich, *The Historical Emergence of the I.*

9 Charles Ess, "A Brave New World? The Once and Future Information Ethics," in *International Review of Information Ethics 3*, no. 12 (2010): 36.

10 Ess, 36.

11 Ess, 37.

12 Ess, 38–39.

13 Ess, 40.

14 Wolfgang Giegerich, "The Opposition of 'Individual' and 'Collective'—Psychology's Basic Fault: Reflections on Today's *Magnum Opus* of the Soul," in *The Collected English Papers of Wolfgang Giegerich*, Vol. 5 (New Orleans: Spring Journal Books, 2013).

15 Friedrich Nietzsche, *The Gay Science*, trans. Walter Kaufman (New York: Vintage Books, 1974), 181.

16 Wolfgang Giegerich, *What Is Soul?* (New Orleans: Spring Journal Books, 2012), 10.

17 Giegerich, "The Opposition of 'Individual' and 'Collective.'"

18 Jacques Derrida, "Structure, Sign and Play in the Discourse of the Human Sciences," trans. Alan Bass, in *Modern Criticism and Theory: A Reader* (London: Longman Press, 1988).

19 Derrida, 109–110.

20 Wolfgang Giegerich, "C. G. Jung's Psychology Project as a Response to the Condition of the World," in *The Collected English Papers of Wolfgang Giegerich*, Vol. 5 (New Orleans: Spring Journal Books, 2013), 10.

21 Karl Marx, *The Communist Manifesto*, trans. Samuel Moore (Independently Published, 2022), 27.

22 Derrida, "Structure, Sign and Play," 109.

23 Derrida, 110.

24 Giegerich, "The Opposition of 'Individual' and 'Collective,'" 358.

25 Derrida, "Structure, Sign and Play," 111.

26 Leonard Lawlor, "Jacques Derrida," in *The Stanford Encyclopedia of Philosophy*, Fall 2022 Edition, https://plato.stanford.edu/archives/fall2022/entries/derrida/.

27 *New Oxford American Dictionary* (2021), s.v., "Deconstruction."

28 Georg Wilhelm Friedrich Hegel, *Elements of the Philosophy of Right*, trans. H.B. Nisbet (Cambridge: Cambridge University Press, 1991), 21.

29 Stephen Mitchell, *Relationality: From Attachment to Subjectivity* (New York: Psychology Press, 2000), 8–9.

30 Wikipedia, s.v. "Masculinity," last modified May 17, 2023, 17:13, https://en.wikipedia.org/wiki/Masculinity.

31 50 Cent, *Get Rich or Die Tryin'*, released February 6, 2003, Interscope Records, compact disc.

32 50 Cent, "In Da Club," track 5.

33 50 Cent, "21 Questions," track 14.

34 50 Cent, "P.I.M.P.," track 11.

35 Dylan Evans, *An Introductory Dictionary to Lacanian Psychoanalysis* (New York: Routledge, 1996), 88.

36 Giegerich, *What Is Soul?* 402.

37 Henri Ellenberger, *The Discovery of the Unconscious: The History and Evolution of Dynamic Psychiatry* (New York: Basic Books, 1970), 484.

38 Bruce Fink, *A Clinical Introduction to Lacanian Psychoanalysis: Theory and Technique* (Cambridge, Mass.: Harvard University Press, 2017), 191.

Chapter 12

"It's Not Art!"

Interiorizing Jung's "Confrontation with the Unconscious"

John Hoedl

In a letter written in 1958, three years before his death, C.G. Jung expressed a concern he had about the longevity of his work after his passing. He wrote: "Now we see what awaits me once I have become posthumous. Then everything that was once fire and wind will be bottled in spirit and reduced to dead nostrums."[1]

Jung's fear was that his work would be entombed into unread books, abstract ideas, "words buzzing about", and lifeless concepts rather than a modern access to the enduring depth of consciousness and soul. Was his fear justified? Has the vitality in Jung's theories now somehow grown stale and flat, "bottled in spirit", that is, confined to positivized versions of themselves?

Jung viewed his psychology as part of a long chain, the *aurea catena*, linking it back through the ages to earlier examples of what he called "Unpopular, ambiguous, and dangerous" gateways to the "other pole of the world".[2] If we think of the "fire and wind" in Jung's psychology as the reigniting and preservation of that perennial living essence for our time, one wonders whether that flame is still detectable or in any way "dangerous" today. Can Jungian psychology, for example, still reach the "other pole of the world" in such a way that it could be comprehended as what Wolfgang Giegerich called "the voice of the abyss"?[3]

To look at this problem clearly, we must ask the fundamental question: What *is* the "soul" in Jungian psychology today? Over 60 years after Jung's death answers to this question remain ambivalent, resulting in a wide swath of understandings of what the provenance and *raison d'être* of Jungian psychology is. Today it seems the main focus is on its application to various disparate areas including personal psychology, biology, ecology, politics, and so on. This is without really a consideration of the point or spirit behind Jung's psychology or how and why it came to be in the first place. It stands to reason that without a living conscious link to its foundational core, Jungian psychology loses its way and no longer maintains its *sublated* viewpoint, which it achieved after realizing it was "doomed to cancel itself out as a science"[4] and realize its object of study, no matter what it is looking at, is always "the inside subject of

DOI: 10.4324/9781003381150-13

all science."[5] Without this awareness Jung's psychology is "demoted" to just one more implement in the toolbox that one can use to help with certain problems in the world.[6]

Perhaps one way to shine a light on this question would be to review, from a psychological viewpoint, Jungian psychology's founding story or "creation image" as recounted by Jung himself in his so-called "confrontation with the unconscious." Jung wrote that everything that was essential was put down during this time and that everything that came afterward was more or less its organization and clarification. We might ask whether or not the events that took place during those years (ca.1912 and 1920) and the power behind their "bursting forth" is still present in or relevant for his psychology today.

In taking up this examination it is important to keep in mind that with a psychological stance our focus is the "soul" of what eventually became Jung's psychology and not the soul of Jung the man. Jung wrote that in any psychological discussion it is the soul that is speaking about itself, which means that Jung himself is interiorized into the process we want to examine, into the dynamic of the soul's self-dialogue or self-movement. What Jung as a person experienced is naturally taken into account, but only as a way to learn what the *soul itself* was doing or "saying."[7] The enduring "fire and wind" of the soul cannot be bottled or inurned, not even in the person of C.G. Jung.

Uncertainty

That a dark chaos descended upon Jung after his difficult parting from Freud is well known. Jung's thoughts about psychology, the unconscious, Christianity, mythology, and even the manner in which he lived his own life up to that point, had reached an impasse, an uncomfortable "dead end." He felt he was stepping away from the known into the unknown and found himself lost and empty-handed.

In MDR Jung described this time as a period of "disorientation" that worsened to almost a breaking point. He wrote that "One thunderstorm followed another..." and at times he felt as if large blocks of stone were tumbling down upon him. So great was the constant inner pressure, he even feared he might have a psychotic break. Certainly, the abyss was making itself present during this time.

One can agree that Jung's fear of going insane was justified and that the stakes were indeed high. For example, on December 18th, 1913, after having a significant dream that he did not readily understand, a voice commanded that either he comprehend the meaning of the dream at once or take the loaded revolver from the night table drawer and shoot himself!

Again, for Jung the person, this was obviously a tremendously difficult time with potentially even fatal consequences. However, from the perspective of psychological *interiority* we look beyond the personal predicament of Jung the man and view these events from the position that had actually been achieved by his considerable effort of working through and consolidating these forces, both at that time and through the many subsequent years during which he formulated his psychology.

When we view these events from this vantage point, we understand that the real conflict that was taking place at that time was on the transpersonal level of the soul. In other words, it was the cultural/historical soul itself, in its own self-unfolding, that had reached a "dead end" and seemed to be "disorientated" and "empty-handed."

We are here taking a theoretical point expressed by Jung, namely that in any *psychological* dialogue the ego/person is not saying anything but rather it is the soul communicating with itself. This is the methodological approach of psychology as the discipline of interiority, which aims at disclosing the soul's logical life, leaving aside (methodologically) the concerns for the private individual's life. Applying this insight (uroborically) to Jung's experiences at that time, we can with hindsight comprehend them as being ultimately the soul's encounter with itself for the eventual purpose of creating out of itself a new orientation or adaption. This new position would, of course, be what we would come to call (Jungian) psychology, which is the matrix from which psychology as the discipline of interiority is rendered possible.

Even Jung himself during this difficult time became aware of the larger dimension of what was happening. He realized that this effort was not limited to himself, that is, his own personal experience, but had implications for a larger context as well.[8] He wrote, "It was then that I ceased to belong to myself alone, ceased to have the right to do so. From then on, my life belonged to the generality."[9]

"Unusual Clarity"

If this difficult time of Jung's was not only his own personal "confrontation with the unconscious" but also a conflict taking place on the level of the objective soul's logical life, what was the basis for this struggle? What was the reason for the soul, at this time in its history, to go through this crisis?

We can get an idea of what this might be from Jung's writing in MDR. During the initial stages of this upheaval, while contemplating how his life had gone thus far, Jung had what he called "a moment of unusual clarity". He thought to himself, "Now you possess the key to mythology and are free to unlock all the gates of the unconscious psyche".[10] He noted that he had written a book about the hero; the myth in which man in the past had always lived. He then asked himself, "But in what myth does man live nowadays?" His tentative answer was that it might be the Christian myth. He then asked himself whether this is the myth in which he himself now lives, and the answer was "no." "Then do we no longer have any myth? No, evidently we no longer have any myth."[11] The realization that the general Christian myth was no longer dominant led to the question: "But then what is your myth—the myth in which you do live?"[12] Any answer that might have been forthcoming was blocked as the dialogue with himself became uncomfortable and he stopped thinking.

In this moment of unusual clarity, there was a deep realization that both the myth of the hero and the Christian myth had ended. Jung's dialogue with himself seemed to be the expression of the fact that these two dominant forms in Western consciousness that had existed for centuries were over. Moreover, there didn't seem to be an obvious replacement for them. This fact was difficult to bear and reflection on it became intolerable, forcing Jung the individual to stop thinking; however, it is clear that the "thinking" on the level of the soul was just getting started. Because Jung the man was not going to be able to think through the impasse, the new position was forced to come through another way, that is, wrapped in dreams, visions, violent images, strong emotions, uncanny events, and so on. The engagement with these forces that lasted seven odd years was in fact the "thinking"[13] out of the new *form* of soul from what Jung recognized as outdated possibilities, namely the Hero and Christian myths.

The Hero Myth

Looking first at the hero myth, we can see its importance for the soul during this time by recounting the powerful and fateful dream Jung had on December 18, 1913. This is the dream that could have proven fatal in that after initially not being able to grasp its meaning and then trying to go back to sleep, Jung was commanded by an inner voice to either understand the dream immediately or shoot himself.[14] Of course we don't know if Jung would have followed through with suicide but we can certainly see here the force and seriousness of the soul's purpose. We also see how, for the *soul's* project, Jung the man is not important. He is dispensable. For the soul, if Jung the individual is not up to the task of working through *its* inner contradiction, then he must go and, presumably, the job would be left for someone else. In any case, faced with this ultimatum, Jung stayed with the dream until the meaning began to come to him. The dream helped bring home to him the position he himself must take vis-à-vis the onslaught of the forces he was dealing with in order to both survive personally and to allow something new to come through. It would prove consequential for his personal life and the formulation of a new understanding of psychology in general.

Jung's dream:

I was with an unknown, brown-skinned man, a savage, in a lonely, rocky mountain landscape. It was before dawn; the eastern sky was already bright, and the stars fading. Then I heard Siegfried's horn sounding over the mountains and I knew that we had to kill him. We were armed with rifles and lay in wait for him on a narrow path over the rocks.

Then Siegfried appeared high up on the crest of the mountain, in the first ray of the rising sun. On a chariot made of the bones of the dead he drove at furious speed down the precipitous slope. When he turned a corner, we shot at him, and he plunged down, struck dead.

Filled with disgust and remorse for having destroyed something so great and beautiful, I turned to flee, impelled by the fear that the murder might be discovered. But a tremendous downfall of rain began, and I knew that it would wipe out all traces of the dead. I had escaped the danger of discovery; life would go on, but an unbearable feeling of guilt remained.[15]

Jung interpreted Siegfried as an embodiment of the hero attitude which at that time he saw as being played out by the Germans[16] and in himself. This attitude no longer suited him, he thought, and needed to be killed. After he killed the hero, he also felt overwhelming compassion for the dead Siegfried; feeling that it was as if he himself had been shot. This indicated a secret identity with Siegfried, thought Jung, and "This identity and my heroic idealism had to be abandoned, for there are higher things than the ego's will and to these one must bow."[17]

Jung wrote that he was not able to understand the meaning of the dream beyond this, giving the hint that there was an even deeper interpretation yet to come. This is significant in that there is certainly a deeper psychological meaning in the dream beyond the personal (the death of Jung's heroic attitude) and cultural (the attitude of the Germans at that time). The dream can also be viewed psychologically as the *soul's* killing its own heroic attitude and the potential birth of something new. What this new quality was, at that time, was not clear. The strong sense of guilt and shame Jung felt after the killing, along with his feeling that there was more to grasp in the dream, indicates that its meaning was not yet entirely understood.

Another clue to what the not yet formulated attitude might be, could be seen in Siegfried's chariot which was made of the "bones of the dead". These bones can be understood as the soul's "dead" ancient traditions, customs, and rituals (the cult of the ancestors) that have carried consciousness down through the ages from one generation to the next, outlining the form it must take in each successive stage. For the modern soul, this particular form needed to be killed "in the first ray of the rising sun", indicating that there was to be a new dawn without the dominant hero standpoint (Siegfried[18]) and without the "bones" of bygone traditions and ways of thinking.

But these ancient forms cannot be left behind entirely, they cannot be left lying in the field, so to speak. As an image of the soul's "dead" past, these "bones" need to be integrated into its new position somehow. Something was left uncompleted in the dream, "*I had escaped the danger of discovery; life would go on, but an unbearable feeling of guilt remained.*"

What is this unbearable feeling of guilt that remained, and how does it relate to the objective level of the soul's logical life, and what was going on at that level? A possible answer might be understood by looking at the second point that came to Jung during his moment of "unusual clarity," that is, Christianity.

Christianity

Of course, an obvious overlap between the hero myth and Christianity exists in the realization of Christ as hero, *par excellence*. Christ conquers death and leads the way to everlasting union with God the Father in heaven. Any wavering from this millennia-old sacred belief structure would elicit profound ramifications in both human culture and the soul. It is no wonder then, that the repercussions of such a momentous historical shift, already achieved on the cultural level but now playing itself out in Jung the person, were so overwhelming that he was forced to "stop thinking."

It is perhaps helpful to remember that there was another time in Jung's life, also in relation to Christianity, when he felt that he must stop thinking in order to avoid an uncomfortable outcome. This happened 25 years earlier when Jung was 12 years old. The situation was also difficult and dramatic, at least as far as the elder Jung remembered it, and perhaps both experiences are connected.

The thought that the boy Jung was forcefully trying to not think was imbedded in the image of God defiling his beautiful church by crushing the Basel cathedral with an immense turd that came from God himself. After much anguish and suffering, the 12-year-old Jung was extremely relieved when he finally understood that the point of his experience was to see deeper into the Christian faith, to see a secret of God's teaching, namely that God could force Jung to think something dark and disgusting in order to understand His grace more deeply. The secret idea was that God could actually work against Himself so that a deeper understanding of His nature could be revealed.

The 12-year old Jung felt on one hand privileged by receiving this insight but on the other hand it also alienated him to the point that at times he felt set apart and isolated from the world. The elder Jung wrote, "... I had the feeling that I was either outlawed or elect, accursed or blessed .... It induced in me an almost unendurable loneliness. ... Thus the pattern of my relationship to the world was already prefigured: today as then I am solitary, because I know things and must hint at things which other people do not know, and usually do not even want to know."[19]

We can see this experience as an illustration of the break that occurred between Jung and the established Church as well as the larger community. Assuming that the larger cultural soul was present in Jung even at this time, we can interpret this event psychologically as the soul's work against itself, against its natural established position.

Jung wrote, "I had heard many religious conversations, many theological discussions, and sermons. Whenever I listened to them I had the feeling: 'Yes, yes, that is all very well. But what about the secret? The secret is also the secret of grace. None of you know anything about that. You don't know that God wants to force me to do wrong, that He forces me to think abominations in order to experience His grace.' Everything the others said was completely beside the point."[20]

With hindsight, we can understand the torment and suffering that the boy Jung endured during that time as a prefiguration or foreshadowing of what was to come during the adult Jung's experiences beginning in 1912. A major difference between the two events is that the boy Jung, after his experience, momentous as it was, stayed within the general structure of the Church, negating only particular aspects of it. Jung's later disorientation began with the uncomfortable realization that he was already living outside the "myth" of Christianity. He could obviously not stay within the confines of the Church anymore because both he himself and the larger collective had reached an endpoint with this "myth." This was the beginning of that chaos that would ultimately lead to the formulation of Jungian psychology.

What is psychologically similar in both experiences is that the soul, in the process of painfully going against itself, gained a deeper and more complex position within itself. In the first case, with the boy Jung, the soul gained insight into its own grace by turning its defiling and desecrating nature against itself, against its own "structure." We might even say it claimed the knowledge of a "sacrilegious contamination" for itself and then used it to work against itself to open up the possibility of new truth.

But this new "truth" stayed local, within the structure of the Church and its dogmas and, most importantly, *within the boy Jung* as his "secret." Later, with adult Jung, the experience was radically different in that the soul's experience was not that of a defilement, but rather of a complete loss, uncertainty, a falling into empty space or a tearing apart and a kind of descent into madness. Here the soul was not simply desecrating its own previous form, it was now in the process of transforming itself completely and not only with respect to Christianity but from a metaphysical orientation per se, into something completely different, that is, psychological interiority.

A crucial link between Christianity and the notion of the hero, as imaged in Jung's Siegfried dream, came in 1916 when after years of enduring this inner crisis, Jung finally sensed that something might be taking shape within him. It was heralded by an intense feeling of "restlessness" and an ominous pressure around him which seemed to expand to the outer world and physical reality. Jung wrote that even his family members were affected by this disturbance and the house became "haunted". Apparently one of Jung's daughters saw a white figure passing through the room while another had her blanket twice pulled away in the night. Jung reports that the doorbell inexplicably started ringing and while people in the household could hear it, no one could see anyone ringing it.

Eventually this intense presence revealed itself to Jung as the "dead ancestors" coming to him and crying out, "We have come back from Jerusalem where we found not what we sought."

When this occurred, something was finally released and over the next three evenings Jung wrote *Septem Sermones* which had the effect of clearing the tension and ending the haunting. Putting aside the specific details of what was written in this text, as well as the other levels of seeing this otherwise complex image, we can simply interpret this as an image of the "empty-handed" and lost objective, cultural soul searching for a new form. Jung "opened the door," so to speak and his subsequent writing assisted in the acceptance and development of this new form.

The "dead ancestors" beckoning outside of Jung's door are both the ancient form that once carried the soul, that is, tradition, custom, ritual,[21] as well as the modern bareness of Christianity,[22] presented as the figures lamenting that they have not found what they were looking for in Jerusalem. Taken together they are an image of the end of the soul's expression of its truth within a metaphysical sphere to its "coming home" to an "earthly" reality and its final transformation to the form of psychology.

Being forced to communicate with the "dead", that is, to let them in and initiate their transformation to the psychological perspective, cleared the atmosphere and ended the haunting. We are not concerned with what Jung actually wrote in *Septem Sermones*, but rather that the writing of the book had the desired effect. Jung wrote, "These conversations with the dead framed a kind of prelude to what I had to communicate to the world about the unconscious: a kind of pattern of order and interpretation of its general contents."[23]

It's Not Art!

The transformation of the objective, historical soul from "dead ancestors" to "a kind of pattern of order and interpretation" was the vital and consequential step during that turbulent period. A key factor that brought about this shift in consciousness is worth looking at, especially with regard to how the modern soul, bereft of its rich historical display, should be conceived and how psychology itself would be understood.[24] It came out of an ongoing dialogue Jung had with an inner figure that he called his "anima" about how what he was doing should be understood.

During the most difficult times in this period, Jung discovered that in order to avoid being swept away by the overwhelming sensations bombarding him and to instead work towards their possible comprehension and integration, the process became more manageable when these forces were embodied or personified. He found that if he painted or carved into stone an overpowering idea or feeling, this would help calm him down and begin a process of understanding or interpreting what the force might be. This became an ongoing activity for him.

Soon he began to reflect on his work. At one point in MDR we read, "When I was writing down my fantasies, I once asked myself, 'What am I really doing? Certainly this has nothing to do with science. But then what is it?' Whereupon a voice within me said, 'It is art.' I was astonished."[25]

Jung wrote that he had not considered that this process had anything to do with art, but also had to admit that it wasn't science either. Initially he couldn't think of a third alternative between the two. He thought, "What then what could it be but art?"[26] Jung continued to feel a strong resistance against categorizing this activity as art and sometime later when the voice came again with the same claim that what he was doing was art, he strongly asserted, "*No, it is not art! On the contrary it is nature.*"[27]

Jung does not specify here what he meant by "nature," but he clearly intimates that the work of transforming the raw forces he was confronting into some kind of conceptual understanding was a "natural" process of the soul.[28] In other words, he was not conceiving it as the deliberate action of "man" or the "ego" but rather nature acting upon nature or, putting it psychologically, "the soul transforming itself".

Jung's insistence that what he was doing was something different from both art and science was an important and consequential moment for his psychology. His adamant "No!" shifts the perspective of how the images and the production of the images are seen. The move takes place on two levels: First, the view that the images were basically on the same ontological level as those produced by other artists had to be negated/sublimated.[29] They could then be perceived in a new way, as self-produced images of the soul.

The second point to be seen through was of Jung viewing himself as "artist," that is, as the true and final agent making the images. His declaration that "on the contrary it is nature" means that he was, in effect, saying, "In doing these images I am not myself but am rather subsumed into the natural process of the soul's self-creation."

The second "negation" is most important for psychology in its highest sense. Jung had to see his own subjectivity essentially as "material" or a "location" in time and space for the creative impulse of the soul to manifest. Even though he as person had been bringing the images into the world with his paint, paper, imagination, and so on, the perspective needed for psychology was that it was truly the *soul working through him*. In other words, Jung the "person" had also to be "negated" in a kind of *self-interiorization* so that all that was left was the soul creating itself. Years later Jung characterized it this way: "This 'other' influence is no longer felt as one's own activity but as that of a non-ego which has the conscious mind as its object. It is as if the subject-character of the ego has been overrun or taken over by another subject which appears in place of the ego."[30]

It is the "not" in Jung's phrase that opens up the possibility for a new psychological perspective. This move interiorizes the world of the ordinary and known into the realm of objective thinking (a thinking without a thinker) or into what Giegerich calls the "land of the soul". Rather than following the impulse to think of his images as art (or science) and himself as artist, the non-ego or soul desire chose the "ambiguous" and "unpopular" route which is, as we already heard from Jung, the "gateway to the other pole of the world."

Self

Once Jung understood how "nature" was working through him to establish a new way of seeing, he felt much more at ease. The images that had been produced and the insights gained could now be seen in their true psychological light, that is, not as "human" artistic achievements in the realm of positivity, but as self-generated products of the soul existing in the realm of absolute negativity. Undoubtedly the new way of perceiving these images added much to the understanding and conception of consciousness and the soul but perhaps the strongest impact came from one particular image: the mandala. Jung was compelled to draw them after writing *Septem Sermones* and it seems he sketched one each day in a book as a kind of morning ritual.

One day it dawned on Jung that the true nature of the mandala was, "Formation, Transformation, Eternal Mind's Eternal Recreation" which he conceived as the "self" and the wholeness of the personality. He wrote,

> My mandalas were cryptograms concerning the state of the self which were presented to me anew each day. In them I saw the self—that is, my whole being— actively at work ... in time I acquired through them a *living conception* of the self. The self, I thought, was like the monad which I am, and which is my world.[31]

We can see here that the interiorization of his mandalas (it's not Art!) shifts Jung's perception away from the personal realm to that of grasping (and being grasped by) the reality that his deepest nature exists as a creative union of subject-object and a living supra-consciousness that contains both himself and the world ("like the monad which I am, and which is my world").[32] The world and objects in it are not things "out there" that I simply observe, but rather are aspects of a comprehensive dialectical unity of which I am part of. Within this perspective Jung ceased to be himself as ego and becomes instead part of the living dynamic of "Eternal Mind's Eternal Recreation."

Psychologically speaking, the soul had now clarified its new form. Premodern expressions of the "monad" were manifest in the rich garments of dogma and displays of faith, ritual, custom, and belief. In modernity, the engine that drove this dynamic, the logical life "behind it", has now been laid bare as the "living conception" of the self, the circle that binds the absolute/conceptual sphere with the "real" that is, down-to-earth realm.

Jung describes the realization of the self as a tremendous relief and the fulfillment of his "confrontation with the unconscious." He wrote,

> This insight gave me stability, and gradually my inner peace returned. I knew that in finding the mandala as an expression of the self I had attained what was for me the ultimate. Perhaps someone else knows more, but not I.[33]

Psychology

Going back to the original question about what the "soul" of Jungian psychology is, we can now give an answer based on the founding purpose which gave birth to it. We can remember that this is not a psychology whose formative tenets and presuppositions were thought out by a "person," (remember that Jung "stopped thinking"). The advent of Jung's psychology was *itself psychological* in the sense that it was the soul itself forging a new status or orientation, a new stage in its historical *opus magnum*. Jungian psychology *is* the historical soul (collective, objective consciousness) now in a modern configuration; its "yearnings and hopes" are "adequately expressed" in a new form resulting from the negation/interiorization of religion, myth, and indeed the pre-modern metaphysical stance *per se*.

What is important to remember is that Jungian psychology was conceived in the spirit of negation/interiorization, not as a finished act completed once and for all by Jung in the past. Rather, that spark is kindled anew every time a prime matter is rendered, through psychological awareness, into the language of soul. Moreover, for there to be "fire and wind," the "not" must be understood as a manner of thinking or a methodological attitude that has the possibility of touching something of the dimension that Jung was dealing with. Of course, not to the same degree but in whatever manner that happens to occur within each individual situation. As Giegerich writes,

> No security. No looking *into* the abyss *that one is* from the safety of a position behind railings (from the ego vantage point). It is the other way around, one's being unpredictably from behind exposed to, and becoming the mouthpiece of, the abyss.[34]

Earlier I noted Jung's fear that after his death his ideas would be interred and relegated to dead nostrums. Certainly a death of the living concept happens as a result of habitual fixation on their abstract and hardened equivalents without a link to how they came about in the first place. The "not" must be applied to psychological concepts as well.

Otherwise the "self," as just one example, becomes a "buzz word" and suffers the fate of identification with the personal realm, ("my" self) instead of being, as it was originally conceived, the equivalent of the *living* monad and "emblem of the *whole* man."[35] Giegerich writes,

> ... being a self is the inevitable and a priori character or logical form of all manifestations of soul ... for psychology each phenomenon is, for the time of its being our subject-matter, a world unto itself, the whole world, the one and only world, the All.[36]

In other words the "not!" of interiorization is the realization of a *living* mandala and overcoming of the subject-object split both within oneself and between oneself and the "world." Certainly, this is an understanding of Jung's psychology that it is the opposite of inurned concepts and dead nostrums.

Notes

1 C. G. Jung, *Letters* 2, to Baroness Vera von der Heydt in 1958, p. 469. Nostrum: a medicine, especially one that is not considered effective, prepared by an unqualified person.

2 MDR, 189.

3 Giegerich, Wolfgang, *What Are the Factors That Heal?* (London, Ontario: Dusk Owl Books, 2020), 35.

4 C. G. Jung, CW 8, § 429.

5 Jung, CW 8, § 429.

6 Of course, the application of Jungian concepts to other areas is not problematic in itself. The question here is whether or not this is understood as psychological, i.e., within the realm of psychology as defined by Jung. Jung was not averse to using psychology in a practical, scientific way, as long as one was aware of the "factors conditioning its judgements". Without this awareness, wrote Jung, psychology was like a "dog chasing its own tale" Jung, CW 18, § 1738.

7 Cf., Wolfgang Giegerich's notion of the "psychological difference" in, for example, *What Is Soul?* 80.

8 Jung wrote, "I myself had to undergo the original experience, and moreover, try to plant the results in the soil of reality; otherwise they would have remained subjective assumptions without validity" (MDR, 192).

9 MDR, 192. Here is Giegerich on this point: "It is a grave mistake to see it [Jung's experiences during this time] primarily as Jung's personal self-exploration, i.e., as belonging to his private biography only. No, it was an achievement for the generality" (Wolfgang Giegerich, CEP Vol 5, 304).

10 MDR, 171.

11 MDR, 171.

12 MDR, 171. The back-and-forth use of the singular and then plural pronouns in this section is interesting in that Jung's memory of that time seemed to go from thinking about himself as person to the collective, a sign that he was thinking of himself as spokesperson for "soul."

13 "Thinking" obviously not in the human sense of sitting down at a desk and calming thinking something through… but *rather the (non-personal) soul's objective thinking, which can be anything but calm for the human in which this thinking takes place, as is obvious here in the case of Jung's experience.*

14 MDR, 180.

15 MDR, 180.

16 This dream occurred 6 months before the start of WW1.

17 MDR, 180–181. Jung does not write about the obvious connection here to Freud's approach (and name), where the theoretical dimensions of psychoanalysis are defined generally with ego consciousness remaining sovereign. In Jung's situation at this time, he *as ego* took a different position, i.e., that of unresisting witness. He described that at times, due to the overpowering nature of the fantasies that emerged, he would be forced to do yoga exercises in order to calm himself down and "find myself again," but would then immediately allow the pressure from his unconscious to rise again so that the "experiment" could continue unabated.

18 Siegfried is an ancient hero within German traditions, including the Nibelungenlied, dating back to the 5th and 6th centuries.

19 MDR, 41–42.

20 MDR, 41–42.

21 That is, the "bones" of the chariot that carried Siegfried in Jung's dream.

22 This was also emphatically stated by Jung years later when he wrote in a letter to Father Victor White, "… we are actually living in the time of the splitting of the

world and the invalidation of Christ" (C.G. Jung, *Letters* 2, 138, 24 November 1953).

23 MDR, 192.

24 Of course, not as academic or technical kinds of psychology but a psychology mindful of this historical lineage, i.e., Jungian psychology or psychology as a discipline of interiority.

25 MDR, 185.

26 MDR, 185.

27 MDR, 186 italics added.

28 Giegerich has stated that Jung's use of the term "nature" does not take into account the fact that for the human mind there is no such thing as raw, unaltered nature. "Nature", by the time it gets to the perceiving and thinking mind, has already been reflected and rendered into concepts. Giegerich's view is that Jung's desire for an *Urerfahrung*, or direct experience of deepest reality, leads to the disregard of pre-reflected, Kantian structures. For the purposes of this chapter, I assume that Jung's use of "nature" in the present context is synonymous with that of "soul" as understood in psychology as the discipline of interiority, even though the mature definition of this notion was obviously not yet worked out in his theory.

29 Giegerich uses the term 'interiorization" to describe this process. Basically, it is not a simple negation where something is canceled or removed and is no longer there. A psychological negation is a "double" negation, i.e., one that keeps the phenomenon in place while revealing its logical or syntactical reality. Jung writes, "*It is not that something different is seen, but that one sees differently. It is as though the spatial act of seeing were changed by a new dimension*" (Jung, CW 11 § 891 italics in original). See also alchemy's famous description of the philosopher's stone as, "the stone that is not a stone." The stone itself does not change but it is perceived in a new way.

30 Jung, CW 11, § 890.

31 MDR p.196 italics added.

32 In writing about the monad or "… the self, like monad which I am …", Jung quoted Hippolytus who compared it to the arcane substance of alchemy and the Son of Man capturing the living dialectic inherent in its nature, "'*This Man is a single Monad, uncompounded and indivisible, yet compounded and visible; loving and at peace with all things yet warring with all things and at war with itself in all things: unlike and like itself, as it were a musical harmony containing all things; … showing forth all things and giving birth to all things. It is its own mother, its own father, the two immortal names. The emblem of the whole man …*'" (Jung, CW Vol. 14, § 38). Also, "Alchemy describes what I call the 'self' as *incorruptible*, that is, an indissoluble substance, a One and Indivisible that cannot be reduced to anything else and is at the same time a Universal…" (Jung, CW 16 § 220).

33 MDR, 197.

34 Giegerich, *What Are the Factors That Heal?* 35.

35 Jung, CW Vol. 14, § 38.

36 Giegerich, *What Is Soul?* 306.

Chapter 13

Bitcoin, Utopia & Soul

Josep M. Moreno

Part 1: Money, Sovereignty, and Emancipation

Money exists as "self-fulfillment of idea," says Makoto Nishibe. The thesis of this essay is based on revealing the key significance of the thought of money and its historical transformations through the vast network of exchanges and institutions called "the market" (the meeting place between supply and demand), a "place" where various goods and services are bought and sold as commodities.

According to Voltaire, paper money eventually returns to its intrinsic value – zero. Where does its social and economical value come from? What is money, to begin with? This is the most fundamental question. Some may say that "money is anything used as money" or "money is money because it is used as money," which is a tautology. Money has had and continues to have various functions beyond the immediate and pragmatic ones, which are, by definition, means of measuring and comparing the value of different things. In past times, religion told its followers that donations would expel the devil's impurities. Throughout human history, almost anything has been used as a material for money: feathers, shells, cloth, iron bars, slaves, wheat, and pieces of paper. According to Graeber,

> The reasons why anthropologists haven't been able to come up with a sim-
> ple, compelling story for the origins of money is because there's no reason
> to believe there could be one. Money was no more ever "invented" than
> music or mathematics or jewelry. What we call "money" isn't a "thing" at all;
> it's a way of comparing things mathematically, as proportions: of saying
> one of X is equivalent to six of Y. As such it is probably as old as human
> thought.[1]

A thought we could add as psychologists, which is an existing concept in its historical process of alchemical transformations. From the psychological approach, Giegerich defends the idea that: "money is all-present and all-mighty. inasmuch as nearly everything can be 'sold' and as everything, even people, are

DOI: 10.4324/9781003381150-14

venal...."[2] In reality it brings out into the open the truth that the author thinks as *Schein*, illusory being, "the former exchange medium on the markets of goods and commodities has now itself become a commodity of its own on the money 'market.' Money has been completely reflected into itself...."[3]

Historically, human exchange has always been and is the most convincing expression of its humanity. Nietzsche's *On the Genealogy of Morals* observed that,

> [t]he feeling of personal obligation has its origin in the oldest and most primitive personal relationship there is, in the relationship between seller and buyer, creditor and debtor... To set prices, to measure values, to think up equivalencies, to exchange things.... Selling and buying, together with their psychological attributes, are even older than the beginnings of any form of social organizations and groupings; out of the most rudimentary form of personal legal rights the budding feeling of exchange, contract, guilt, law, duty, and compensation was instead first transferred to the crudest and earliest social structures.[4]

Beyond the primordial barter, the direct exchange between two parties, the historical emergence of exchange mediated by money between humans manifested not as a merely biological, practical, and survival necessity but as the expression of the fundamental impulse of the soul to unfold and express itself in culture and life through *sharedness*. Sharedness is the quality that is essential for the constitution of meanings, and I would add, for the whole human experience that inescapably follows the same logic. There is no culture or history without exchange. Exchange psychologically includes not only buying and selling commodities by means of barter or money with a more or less pragmatic purpose but also "reciprocity in community," in other words, "mutual help."[5] The need for exchange is intrinsic to the life of soul. The search for any benefit – be it biological, personal, or tribal, is empirically obvious but psychologically not essential. There is no exchange unless there is a tool that makes it possible; this is the concept of the market, the "place" where the exchange takes place. This is money, a manifestation of the soul that unites in an objective act of consent the reciprocal recognition of sharedness. The invention of money represented a sublation, an evaporation of the logic of barter, comparable to the ritualized act of killing[6] in contrast to the activities of procuring food for survival purposes. The existing concept of money is essentially linked to the thought of sharedness whose sublation leads to its emergence and later to the market and the economy that moves the world. We see in Economy, not the sophisticated machine as economists want it, but rather as a manifestation of the logical life of the soul; a structure of consciousness that articulates itself and moves as an existing concept and its historical transformations.

In short, traditionally there have been two types of "money": one based on a hard commodity such as gold and one based on a promise, such as the euro. In

Goethe's Faust (1808), the hero pays a visit to the Holy Roman Emperor. The Emperor is sinking under the weight of endless debts that he has piled up paying for the extravagant pleasures of his court. Faust, and his assistant, Mephistopheles, convince the Emperor that he can pay off his creditors by creating paper money. It is represented as an act of pure prestidigitation. "You have plenty of gold lying somewhere underneath your lands," notes Faust. "Just issue notes promising your creditors you'll give it to them later. Since no one knows how much gold there really is, there's no limit to how much you can promise."[7]

Cox[8] notes that it was only with the creation of the Bank of England that one can speak of genuine paper money, since its banknotes were in no sense bonds. They were rooted, like all the others, in the king's war debts. The fact that money was no longer a debt owed to the king, but a debt owed by the king, made it very different from what it had been before.

The key aspect of money in modernity is that money and value are by definition scarce, expensive, and difficult to access.[9] In a further distinction, when the interchange is not mediated by money but by a promise, it opens up a new dimension of the interchange: the debtor and the creditor relationship. As Cox says:

[t]he word "creditor" is based on the Latin word "*credo*," which means "I believe." The creditor needs to believe in whatever the debtor is willing to pay and therefore the debtor needs the confidence and trust of the creditor.... The two sides have a mutually binding relationship.[10]

The author is convinced that the debtor/creditor relationship is the basis of human collaboration and a key reason why the human race has advanced so far. Whether we agree or disagree, this opinion is interesting enough to make us consider the soul logic of this type of experience, whose fundamental impulse is represented by the notion of debt. In the mythological and religious eras, the debt is coined as pertaining to the gods; in all Indo-European languages, words for "debt" are synonymous with those for "sin" or "guilt," illustrating the links between religion, payment, and the mediation of the sacred and profane realms by "money."

Graeber notes that,

[the] difference between a debt and an obligation is that a debt can be precisely quantified. This requires money. Not only is it money that makes debt possible: money and debt appear on the scene at exactly the same time.... Some of the earliest works of moral philosophy, in turn, are reflections on what it means to imagine morality as debt—that is, in terms of money.[11]

Etymologically there is a connection between money (German Geld), indemnity or sacrifice (Old English Geild), tax (Gothic Gild) and, of course, guilt.[12] It is believed that in those times it was the king who took over the guardianship of this primordial debt, while today the State is its continuator through the medium of taxes, which are the measure of our debt to society. The thesis that debt is the origin of the positivistic invention of money has been discussed by some authors, but psychologically I retain the idea that the notion and the experience of debt have had and continue to have a relevant meaning that blossoms from the logical life of the soul, having a profound impact on the psychic structure of mankind. The notion of debt is deeply embedded in Western culture by the Judeo-Christian religious tradition; the primordial beginning portrays the debt, the original sin performed by Adam and Eve, and ever since then, Christianity has been compelled to ask for and implore the redemption of our debts in its prayers.[13]

In our contemporary history, it is pertinent to mention a political and economical event that initiated a new era in the logic of exchange. Richard Nixon's decision in 1971 to unpeg the dollar from precious metals, eliminate the international gold standard, and introduce the system of floating currency regimes that have dominated the world economy ever since, meant that all national currencies were henceforth, as neoclassical economists like to put it, "*fiat money*" backed only by the public trust. This marked the beginning of yet another phase, another step in the sublation of the concept of money: virtual money.

The story of the origins of capitalism is the story of how an economy of credit was converted into an economy of interest; of the gradual transformation of community networks by the intrusion of the power of the state whose core argument is that any attempt to separate monetary policy from social policy is ultimately wrong. Governments use taxes to create money, and they are able to do so because they have become the guardians of the debt that all citizens have to one another [to society and the State]. This debt is the essence of society itself.[14]

According to Cox,

[t]his is a staggering thought. We are completely dependent on the commercial banks. Someone has to borrow every dollar we have in circulation, cash or credit. If banks create ample synthetic money we prosper, if not we starve. We are absolutely without a permanent money system. When one gets a complete grasp of the picture, the tragic absurdity of our hopeless position is almost incredible. But there it is.[15]

In our current situation, consumer debt is the lifeblood of our economy. All modern nation-states are built on deficit spending. Debt has come to be the central issue of international politics. Bankers can produce money by issuing book credits for more than they have in cash reserve. This is considered the very essence of modern banking. Today, debt has become the equivalent of the atomic bomb in the realm of political, economic, and social life. Public and private debt has inflated a gigantic bubble whose explosion might destroy the entire financial system and our lives with it. This leads us to the actual financial system and the monetary policies that go together, and according to Cox, succinctly might be described as follows:

> [T]he Treasury creates the bond and the Fed creates the dollar and they swap them. The Treasury is now able to spend its dollar via the government; this is done through the banking system. The fractional-reserve banking system requires that they only have to hold onto a fraction of the paper money. And so the next layer of banks can multiply the amount of credit and the process can be repeated. Finally, the credit appears in the loan-deposit accounts of the general public. And that is the currency supply.... When you get a loan for a car or a house, neither you nor the bank had the money. Instead, the bank simply wrote the numbers into the computer and you can see them on your screen.... But what gives all of these numbers value? The answer is you.[16]

Of course, as psychologists, our answer has to take into account the soul and its *opus magnum* that allow us to think that the value of money is not only based on calculations and the egotistical search for profit but also on the whole syntactical structure and the internal contradictions that inform the logical soul life in modernity. The concept of debt has been and still is sustained and enforced by the State through rules, laws, norms, and regulations via the medium of hierarchical sources of authority of bureaucracies.[17] Historically, the concept of debt has been transformed from a meaning of divine faith to one of social trust, an existing concept that today supports the logic of the civil organization of life; a social trust that nowadays is being corrupted, evaporated as evidenced by the social and cultural symptoms that surround us. This is an idea that I will develop further.

According to Giegerich, money, following a logic of dialectical negation, has been emancipated from human decisions; I believe that the notion of debt that I have analyzed must be taken into account given that its substantial growth toward infinity[18] is only leading to the possibility of its radical annihilation. Viewed psychologically, the process of sublation of the ideas that underpin the forms of the crisis of the current social organizations in which this phenomenon occurs, and the same forms of incessant technological innovation, seem to express a continuous sublation whose direction and scope are still incomprehensible but that invite us to reflect on the emancipatory teleology of the soul.

Utopia Revisited

[T]he essential, but formally essential, feature of mind is Liberty....

G. W. Hegel

Utopia has been referred to as desire, the desire for a better world and/or society, and as such it has been embedded in the core of human experience and implied in political programs and constructing alternatives for a just, equitable, and sustainable society which provides the conditions for an earthly kind of paradise. Thomas More coined the word as the title and locus of his 1516 *Utopia* in a pun that conflates *ou topos*, or no place, and *eu topos*, or good place. Giegerich argues, "Ideology is the counterfactual giving out of subjective wishes as objective reality. It is a – structurally – metaphysical hypostasis that posits as actually existing what in truth is only sorely missed. It is the substantiation and objectification of subjective functions. Mystification, 'fetishism.'"[19] Consequently, utopia is widely understood as a chimera, a panacea, an instance of wishful thinking, an imagined perfect society or constructed place which does not and cannot exist.

The 19th and 20th centuries were *par excellence* the epoch of social, political, and cultural utopias. Socialism, communism, anarchism, and liberalism, all were a set of utopian programs and redemptive promises that stemmed from profound schisms in society and cultural life, whose consequences were highly contradictory. They were "utopian schemes, to provide a new, ultimate goal of life."[20] My stance is that political utopias have been the first instance of the emergence of a new status of consciousness pushing off from the old in-ness into the born man, but with the first immediacy still very weighed down by the old style of consciousness.

Among the several dominant ideologies in modernity, I will focus on anarchism because its root concept entails a negation, *an-arche*, intimately related, in my view, to the negativity of the life of soul. The root concept in the thought of anarchy entails the idea that a human being loses their essence when their decision-making capacity (as the foundational mark of their self-sovereignty) is captured by any instance external to themself. The delegation or exteriorization of this dimension accounts for the old form of in-ness that displayed a concept of verticality whose dynamic was of submission to the numinous powers. This form of in-ness that has not yet been distilled and evaporated is now displaced to the social institutions called State and Corporation. Since the dawn of modernity, both institutions are believed to be essential to human life, human progress, and social development; I contend that they follow a logic that preserves a collective state of consciousness that stems from the longing for in-ness of the neurotic soul of modernity.

Both institutions were erected as a form of neurotic resistance against the "death of God" and the collapse of the vertical axis that sustained the premodern man.[21] They caved its foundations in a schism, an irreducible dissociation or the contradiction between order and chaos (State), and between prosperity and poverty or growth and decay (Corporation) together with other schisms and irreducible contradictions between moral opposites. In my view, this concerns not only the totalitarian states but also the contemporary democratic states. Despite the appearances that stem out of their predicates (human rights, freedom of speech, etc.), the Corporation as a psychopathic creature and the State, according to Bakan, as the Hobbesian Leviathan, are essentially

sustained by pyramidal, vertical, hierarchical logical structures. Such structures constitute bureaucratic organizations that are supposedly legitimized by
the social contract[22] whose *de facto* job is to create a logical coercion informed
by the split of social reality into irreducible opposites, through the compulsive
fight against their external too-awful-Other (the State monopolizes the use of
force against any Other that questions it).[23] The weakness of our current
democracy is the exercise of a vertical authority sophisticatedly disguised in
doctrines of the Welfare State, human rights, and the ritualistic practice of
periodic exercises of electing governments. This disguise covers up a structural
violence that is an expression of the contemporary consciousness still rooted
in the dissociation of a logically outdated psychological inwardness, which
feeds a social trust blind to its own absence of truth, the signature of today's
homo absconditus.

Žižek affirms that

> one of the main forms of the analysand's resistance is his insistence that his
> symptomatic slip of tongue was a mere lapse without any signification, up to
> the domain of economics, in which the ideological procedure *par excellence* is
> to reduce the crisis to an external, ultimately contingent occurrence, thus fail-
> ing to take note of the inherent logic of the system that begets the crisis.[24]

This contingent occurrence is usually ascribed to the antagonist external Other.
Its vertical articulation resists its sublation into the horizontality of today's
consciousness of emancipation. The collapse of the vertical axis of the Absolute is resisted. The in-ness staged by it is similar to any neurotic symptom,
based in the absence of truth. Giegerich notes that " [i]deology is a less real and
powerful, more vaporized version of the neurotic Absolute ... its syntactical
character must not be noticed, ideology as 'false consciousness'(Marx)."[25]

The author says: " [t]he kind of in-ness that [in the modern period] is longed
for, if it were indeed realized, would be intolerable for the modern subject ... it
would be felt as imprisonment, as a nightmare, of which the 20th century experience in totalitarian states and with fundamentalists sects has given us a
taste."[26] This taste is also offered by not only totalitarian states. At the beginning of the 19th century, Proudhon, one of anarchism's most influential theorists, claimed that

> [t]o be governed is to be watched, inspected, spied upon, directed, law-
> driven, numbered, regulated, enrolled, indoctrinated, preached at, con-
> trolled, checked, estimated, valued, censured, commanded, by creatures
> who have neither the right nor the wisdom, nor the virtue to do so. To be
> governed is to be at every operation, at every transaction noted, registered,
> counted, taxed, stamped, measured, numbered, assessed..., punished. It is
> under pretext of public utility, and in the name of general interest, to be
> placed under contribution, drilled, fleeced, exploited, monopolized....[27]

A prophetic claim that anticipates the surveillance mode of capitalism in medial modernity. His motto: " [w]e do not admit the government of man by man any more than the exploitation of man by man"[28] is, in my view, the first immediation of the thought of emancipation expressed in the externality of the political and social milieu. Psychologically, the thought of anarchy is an expression of the logical concept of emancipation, in its historical process of reaching the truth of its own notion. Historically it has its expression in the negation of the notion of authority (submission) in its vertical structuring.

The thought of anarchy has been accomplished in the axis of the Absolute (metaphysics and religion) and currently in the ongoing process of corruption, dissolution, and putrefaction of the secular, social, and civil authoritarian structures congregated around the State and the Corporation that are manifested in the empirical level as social crises, and at the logical level, as the dissolution of the subject in its concrete and positivistic identity (including with it the positivistic concept of nation-state, the dissolution of its sovereignty forced by the transnational character of ecological crisis and of nuclear threat, etc.). All the emphasis on autonomy and human self-determination in modernity is tempered with an equally intense pull to obey the State at its expense.

Anarchy cannot exist empirically as long as it is imagined from its exteriority as a social and political state to be achieved through struggle, an effort of will, a program to be carried out. We understand it as the process of emancipation in its historical journey of the unfolding of its contradictions and the various stages and sublations that correspond to each one of these in approaching the fulfillment of its truth. The thought of anarchy entails a teleology, the logical obsolescence of any positive authority other than the soul truth of the Man for himself. Our position as psychologists invites us to think about the immanent telos of the phenomenon of the soul without having to applaud or condemn it. The question of whether this logical utopia that I analyze in the present work will turn into a positive and empirical utopia in the near or distant future does not concern us. As psychologists, we only have to admit that, in the words of Giegerich,

> Emancipation in the sense of 'individuation,' freeing oneself from illusions, facing oneself objectively, is nowadays a *task* of the individual... But emancipation is also a historical process that has already taken place so that we find ourselves in the accomplished situation of emancipation (emancipatedness) as a fact. It is a world condition, the condition of psychologically *born* man.[29]

Ultimately, the delegation, the surrogation, the giving away of the thinking moment of decision-making is an act logically and necessarily linked to the prevailing flight from thought (Heidegger) that characterizes contemporary man. Our contradiction is: we are born as free, sovereign, autonomous, and conscious individuals and at the same time we live in a neurotic submission instantiated by external forms of "freely chosen" authorities, that control us and demand absolute obedience, "... in concert with the demands of a market-place, political sphere, and power structure that depend on human isolation and predictability in order to operate."[30]

Although earlier I have affirmed that the State and the Corporation are analogous in their psychological structure, today the State and its legion of politicians – officials who, directly or indirectly, conscious or unconsciously – end up being mere employees/stooges of the all-powerful corporations. In other words, the only institution that reigns is the latter, which brings us back to the aforementioned Giegerich idea: money is God, therefore the changes that occur in the sphere of money seem to point to the very core of contemporary life, an issue that I develop in the following.

Utopia in the form of anarchy is a negative concept that compels human consciousness to exist in the Heideggerian *nameless*,[31] in the "nearness of Being" which is, in the words of Vieira,

> Heidegger's designation of utopia, the promise of a new name that, instead of replicating the old semantic power-structures of the world, would keep its existential-utopian commitment to a name without mastery, retaining a modicum of namelessness ... a fluidity of semantic-ontological complexes and their readiness to dissolve as soon as they have been brought into existence in the new world shaped by the utopian impulse.[32]

Bitcoin; De-Centralized Networked Consciousness

Since the beginning, the creation of the digital world – which as such is destined to make the natural world logically obsolete – entails a soul process that is sublating the positivistic notion of identity. This has resulted in a wholly modern concept entangled in the logic of a hierarchy sustained in social trust. Technology has made possible the emergence of a digital system that sublates into itself the trust and hierarchy that until now has been an inherent part of the substantial identity of people and institutions. The digital system reveals itself as being the trustee of that trust, thus expressing the work of the magnum opus of the soul. The interaction and interpenetration of the economy and techno-science functions as a great universal solvent diluting identities and barriers, like a great torrent relentlessly directing human endeavor toward an unknown direction. This new movement in culture and human beings' psychic structure is forcing us to leave behind the old and obsolete logic that still remains.

The first serious attempt at digital currency was born on a paper signed by Satoshi Nakamoto in 2008.[33] The idea that underlies the project was to create a de-centralized and alternative system for the circulation of money, for exchanges beyond the control of the current financial-economic system. Nakamoto started a revolution by deploying a decentralized and anonymized financial system, allowing people to operate independently of governments and central banks. Antonopoulos argues that Nakamoto's main invention was making all the properties of Bitcoin, including currency, transactions, payments, and the security model, derive from its decentralized mechanism for emergent consensus. Such a consensus is not achieved explicitly – by decision-making from some central authority – nor by any inherent complexity or trust in any single node. Instead, it is an artifact of the asynchronous interaction of a resilient network of thousands of uncomplicated, independent nodes, all following straightforward, algorithmic rules to accomplish a myriad of financial processes.[34] We read in a crypto manifesto,

> These developments will alter completely the nature of government regulation, the ability to tax and control economic interactions, the ability to keep information secret, and will even alter the nature of trust and reputation.[35]

The concept of anarchy presents interesting etymological links with the negativity of the logical life of the soul, *an-arche*, a determinate negation of any principle or imposition of authority or positive power which emanates from any externality. This is the logic of Bitcoin the digital currency, whose anarchy is reflected and embedded in its *logical* structures (encryption technologies, anonymous digital networks, and decentralized peer-to-peer instruments). In Nakamoto's foundational document, "Bitcoin P2P e-cash paper" we read, "I've been working on a new electronic cash system that's fully peer to peer, with no trusted third party,"[36] opening up a new horizon that spawns horizontally across permission-less financial applications, which together support a permission-less economy. The key idea here is "no trusted third party" inscribed in the logical-binary structure of Bitcoin which entails the absolute denial of any external authority, banking institution, or government. There is a determinate negation of having trust linked to any empirical third party:

- Give everyone a piece of the pie by giving away the software to create more Bitcoins. This is Bitcoin mining.
- Have no central authority, or founder, that controls the currency.
- Make it operate like cash with irreversible transactions.
- Keep the whole system honest and transparent. Everyone has a record of all the Bitcoins, or what is known as the ledger.[37]

Here, the ledger can be imagined as a manifestation of the soul's logos incarnated as software code; it is emancipation in its continued motion of coming home to itself, liberated from identification with any positivity (individual or institutional). Vigna notes, "the public ledgers used by cryptocurrencies can bring into the open the inner workings of an economic-political system that was previously hidden within impenetrable, centralized institutions."[38] I posit that we are facing a phenomenon that is not merely a technical-practical transformation, but a soul movement that sublates a previous state of consciousness in relation to the articulation of a social life still embedded in the verticality of the in-ness of the past eras. Trust is a soul value that allows consciousness to open up and commit to whatever or whoever demands it. Trust lies at the very foundation of every act of value. Premodern man trusted the numinous, and this experience articulated his being-in-the-world as much as modern man trusts the discourse of democracy and prosperity coming from the liaison between the Corporation and the State.

Bitcoin denies the three current concepts and uses of money:

• As a reserve of value guaranteed by the state.
• As an accounting unit carried out by corporations and
• As a payment system controlled by governments and banks.

It refutes all three determinations of external control and integrates them into a horizontal structure, a network of distributed code that inherently creates and confers sovereign control to the anonymous user. Bitcoin is a symbol of a new era of computer applications whose philosophy is animated by the core concept of de-centralisation. These applications compose an ecosystem of services that are developed with enormous power and passion. Its telos is to preserve the freedom of movement and the dissolution of individual identities into group experience, anonymously absolved from identity chains. These applications carry in their logical system a form of emancipation of creative human faculties and the creation of networks of solidarity beyond identity constraints and the obsolete logic of the containment in vertical authoritarian forms of submission. I consider Bitcoin's code to be a great contemporary work of art, in the sense of considering art as an expression of the soul that reveals a truth of the historical locus in which technology is born. Its beauty is neither sensitive nor does it follow orthodox aesthetic canons; rather, the "genius" of its author or authors is manifested in the psychological impact it implies for the logic in the way humanity experiences its social reality. The "legend" that revolves around its authorship (anonymity, group-produced work) seems apropos because we know that the name, Satoshi Nakamoto, is a pseudonym, and it is also suspected that there is not a single author, but rather a group that hides behind it. Such anonymity, be it of one or more authors, reflects the spirit of soul's *opus magnum* that today seems to "indulge" in the dissolution of identities and substances into pure syntax. As Giegerich observes: "[w]hat we call creativity is precisely the capacity to become used by works that want to be produced. It is the capacity to build castles *in the air*."[39] How better to describe algorithmic functions and cloud software code! The beauty of the code resides in the elegance with which some lines of binary logic radically and without any empirical violence question what the great ideologies were looking for, and favor a transformation of the logic of our current financial and political system and the neurotic state of consciousness that sustains it.

Bitcoin represents a new dimension of the logical negativity of emancipation because it is not based on the positivistic realm of trusting an institution;

rather, it depends on a concept of trust in that it is logically transparent for everyone to see and control given the open source nature of its code. This is interesting because it literally negates trust in established authority yet places complete trust in its own logic/concept, its own truth.

The Code Speaks for Itself

Soul truths need to be *made true*.

W. Giegerich

The concept for a DAO – an acronym that stands for decentralized autonomous organization -[40] is derived from Bitcoin, which might be viewed as its precursor. Its central points are anonymity, peer-to-peer relations, and communications that favor horizontal governance, and many of them, and in many cases, support the dissolution of identities and external power structures. The emergence of DAOs constitute a happening (in the Heideggerian sense) that herald a logical revolution, subjecting humanity to a global transformation – a transformation that entails the collapse of the classical forms of community, nation, and state, and thus leaves subjectivity in a state of "transcendental homelessness," as Lukacs once described it. As psychologists, we are not able to predict any empirical outcome; instead, we rather need to concentrate our efforts, as Giegerich suggests, on imitating Minerva's bird and her night flight. What I have analyzed is already here, in the tense of the past perfect; it has become visible and seems to follow an unstoppable evolution. The soul today presents its thought to us and pours its dynamism into the binary code, the ethereal substance (embodied logos) that marks the course of our existence and creates a new emancipated reality, internalized in its truth, carrying out the inherent logic of the notion of the old anarchist negative lemma, "Neither God, nor Country, nor King."

The notion of anarchy, which I have discussed in this work, emptied of any positivistic meaning is, I maintain, one of the core concepts that operates at the heart of the soul's emancipation teleology in "the actual historical moment of the radical reversal from man's embeddedness in something expansive surrounding him to a state where that which used to surround him has shrunk to a limited object now encircled by man."[41] Utopian emancipation, so considered, is aiming at the explicit birth of the soul out of itself for the emergence of a born soul as entirely human consciousness and its infinite interiority. That emancipation is not ready-made. As Giegerich says "it requires the continuous work of a stripping off piece by piece of whatever concept that modern man shows himself to be *still* cloaked in despite all previous emancipation efforts."[42]

At the light of the ongoing soul emancipation acting through the technological logic as an *opus* of the soul that points to sublation and interiorization of the notions of identity and subjectivity in a web of de-centralized and anonymous networks of mutual interdependence that have the syntactical quality of the horizontal reciprocity of receiving and giving that leaves aside the Cartesian subject: an "independent" self, set in dualistic opposition to the external world, self-enclosed in the obsessive centrality of its ego-consciousness. Another kind of trust is emerging, which is not conceived as a moral virtue, but rather as the logic of sharedness and togetherness embedded in the technological structures that determine our life.

The blindness and avertednes of the modern ego should not be fought but allowed to go through its own sublation that is negating the powerful ideas that sustain the current social institutions, and by turning human sharedness itself into debts, information, and numbers, incarnates the neurotic constitution of the epoch. According to the notion of anarchy embedded in the concept of Bitcoin with its negative logic, our consciousness is now exposed to the truth that money is *not* ineffable, that paying one's debts is *not* the essence of sharedness, that just as *no one* has the right to calculate our true value, *no one* has the right to impose what we truly owe.

There is no call for political action sustained in my arguments. I agree with Giegerich when he says in relation to the nuclear bomb and the collective fear of extermination, "I am not just talking of the actual physical ridding us of problems, but much rather of the prior and more subtle extermination in our way of thinking about them, in the sense that unwelcome things are looked at exclusively as problems to be done away with."[43] It's not about an undialectical negation and throwing away of the concept of society; rather, I consider it a determinate negation,[44] the other of utopia rid of the weightiness of positivity. Bollier and Clippinger affirm that "If networked technologies could enable people to negotiate their own social contract(s) and meet their needs more directly and responsively, they would enable the emergence of new sorts of autonomous governance and self-provisioning"[45]. Žižek would also agree, stating

> [t]he passage to the next "higher" stage of the dialectical process occurs precisely when, instead of continuing to search for a solution, we problematize the problem itself, abandoning its terms—when, for example, instead of continuing to search for a "true" State, we drop the very reference to the State and look for a communal existence beyond the State.[46]

Bitcoin's logic reveals "the soul's pushing off from a given status of consciousness and reaching out for something that is still in the future, still an unreal projection through which the soul is ahead of itself...."[47]

And, last but not least, we cannot fail to bear in mind that this psychological analysis of the State and the Corporation is intimately related to the notion of the neurosis that infects our contemporary ego.[48] Both institutions that now direct our lives are its reflection, the expression of the collective insanity, via the dissociation of their *modus operandi*, the hierarchization of their governance rituals that echo the same lack of adaptation to the world (ecological crisis) as that produced by any neurotic symptom. And as Giegerich points out, there is nothing redeemable in neurosis; only the "dream" of freeing one-self from it, only an iron utopian will to overcome its logic has to be taken into account.

Technology as a psychological machine[49] is working at the transformation of our being-in-the-world. Its recent production, Bitcoin, and its whole ecosystem of applications is a step into a new logic of the concept of authority sublated into itself, into the logical transparency and objectivity of the horizontal networked togetherness.

Notes

1 David Graeber, *Debt: The First Five Thousand Years* (New York: Melville House, 2011), 151.
2 Wolfgang Giegerich, *Technology and the Soul (Collected English Papers, Vol. II)* (New Orleans, LA: Spring Journal, Inc, 2007), 274.
3 Giegerich, CEP vol. 2, 275.
4 Friedrich Wilhelm Nietzsche and Reginald John Hollingdale, *On the Genealogy of Morals* (Vintage Books, 1989), 154.
5 Makoto Nishibe, *The Enigma of Money. Gold, Central Banknotes, and Bitcoin* (Singapore: Springer, 2016), 9.
6 See Wolfgang Giegerich, *Soul Violence (Collected English Papers, Vol. III)* (New Orleans, LA: Spring Journal, Inc., 2008).
7 Graeber, *Debt*, 999.
8 James Cox, *Bitcoin and Digital Currencies: The New World of Money and Freedom* (Laissez Faire Books, Baltimore, Maryland, 2013).
9 David Hoffman, *Ether: A New Model for Money* (2019), in: https://medium.com/pov-crypto/ether-a-new-model-for-money-17365b5535ba.
10 Cox, *Bitcoin and Digital Currencies*, 5.
11 Graeber, *Debt*, 62.
12 Graeber, *Debt*, 171.
13 " [T]he Christian god, who, as the maximal deity, necessarily 'brought about the maximum feeling of indebtedness on earth.' Even our ancestor Adam is no longer figured as a creditor, but as a transgressor, and therefore a debtor, who passes on to us his burden of Original Sin.... Why, for instance, do we refer to Christ as the 'redeemer'?... It is rather striking to think that the very core of the Christian message, should be framed in the language of a financial transaction" (Graeber, *Debt*, 154–162).
14 Graeber, *Debt*, 162–163.
15 Cox, *Bitcoin and Digital Currencies*, 58–59.
16 Cox, *Bitcoin and Digital Currencies*, 57–58.
17 Max Weber argued that rational bureaucracy was in fact the very essence of modern life.
18 "After all, we do owe everything we are to others.... The language we speak and even think in, ... the kind of food we like to eat..., even the style in which we carry out our gestures of defiance and rebellion against social conventions—all of this, we learned from other people.... If we were to imagine what we owe them as a debt, it could only be infinite." (Graeber, *Debt*, 128).
19 Wolfgang Giegerich, *Dreaming the Myth Onwards C.G. Jung on Christianity and on Hegel Part 2 of the Flight Into the Unconscious (Collected English Papers, Vol.VI)* (Spring Journal, Inc., 1861), 400.

20 Wolfgang Giegerich, *The Soul Always Thinks (Collected English Papers, Vol. IV)* (Woodstock, Conn.; Lancaster: Spring Journal, Inc., 2010), 190.

21 Giegerich notes that "the sense of verticality is absolutely gone; modern thinking is decidedly horizontal" (CEP vol. 4, 300), but I argue in this paper that a kind of verticality is still present in the form of the modern State and the Corporation.

22 "All of this is said to go back to some sort of original 'social contract' that everyone somehow agreed on, though no one really knows exactly when or by whom, or why we should be bound by the decisions of distant ancestors on this one matter..." (Graeber, *Debt*, 160).

23 "A State claims a monopoly on deciding who may use force and when, it reserves to itself the sole right to pass on the legitimacy of any use of force and permissibility in its boundaries." Robert Nozick, *Anarchy, State and Utopia.* (Oxford: Blackwell Publishers, 1974), 23.

24 Slavoj Žižek (ed.), *Mapping Ideology* (London; New York: Verso, 1994), 4.

25 Wolfgang Giegerich, *What Is Soul?* (New Orleans, LA: Spring Journal, Inc., 2012), 334.

26 Giegerich, CEP vol. 4, 193.

27 Pierre-Joseph Proudhon, *General Idea of the Revolution in the Nineteenth Century* (London: Freedom Press, 1923), 293–294.

28 Cited in: http://www.davidmhart.com/liberty/OtherLiberals/Gray/index.html#link-1167. Accessed June 25th 2023.

29 Giegerich, *What Is Soul?* 323.

30 Douglas Rushkoff, *Team human* (Ledizioni: Apple Books, 2020), 13.

31 Martin Heidegger, "Letter on Humanism," in *Basic Writings* (204: 189–242), 223.

32 Patricia Vieira and Michael Marder, *Existential Utopia_ New Perspectives on Utopian Thought* (Bloomsbury Academic, 2011), 40.

33 https://bitcoin.org/bitcoin.pdf

34 Andreas M. Antonopoulos, *Mastering Bitcoin: Unlocking Digital Cryptocurrencies*, 1st edition (Sebastopol CA: O'Reilly Media, 2014), 177.

35 Timothy C. May, cited in https://www.paralelnipolis.cz/wp-content/uploads/2022/06/The-Crypto-Anarchist-Manifesto.pdf. Accessed Oct 2021.

36 https://www.diariobitcoin.com/glossary/bitcoin/. Accessed Sep 30 2021.

37 Daniel Forrester and Mark Salomon, *Bitcoin Exposed: Today's Complete Guide to Tomorrow's Currency* (CreateSpace, Apple Books, 2013), 44.

38 Paul Vigna, *The Age of Cryptocurrency* (Apple Books, 2016), 20.

39 Vigna, *The Age of Cryptocurrency*, 184.

40 According to Merkle, they are, "... decentralized organizations, which means they aren't governed by one person or entity. The rules and governance of each DAO is coded in smart contracts on the blockchain and cannot be changed unless voted upon by the DAO's members." (Ralph Merkle, "DAOs, Democracy and Governance" in *Cryonics Magazine*, July- August 2016, Vol 37:4, pp 28--40; Alcor, www.alcor.org. https://alcor.org/cryonics/Cryonics.)

41 Giegerich, CEP vol. 2, 30.

42 Giegerich, *What Is Soul?* 328–9.

43 Giegerich, CEP vol. 2, 26.

44 According to Heidegger, who speaks of a negative concept of freedom, is to focus in its essence which is negative, where it refers primarily to "autonomy, independence, the absence of dependence, involves the denial of dependence on something else." Martin Heidegger, *The Essence of Human Freedom* (London: Continuum, 1982), 5.

45 David Bollier and John Clippinger, *From Bitcoin to Burning Man and Beyond. The quest for identity and autonomy in a digital society* (Published by ID3 in cooperation with Off the Commons Books, 2014), 24.

46 Slavoj ŽiŽek, *Menos que nada. Hegel y la sombra del materialismo dialéctico* (Madrid: Akai, 2012), 239.
47 Giegerich, CEP vol. 4, 323.
48 See Wolfgang Giegerich, *Neurosis: The Logic of a Metaphysical Illness* (New Orleans, LA: Spring Journal, Inc., 2013).
49 See Giegerich, CEP vol. 2.

Chapter 14

How Does Music Think?

Pamela J. Power

Introduction

The title of this chapter might strike the reader as odd since music is closely associated with emotions and feelings. Nothing in the arts can move us so deeply, bring us to tears or even despair, quite so much as music. Addressing how music "thinks" addresses the underlying forms and structure of music. The syntax tells the story of the autonomous process propelled by the spiritual unfolding of Western culture. It is a process that includes the development of technology, science, and psychology. This autonomous process, this evolution, this shift in the syntax and structure of music is best described as "how music thinks." It may also be described as the logical life of music.

At the outset, it is essential to differentiate between emotion and feeling. The latter, described by Jung, is an ego evaluative function of the psyche, whereas emotion is a physiological response such as joy, pleasure, revulsion, fear, and so on. Feeling may have no emotional or physical component, and one might not even know what one feels. Furthermore, rather than thinking and feeling as discrete functions of the ego, as Jung describes them, they are better considered as aspects of a whole. Giegerich writes, "... the concept of the typology of functions not only condones but also itself decrees and 'institutionalizes' the popular absolute split between thinking and feeling, their mutually excluding each other."[1] Throughout history, there has been continual development of thinking and feeling, and refinement of both through science, philosophy, religion, technology, and the arts.

My interest in the development of music dates to undergraduate studies, during which I found myself particularly interested in how music changed through the ages from one formal structure to another, very different one. How did Renaissance music change into Baroque music, and the latter into Classical? While there were towering figures in all eras, the changes were gradual and often made by composers who are long forgotten. The great composers seemed to solidify a period rather than create it; they coagulated the trends into a definite form and style.

DOI: 10.4324/9781003381150-15

Those studies were in the background of my experience when I first read "Burial of the Soul in Technological Civilization" by Wolfgang Giegerich.[2] Quickly I came to see that in addition to technology being a unique development of Western culture—so, too, was music. The history of Western music is inextricably bound to the history of science and concurrent achievements in technology. For this chapter, I have chosen to focus on a few aspects unique to music to demonstrate how music had its own "logical life" within the context of the broad development of Western culture, or rather, how the soul's logical life manifested in music.

A less than obvious aspect of the development of music is that it was accomplished with and through negation. By the term "negation" I do not mean an evaluation as bad or as a nullification, as when a proposition is negated. Rather, it is a negation as in alchemy when a substance is negated in its current form and is sublated to become something else. It becomes transformed so that the original is preserved in a different form. This is merely an analogy. In music, negation occurred because of inherent contradictions in the nature of musical tones, as I will demonstrate in what follows. These contradictions and how tones relate to each other forced music to work with itself, against itself, with the Church, against the church, with the natural scale, against the natural scale, with consonance, against consonance. I shall briefly describe these as making up how music thinks.

Incarnation: The Spirit of Western Culture

Music is ubiquitous around the world. As far as we know, it has developed in all cultures. But the only place where complex, systematic harmony originated and manifested as a major phenomenon was in Western music. Science, technology, mathematics, and music developed in a particular way that is more complex—not better—but more complex than other places.

Certainly, there was and is music in other cultures that is far more complex and developed in terms of scales, melody, or rhythm. But only in Western music did harmony take on something of a driving force and become extensively developed. The earliest music, of the Greeks and of most tribal cultures, was based on rhythm and the horizontal line of melody. Over the centuries, melody gained simple harmonies that led to polyphony. Gradually, chords, chord progressions, and major-minor tonality developed, and the vertical dimension of harmony replaced the melodic line as the determining syntax.

The driving force was the spirit of incarnation that was embedded in the early doctrine of the Western Christian church. Και 'ο λογος σαρξ εγενετο—and the word became flesh. These words from the Gospel of John (1:14) became the formulation for the doctrine of the Incarnation. The creative logos, God the spirit of heaven, took on the human form in the figure of Jesus, the son. Although the book of John was written in the first century CE, the doctrine of the incarnation became worked out as dogma during the ensuing centuries. Through numerous controversies, heresies were defined, and doctrines were accepted and rejected. Differences between the Eastern Greek Church and Western Roman Church began to drive them apart as early as the 4th century, and the division between them was made final in the Great Schism of 1054. While issues of political power and influence played a major role, the crucial doctrines in dispute were the following: Are the father and the son of the same or similar substance? This is the "*homoousia* v *homoiousia*" controversy, are they of the *same* or only *similar* substance? And the corollary: does the Holy Spirit emanate from father *and* son or only from the father, the "*filioque*" controversy. Both pieces of doctrine have to do with the role of the flesh and blood human figure of Jesus in the religious theology of the early Christian church. This became highly significant with implications for the eventual dogma of the Incarnation. If Jesus, as a man, is of equal importance to God, then God *really* becomes man, and man *really* becomes God. As dogma, this was fought for, firmly established, and incorporated in the Creed of beliefs by the Western Church. However, the Eastern Church rejected the *homoousia* (same substance) and *filioque* (and the son) additions and these are not included in the Eastern Orthodox Creed.

The result is that in the Western Church, the incarnation as dogma, that is, revealed truth, was realized, and over the following centuries incarnation was applied to itself. *Incarnation became incarnated.* In the Eastern Church, incarnation remained as an idea that was not applied to itself, not interiorized into itself. The incarnation was merely "worshiped and adored but not incarnated."[3]

It is curious that these matters of dogma played such an influential role. Giegerich wrote, "Incarnation means nothing less than the systematic undoing of the Heaven-Earth distancing.... Heavenly Logos has now been interred in earthly flesh."[4] "The Incarnation is ... indeed the myth of the unmythological...."[5]

All the prerogatives once belonging only to God became—in the process of incarnation—available to humans. Mankind would become creative. He would investigate nature, unlock God's secrets of the universe, and look behind the curtains of God's mysteries. And for these purposes, he would invent telescopes and microscopes to look beyond the visible. These were done *against* the resistance of the Church that had determined and affirmed the dogma of the Incarnation in the first place! God becoming man means that Man would place himself at the center of all things. Man would become creative and put his own fleshed-out image in the human-like images of Madonna and the Christ child of the early Renaissance. Human emotions would become the center of all things as they did in the music of the Classic and Romantic periods.

Giegerich wrote about the Incarnation and the immurement of soul in technology. The development of music was inextricably intertwined with the development of technology through the inventions and innovations of musical instruments. The driving spirit of music required new technological advancements and those advancements further served the propulsive movement of that spirit. If the "Incarnation is the burial of soul in technology,"[6] it is also the burial of soul in all things as man becomes the creator, in the arts, in music, in crafting telescopes, building steam engines, and making computers.

Beginnings of Music

The spirit of incarnation was locked up during the centuries of the early church that first sought to wean its adherents from any residue of the pagan past. Early church music was continuous with traditions from the Israelites, through chanting psalms, scripture, and prayer. Instruments were distrusted and discouraged in church music and it was not until the 9th century that the church organ, against much resistance, was incorporated into the Church. What we think of as plainchant, the monophonic chanting of liturgy, was varied throughout regions and then consolidated by Pope Gregory in the 6th century. The Gregorian chant is the body of liturgical music that provided the basis for further development over the next several hundred years.

The beginnings of harmony occurred around the 10th and 11th centuries, first by the addition of single notes moving in parallel to the chant. However, rather quickly came the invention of more elaborate melodies that moved in contrary motion, as well as the interweaving of different melodic lines. "The possibilities of harmony that resulted from the combination of separate lines represented undiscovered territory, as promising and mysterious as the interior of a newly discovered continent."[7]

Rudimentary harmony at first used the octave, perfect 5th and 4th as these were the most pleasing and consonant intervals. The 3rd and 6th, for many years considered too sensuous for music that was designed for devotion to God, were later incorporated. Polyphony emerged during the Renaissance and is familiar to us in its most developed form in the music of such figures as Josquin, Monteverdi, and Palestrina. But still, in that music, the horizontal, melodic lines predominated, as rudiments of the plainchant (the *Cantus Firmus*) formed the structural basis of that music (the syntax).

However, with the push for more complex polyphony, there emerged a serious conundrum that music had to "think through." An implicit problem, a contradiction is built into the very nature of music within the natural laws of musical tones. For music to continue to evolve this problem would have to be taken up, and it did so with contentious dispute for over 600 years.

The Conundrum of Musical Scales

The conundrum is that music, as scales, does not fit itself, and attempts to do so resulted in some kind of negation of itself. Music in its natural, God-given state, music of the spheres, the perfect intervals determined by exact proportions, as discovered by Pythagoras, only worked as long as it stayed away from anything but the most simple harmony and relied on melody as the determinate structure.

Here is a simplified description that I hope will make the point. You all know that any note, let's take a middle C, has an octave above, also a C, and this note vibrates at twice that of the middle C. The ratio is 2:1 for this higher C. A fifth, the interval sounded by the first four notes of "Twinkle Little Star," has the ratio of 3:2. A fourth by the ratio of 4:3, the first notes of "Here comes the bride." The interval of a major 3rd is produced by a vibration ratio of 5:4 and makes up the first and third notes of "Doe a Deer" from *The Sound of Music*.

Let's take a perfect 5th and build a perfect 5th on top of that. We will do a circle of 5ths going through all the notes and eventually come back to C, many octaves above where we began. It turns out it is too big, too wide. That C would be out of tune with the C we began with. If instead, we begin to build with major 3rd intervals, this results in a scale that is too small. C to E, E to G#, G# to B#. Anyone who knows a slight amount about music knows that a B# is the same note on the piano as a C. But using the exact Pythagorean intervals, it is not—it is lower. Three major 3rds do not fit neatly into an octave; they are too small, too narrow.

Of course, *we know* they fit because our modern piano makes them fit. This is because of what musicians and particularly piano tuners call Equal Temperament tuning. This means that the distance between any two notes is exactly the same throughout the keyboard. The struggle over Equal Temperament was fought out over many centuries. The natural, God-given, music of the spheres, was eventually negated for the sake of Equal Temperament syntax, a nearly completely out-of-tune system that we have grown accustomed to for almost three centuries.

To better understand the struggle over this matter, the laws of music, as well as of geometry, astronomy, and mathematics, were considered to be the fingerprints of God, sacred and immutable. In a word, those laws were *numinous*. Therefore, what devoutly religious person would dare to tamper with God's fingerprints? There was great resistance to tempering, meaning lowering or raising a note in a scale, in order to create artificial intervals that would not clash with each other. Many different tempered scales were attempted; most tried to maintain the perfect 5th or the major 3rd. The idea behind these different systems of temperament was to alter as few notes as possible in order to retain as many intervals that maintained the ideal ratios. One later system was called "well-tempered tuning" that J.S.Bach utilized in his *Well-Tempered Clavier*. But gradually, perfect 5ths were lowered, major 3rds raised, and all other notes altered so that each note was equidistant from the adjacent note. The adoption of Equal Temperament amounted to a nearly complete negation of the God-given, natural intervals in favor of a cultural invention. In Equal Temperament tuning, the only interval that remains truly acoustically consonant is the octave. This technological change allowed music of the classical and romantic periods to explore musically in ways previously impossible. This transition allowed man to become God in music, to master full creative invention.

Once equal temperament was established, modulation throughout the 12 major and minor keys became possible on one keyboard instrument. No longer was a musician restricted to playing in one key and closely related keys. The diminished 5th (augmented 4th), called in early times "the devil in music" [*diabolus in musica*] because of its harsh and unpleasant sound, rather than being avoided as it was *in the melodic line*, now *in the vertical line* became utilized as a driving force to create tensions and color in the new harmonic system. All sorts of enharmonic modulations became possible, freely moving between keys, major and minor, to produce an expanded variety of nuances, musical colors, and subtle differences. This revolutionary change, this out-of-tune scale system, enabled music to engage on a major thrill ride of harmonic expression that exercised itself from the classical, through Romantic and late-Romantic music.

Soul was working out new territories for itself. Music was a means and expression of new soul truths, of soul-making, in the area of emotions, feelings, and sentiments. The self-negation of music allowed the creation of new soul continents. Perhaps nature reveled in nature during earlier times when music was simple melody and rhythm. When the spirit of harmony was unleashed upon natural musical tones, something was set in motion, slowly at first. With the spirit of invention, discovery, and creation, the human drive overrode and overruled the fingerprints of God.

Emotions and Feeling

We cannot know with any certainty the aesthetic sensibilities and emotional experiences of humans throughout the centuries. We can only infer feeling values by what was revered at any given historical time and that these values changed, evolved, and expanded over the centuries.

Cultural development is soul-making. Giegerich wrote, for example, about the re-purposing of philosophical Eros during medieval times:

> [T]hrough the almost cultic devotion of the Minnesingers to an idealized woman, slowly the feminine had acquired a totally new soul aspect unknown before. This was a truly new *conquest*, an extension of the range of feelings beyond what previously had been possible: an *invention*.... [S]o the repurposing of the philosophical eros, by directing it all of a sudden to 'the feminine,' invented and established the inwardness and depth of *feeling* as a totally new addition to the inventory of psychological possibilities and regions of experience, making mystical as well as romantic soul love possible."[8]

Feelings of all sorts came into being as part of overall Western cultural development, extensions "of the range of feelings beyond what previously had been possible."[9]

Music, so associated with emotions today, most likely was unlike earlier periods. Early music was about devotion and the worship of God. Except for secular music, it was frowned upon for pure enjoyment. What began as Liturgical chant for the Church evolved over hundreds of years to a differentiated expression of human emotions. Here is what a musicologist wrote in 1691: "Music is a gift of God, to be used only in His honor."[10]

By contrast, here is a quote from another musicologist writing in 1776: "Music is an innocent luxury, unnecessary, indeed, to our existence, but a great improvement and gratification to the sense of hearing."[11] What happened during those 100 years was the Enlightenment. "This complex movement known as *the Enlightenment* began as a revolt of the spirit: a revolt against supernatural religion and the church, in favor of natural religion and practical morality; against metaphysics, in favor of common sense, empirical psychology, applied science, and sociology; against formality, in favor of naturalness; against authority, in favor of freedom for the individual."[12] I find it interesting that the conclusion of the long contentious fight for Equal Temperament in music was coincidental with the age of The Enlightenment.

The apex of identity between personal, subjective emotions and music occurred during the Romantic period, a relatively brief period early in the 19th century. Here is a description, by a modern music critic, written in 2007, about one composer of that period.

Schubert is at the very heart of music. More: definition of what he is, account of what he did, in music, are tantamount to a description of music itself in its more normative and widely shared sense—what it is, how it works, what it is *for*. No composer is less dispensable, more essential and intrinsic. 'Essential' meaning closest to the art's grammar, syntax, language, which he employs with extraordinary purity and exactness even while they undergo in his hands the most radical extensions ever made by one individual. Their purpose, of course, to expand, to deepen, intensify expression: to which the same superlative applies—no single composer has added so largely to what music, in its innate nature, not foisted upon it, can *say*. This is just as essential and intrinsic as the linguistic usage. They can't be separated: the wider key-relationships, the major/minor ambiguity, the enharmonics, the enhanced dissonances, equally with the exploration of the most basic facts of diatonicism, and every motive, melodic, rhythmic, textural element; all this is in such perfect fusion with the affective ends that he has to be called Apollonian, whatsoever is being expressed — amiable/convivial, frenzied, doom-laden, *angstvoll*, erotic, pantheistic, radiant, desolate, God-forsaken, weary-unto-death, furious, frustrated, fragmented, nihilistic, nostalgic, or just *cold!* Many more words could thus be adduced, for Schubert covers a wider range of emotion than any other composer and most other artists in any medium; but they would be mere signs and ciphers apart from the way their every nuance within the comprehensive coverage is imprinted into the notes.[13]

Through internal self-movement, music as a soul phenomenon displayed itself at its fullest in emotional expression during this period. However, beginning with the late 19th century and into the early 20th, (concurrent with the "death of God," the beginning of modernity, and the rise of psychology) music exsanguinated itself. It was as if music had had enough of all the sentiment, over-indulgence, emotional excess, grandiosity, and even mysticism. The bottom dropped out, rhythmic intensity was reasserted, and the rigors of 12-tone (atonal) music moved in for a period and tried heroically, but in vain, to clear the decks of the dominance of tonality and tonal-based harmony. "Music is, by its very nature, powerless to express anything at all," wrote Stravinsky.[14] These values began to be asserted by early 20th-century composers such as Stravinsky and Schoenberg. American composer John Cage (1912–1992) said, "Emotion doesn't fit into my work. It exists in each person, in his own way; but I'm not involved with that. I have emotions, but I don't put them into my work."[15]

Music wrung itself out; the emotion of music got used up. But like a fire that burns itself out, there is a residue, something that is not something, the white ash of alchemy. Thought is sublated emotion, but so is feeling. Music "thought" through the paradoxes of scales and harmony, and it "thought" through its overweening talent for emotionality. Soul did its work. It distilled feeling. Concurrent with the loss of soul for modern man came the bridge to soul, the ability to "feel" the soul dimension, feel the "departed soul."[16]

Giegerich wrote that feeling is the bridge to soul:

Without feeling, the soul cannot be apperceived. Feeling in this sense is what has the power to connect modern consciousness with the soul-in-the-real across the gap of our fundamental alienation from it. The capacity to feel is the bridge across the psychological difference, the bridge also across and beyond our subjective positive or negative feelings, so that we may become open to the heart of what *is*.[17]

In a footnote to that statement, Giegerich wrote:

My term feeling is different [from Jung's feeling function in his typology]. I call it 'rational' mainly to ward off any sense of emotion or sentiment, and for me it is not a merely processing or evaluating function (e.g. according to the "good-bad, pleasant-unpleasant etc." categories which are always measured from the ego point of view), but it also makes something new accessible and, as in this way providing us with new "input," has thus a kind of "irrational" aspect, too. However, this new material is not, horizontally, new empirical data as in the case of the sensation and intuition functions, not "what the eyes can see," but vertically a new *dimension* ("what opens the eyes"), the depth dimension of what has already been made available by sensation or intuition.[18]

Feeling, in Giegerich's sense, had always been *implicit* within music even as soul enjoyed itself in the display and emotionality of music, the sensuous delights of music. Eventually, music freed itself of the conflation and preoccupation with the expression of emotions. Soul, through the medium of music, created a sundering, a negation of deep emotions for the sake of deep feeling. The detritus of music is feeling as a "judgment of taste," as a capacity to discern the soul dimension, and as an act to create the bridge across the "psychological difference."[19] With the departure of soul from music, feeling as cool discernment became an *explicit* possibility.

But wait! How can one even think of music without emotion? The potency and power of music is that it evokes emotional states that take one out of and beyond oneself. Isn't *that* the soul dimension that Giegerich refers to when he writes about feeling as a bridge to soul? No, and this point is key, or rather, at this point we are in the key of soul, a sublation of literal music. Soul, as we know, is no longer *something* to connect to, out there or inside, but a dimension, a perspective, a methodology, a way of seeing, hearing, or listening.

Igor Stravinsky was aware of this shift in music which he described in the following comments:

> Most people like music because it gives them certain emotions such as joy, grief, sadness, and image of nature, a subject for daydreams or – still better – oblivion from "everyday life". They want a drug – dope – .... Music would not be worth much if it were reduced to such an end. When people have learned to love music for itself, when they listen with other ears, their enjoyment will be of a far higher and more potent order, and they will be able to judge it on a higher plane and realize its intrinsic value.[20]

In much of the classical music written in the 20th century, I hear nostalgia, sadness, and a longing for something that has passed. The English novelist, Julian Barnes, wrote, "I don't believe in God, but I miss him."[21] For me, much of 20th-century and contemporary classical music expresses this sentiment. It is a partial recognition, a reluctant recognition, of knowing "God is dead" but not yet realizing it as an accomplished fact, instead, continuing an emotional attachment to and longing for the past. Some of the *most* interesting later 20th-century music reflects the *best* attempt to display the coolness of feeling—in Giegerich's sense—that is possible within the medium of sound.

Western music was not the only avenue for the development of feeling. All aspects of life, philosophy, science, politics, as well as the arts, are domains conducive to the cultivation of feeling. In music, the expression of emotions was especially forceful and compelling. Soul was music in its fullest emotional experience—and still is. But now soul has both abandoned music *and* absconded *with* music into the realm of the media with the result that except for live music in concert halls, clubs, and pop venues, all music today is entirely in digital form. Furthermore, the main thrust of music *today* is not about the *expression* of emotion through music—but about the *manipulation* of emotion *by* music, which is so obvious and common in television, movies, and commercials.[22]

Listening to "classical" music today "is like going to a museum. However, museums are a part of the modern soul! Former ages and other cultures did not have museums in our sense. I think this has something to do with 'the birth of man,' which means the end of immediacy and the explicit emergence of Mnemosyne."[23]

Soul has finished its work in and through the medium of music. In the wake of the departed soul, there is a residue, the alchemical "white ash," a sort of "arcane substance," a something that is not something: "feeling as a bridge to soul." Feeling in this sense (refined and distilled from emotion) allows apperception of soul in the real and is, paraphrasing the Kena Upanishad, "not *what* the ears can hear, but what *opens* the ears."[24]

Notes

1 Wolfgang Giegerich, *The Soul Always Thinks* (New Orleans: Spring Journal Books, 2010), 3.
2 Wolfgang Giegerich, "The Burial of the Soul in Technological Civilization," in *Technology and the Soul* (New Orleans: Spring Journal Books, 2007), 155–211.
3 Wolfgang Giegerich, Personal communication via e-mail, 2013.
4 Giegerich, "The Burial of the Soul in Technological Civilization," 167.
5 Giegerich, "The Burial of the Soul in Technological Civilization," 171.
6 Giegerich, "The Burial of the Soul in Technological Civilization," 159.
7 Thomas Levenson, *Measure for Measure: A Musical History of Science* (New York: Simon & Schuster, 1994), 55.
8 Levenson, *Measure for Measure*, 180.
9 Levenson, *Measure for Measure*, 180.
10 Andreas Werckmeister in Grout, D, *A History of Western Music* (New York: Norton, 1973), 447.
11 Charles Burney in Grout, *A History of Western Music*, 447.
12 Grout, *A History of Western Music*, 447–8.
13 Composer/critic Robin Holloway writing in 2007, quoted in Scruton, R, *Understanding Music: Philosophy and Interpretation* (London: Continuum Publishing, 2009), 49.
14 Igor Stravinsky, *An Autobiography* (Calder and Boyars ed., 1935/1975), 53.
15 Richard Kostelanetz, *Conversing with Cage* (New York: Limelight Editions, 1987), 213.
16 Wolfgang Giegerich, *What Is Soul?* 1st ed. (New York: Routledge, 2020), 130–131.
17 Wolfgang Giegerich, "Psychologie Larmoyante" in *The Soul Always Thinks* (New Orleans: Spring Journal Books, 2010), 510.
18 Giegerich, "Psychologie Larmoyante," 510, note 8.
19 Giegerich, "Psychologie Larmoyante," 512.
20 Stravinsky, *An Autobiography*, 163.
21 Julian Barnes, *Nothing to Be Frightened Of* (New York: Knopf, 2008), 1.
22 Peter White, "Some Reflections on the Commercialization of Music in the Light of the Syzygy" Inaugural Conference of ISPDI, 2012. Website ISPDI.org.
23 Giegerich, Personal communication via email, 2013.
24 Kena Upanishad: "Not *what* the eyes can see, but what *opens* the eyes, that is the Brahman."

Chapter 15

Churchill's Shroud
Archetypal Forces in the Rise and Fall of the Great White Male

Robert Dommett

Introduction

At the time I started writing this chapter in mid-2020, much of the world was consumed by protests under the banner of Black Lives Matter (BLM). This movement followed rapidly on the heels of protests associated with the COVID-19 lockdowns, climate change, and the #MeToo movement.

With this as a backdrop, the impetus for my investigation was the image of Winston Churchill's statue on London's Parliament Square shrouded in a steel cage to protect it from defacement and possible destruction by protestors.[1]

To me, this begged the question of why we were all of a sudden being confronted by protests of this magnitude. Was there a common thread linking them and why was the once revered Winston Churchill, arguably the greatest statesman in recent British history, suddenly so out of favor?

At one level, it's not hard to see why Churchill became a target for BLM. His own words point to his being a serial offender against our modern-day standards of what constitutes racist statements. Here are a few examples:

In 1919, in relation to using chemical weapons—primarily against Kurds and Afghans—the following is often quoted:

I cannot understand this squeamishness about the use of gas.

Churchill continues by saying:

I am strongly in favor of using poisoned gas against uncivilized tribes.[2]

And on the four million deaths during the 1943 Bengal famine, he said:

I hate Indians. They are a beastly people with a beastly religion.[3]

And, finally, his words on how to deal with Egypt in 1951 were:

Tell them that if we have any more of their cheek, we will set the Jews on them and drive them into the gutter, from which they should never have emerged.[4]

DOI: 10.4324/9781003381150-16

Whilst Churchill's history of racist statements makes him a natural target for BLM protestors, at the same time these protests have also attracted a defensive counter movement, popularly characterized as being driven by right-wing reactionaries. To quote one of Churchill's defenders, former Prime Minister Boris Johnson:

> The statue of Winston Churchill in Parliament Square is a permanent reminder of his achievement in saving this country—and the whole of Europe—from a fascist and racist tyranny.[5]

So, what is really happening here? Are these simply developments at the ontic level or do they indicate some significant ontological phenomenon, a profound movement in the Soul's logical life?[6] Our ability to understand such a phenomenon is very much dependent on the perspective from which we are viewing it. Nietzsche has provided a framework of three perspectives that can help us in this regard.[7]

The Phenomenon from Three Perspectives

Firstly, in Nietzsche's framework, the BLM protestors represent the Last Man or, more correctly nowadays, the Last Human. They exemplify humankind in decline and naively and un-reflectively embrace the idea of change, or negation of the current position. On the other hand, Churchill's defenders represent Nietzsche's Good and the Just or preserver type, who have an unquestioning ideological commitment to the current position.

Together, these two seemingly opposing groups represent the substrate in which an actuose dialectical evolution is playing out. Both are held in the thrall of what appear to be diametrically opposed positions, but which in reality are contradictory aspects of a single evolving notion.

In seeing these two positions as part of an unfolding dialectic, we are adopting the perspective of Nietzsche's third type, the Noble [Hu]man, who is the embodiment of Zarathustra's high moral and spiritual ideals and has the energy and capacity for creation, destruction, adaptation, and direct participation in the process of dialectical thinking.[8]

Allowing the dialectical process[9] to internalize itself in us as Noble Humans should enable us to travel with the dialectic across time and to understand the interplay of teleology and contingency within its unfolding. For this to occur, we need to find the un-understood question that is the key to interiorizing the dialectic within us.[10]

But what could this question be? Maybe we should ask what Churchill's statue represents symbolically. With this question in mind, it's not hard to see that there are a lot of statues around from the colonial era, predominantly of white males who were in some way or another 'great' like Edward Colston, Cecil Rhodes, Christopher Columbus, and James Cook.

This was the era when Great White Males reigned supreme. They explained the universe, developed science and commerce, and built vast empires as the fonts of wisdom and bearers of *Logos*. For the Pharaohs, this would have been *Maat*, while the Persian kings were similarly imbued with *Xvarnah*, the divine light of glory.[11]

For a time, the perichoresis or mutual interpenetration of the divine and human nature, God and Man, Logos and Sarx, came together in a single point—Great White Males. This followed a transference process in which the Great White Male enlightenment killers of the Jesus myth subsumed his role and collectively inherited his mantle or divine shine.[12] At this time, a lot of new statues of Great White Males were being placed in public squares—but not so many of Jesus.

With the enlightenment and the associated conquests of knowledge and the new world, Great White Males ascended to the penultimate rank in the Great Chain of Being, to become the Neoplatonic divine intelligence, the Sun, and humanity's guiding light. As such, collectively they became the new translators of God's intelligence into everyday human knowledge and law. They were the angels who, supported by Christianity's vestiges and the military and financial power derived from their control of the industrial revolution, spread divine knowledge across the world (at least from their perspective at the time).

Great White Males became the apex of consciousness and embodied the power of the transcendent God, which, as Giegerich tells us, has taken the form of money.[13] The accumulation of money provided the rationale for transporting slaves, taking Inca gold, poisoning American natives, wholesaling opium to the Chinese, and many other brutal and racist atrocities.

But nowadays, the previously unchallenged prerogatives of these once mighty angels are under attack on many fronts—BLM, climate change, coronavirus response—and they appear to be in decline.

The kingly crown and its golden glow, representing the shine bestowed on God's vice-regents, certainly seems to have dulled as we look at the finest specimen of Great White Male leadership available at the time of writing, Donald Trump. In mid-2020, Trump was the most powerful Great White Male on earth. He held the thermonuclear button and the fate of all humankind in his hands—those same hands which, to quote his locker room talk, he also uses from time to time to "Grab 'em by the pussy,"[14] so he really represents a sad vestige of Great White Male colonialist exploitation.

We can see that, as of today, the Great White Male shine has more than dulled; it has morphed into a grotesquely degraded carnival of confusion, lies, and poisonous self-interest—the very embodiment of the cunning and devious modern soul as described by Giegerich.[15]

But why is this happening? Where have the ideals of great past leaders like Franklin Roosevelt and Robert Kennedy gone? In 2010, James Wolfensohn, former head of the World Bank, gave one clue to this in a lecture to Stanford graduate students:

> A huge power shift will occur in the next 40 years that will reduce the influence of the wealthiest countries. As population and GDP grow in countries such as China and India, they will assume a larger role in their relationship to the United States and Europe. The developed countries will drop from having 80% of the world's income to 35%. There will be a monumental shift of economic power.[16]

Along with economic power, we are witnessing a massive transfer of scientific, technological, and financial expertise and influence from the West, which has traditionally been led by Great White Males, towards a globally integrated economy and convergent, materialist world culture. This transfer is on the scale of the colonialist's rape of the new world, only this time it is in the opposite direction.

The divine glow or shine associated with the accumulation of money in modern times has a parallel to the ancient Persian concept of *Xvarnah*. While the Great White Male colonialist angelic viceroys controlled the global economy, they basked in the radiance of the *Xvarnah's* divine glow.

However today, along with their monopoly on economic power, Great White Males have lost their divine glow. We can turn to the Persian myth of Jamšid to see what happens when the *Xvarnah* is lost. According to the myth:

> Empowered by his *Xvarnah*, Jamšid rules the world. He went into the heaven of the sun every day and brought back the science of the stars. However, he loses his *Xvarnah* when he strays from the righteous path and tells lies. After two preliminary encounters, his *Xvarnah* is taken by a falcon, Vareyna, to Apạm Napāt, who hides it for safekeeping in the waters of Lake Vouroukaša, where it lies underwater in a dormant state.[17,18]

Given the deceitful behavior of the former POTUS and the influence of the devious Western Soul more generally, it is not hard to see where the lies come from. But what is the lie that caused the Great White Males to lose their *Xvarnah*?

It is simply this: They told us that the Enlightenment, Colonialism, and Western Modernity more generally was an optimal model for human society and that we should just ignore the impact of industrial farming, gene splicing, colony collapse, devolved oceans, denatured forests, global warming, uber jobs, lost traditions, pedophile priests, humanity as matter, life as information, the robot apocalypse, encroaching Taylorism, recreational oxycodone, Trumpism, and the Kardashians. We should just tuck our heads down, make more money for them, and everything will be just fine.

The lie was always there as the Ahrimanian shadow of Western civilization's rise under the tutelage of the Great White Males; however, we couldn't see it because we were blinded by the shine of their divine *Xvarnah*.

However, once their monopoly on economic power and with it their claim to divine intelligence was lost, the blinding shine of the Great White Males' *Xvarnah* dimmed and their fundamentally flawed, twisted, and perverted nature was revealed for all to see. Plainly, we now know that everything isn't just fine, as evidenced by today's many protest movements.

So, where is the *Xvarnah* now? Has it been distributed to the newly wealthy non–White-Male plutocrats who are now spread across the world? While these plutocrats have accumulated great wealth, this transfer to them has been horizontal, and it is a long stretch to see them as a new divine intelligence. More likely, they are just rich people working within an extension of the Great White Male's colonial and post-colonial envelope.

Given all the chaos in the world, maybe the *Xvarnah* is still dormant in Lake Vouroukaša. However, there are exceptions to this prevailing state of chaos. In fact, the world of cloud-based technology is highly organized. It is also growing rapidly, by absorbing many aspects of the human and natural worlds into a new technological envelope. And this is a development that is of much greater significance than the horizontal transfer of economic power.

Giegerich tells us that if there is an absolute or a 'god' today, it would have to be produced by human acts,[19] an idea that he associates with the soul's migration into technology.[20] In the context of this fundamental shift, we can see that the Great White Male emanation of divine intelligence is rapidly being replaced by a new technological version—a cybernetically blended hive mind that is operating in hybridized human/machine substrate. It comprises a massive web of nested feedback loops and has an underlying objective function (teleology), the nature of which is difficult for us to discern from our perspective—as humans embedded within it.

This is "Godgle" (the conflation of God and Google), who along with the technological archangels Amazon, Facebook, Alibaba, We Chat, and Apple is our new source of divine intelligence and humanity's ultimate guide. This is where we modern humans go for answers to our problems, where we go to pray through our screen shrines, and where statements like "Hey BMW"; "Alexa, could you please"; and "Siri, what is the meaning of life?" are the opening lines of our new prayer book.

The human contribution to this hive mind is coming from all races, genders, cultural backgrounds, religious denominations, and social strata, while the technology comes from sources like social media databases, search histories, mobility patterns, and purchase behavior and their associated platforms and AI algorithms.

Depotientiated white males are still part of this modern-day platonic cave but, like everyone else, they have to fight for their place, with their spawn now actively renouncing their inherited 'white privilege.' The once undisputed moral authority of Great White Males has moved to a multicultural, multi-gender, multi-class, multi-substrate, cybernetically driven collective in which it is represented by the perspective of Nietzsche's Good and the Just preservers who are under challenge from the forces of negation, represented by Nietzsche's

Last Humans. This is happening in a huge dialectical machine that, to quote Swiss poet C.F. Meyer,

> ... is the battleground of what was and what will be, a pair of interlocked and panting wrestlers.[21]

Giegerich tells us that it is through this battle of subjective souls representing past and future that "the objective soul is trying to wriggle out of its old skin and work out for itself an entirely new self-definition as its new 'skin'."[22]

According to Giegerich, there is no master plan and no antecedently known goal to this process. The new skin represents a "form change of truth"[23] that is simply what arises as a result of the battle and has no inherent sense of what is right or wrong. This was originally written by Giegerich to describe the inner turmoil of Martin Luther, but it seems to apply equally well to the wretched inner struggle of the Google and Facebook content algorithms as they assimilate Fake News, the industrial scale obfuscation of conspiracy theories like QAnon, the sacralization of traditional values by conflating them with religious beliefs, and the demonization of political movements like Antifa.

The Great Chain of Being has been reconfigured, with Godgle's cybernetically blended hive mind now firmly occupying the privileged place that was once held by Great White Males. Far from dormant, the *Xvarnah* has left Lake Vouroukaša and its divine radiance now illuminates the new technological viceroy and divine intelligence with brilliant intensity.

The reign of Great White Males as Jesus's replacement is over. They are now as dead as the sugar cube wrapper that Giegerich says is what remains of formal religion, mere decals of their once glorious past selves.[24] And now, following the Zoroastrian tradition, three days post-mortem, they are meeting their judgment at the *Chinvat* Bridge.[25]

The dead Great White Males are not being greeted by their *Daena* or guardian angel, a "heavenly maiden whose beauty surpasses all imagination,"[26] but rather they are being met by an atrocious figure made up of their own negativity, an abomination that embodies all the reprehensible things they have done throughout their reign.[27] If we build on an idea from Giegerich, the collective "I" of the Great White Males that is being judged at the "Bridge of the Requiter"[28] is an amalgam of slavery, genocide, deception, brutality, racism, and so on, and the many other facets of the Great White Male's fatal lie.

Continuing this analogy with the Zoroastrian tradition, the souls of the dead Great White Males are faced not only by this abomination but also by a demon called "the loosener of bones"[29] (manifest as the BLM protestors), and their bones of bronze are being loosened from their pedestals all across the world.

So, what should we do, as individuals living in these momentous times? Should we person the barricades and encase our proud colonialist history and fond memories of Churchill and the other Great White Males in a protective shroud or should we rip down the last vestiges of the evil beasts? It may be that the answer depends on which of Nietzsche's perspectives is dominant in us.

If our dominant perspective is that of "the Noble Human," we would probably prefer that the statues were moved to a museum, consistent with their role as carriers of colonialism's full meaning, incorporating its sublated shadow elements of slavery, genocide, and exploitation. Great White Males would then become "known" in the fullest sense of the word and, once known, would lose their symbolic power.[30] They would become mere historical curiosities, and we could all move on and come to grips with the cybernetic future that awaits us beyond the dawning of this new stage of consciousness.

One of the roles of the Noble Human is to stand above the hive mind and bring an understanding of the forces shaping our future into contemporary consciousness. This is of critical importance, as having a cybernetic hive mind that's driven by an opaque objective function as our divine guide points to a very uncertain future for humanity. Navigating this uncertain future will require the highest level of understanding available to Nietzsche's energetic type.

Maybe this higher-level understanding can help us work our way through the legacy of the Great White Male's lie and lead us on to a better world, at least until Godgle more fully manifests itself in empirical reality and there is no longer any need for human leadership at all.

Notes

1 The statue was covered in metal sheeting on 12th June, 2020 amid protests by members of the Black Lives Matter movement, following the killing of George Floyd in Minneapolis on May 25.
2 Tom Heyden, "The 10 Greatest Controversies of Winston Churchill's Career," *BBC News*. Last modified January 26, 2015, accessed August 3, 2020, https://www.bbc.com/news/magazine-29701767.
3 Crimes of Britain, *"The Crimes of Winston Churchill,"* Last modified January 26, 2018, accessed August 3, 2020, https://medium.com/@write_12958/the-crimes-of-winston-churchill-c5e3ecb229b3.
4 Heyden, *"The 10 greatest controversies of Winston Churchill's career."*
5 Bevan Shields, *"'Absurd and shameful': Winston Churchill statue sealed in steel ahead of protests,"* in *The Sydney Morning Herald*, last modified June 13, 2020, accessed August3,2020,https://www.smh.com.au/world/europe/absurd-and-shameful-winston-churchill-statue-sealed-in-steel-ahead-of-protests-20200613-p55282.html.
6 This concept is explored extensively in Wolfgang Giegerich, *The Soul's Logical Life: Towards a Rigorous Notion of Psychology* (Berlin: Peter Lang, 2008).
7 Hugo Reinert and Erik Reinhart, *"Creative Destruction in Economics: Nietzsche, Sombart, Schumpeter"* in Friedrich Nietzsche 1844–1900: Economy and Society, Ed: Ju"rgen Backhaus & Wolfgang Drechsler (Berlin: Springer, 2006) 55–85.
8 Giegerich, *The Soul's Logical Life*, 136.
9 Wolfgang Giegerich, David Miller, and Greg Mogenson, *Dialectics & Analytical Psychology: The El Capitan Canyon Seminar* (Louisiana: Spring Journal Inc., 2005), 5.
10 Robert Henderson and Janis Henderson, *Living with Jung:"Enterviews" with Jungian Analysts*, Vol. 3, (Wolfgang Giegerich) (New Orleans, LA: Spring Journal Books, 2010), 264.
11 Encyclopædia Iranica, *Farr(AH) ii. Iconography of Farr(AH)/Xᵛarənah*, Accessed, August 3, 2020, http://www.iranicaonline.org/articles/farr-ii-iconography.

12 The substantial reality of this act was similar to the one described in Wolfgang Giegerich, "Blood Brotherhood, Blood Revenge, and Devotion: Glimpses of the Archaic Psyche," in *Soul Violence (Collected English Papers, Vol. III)* (New Orleans, LA: Spring Journal, Inc., 2008), 290–291.

13 Wolfgang Giegerich, "Once More the Reality/Irreality Issue" in *Soul Violence*, 334.

14 Wikipedia, *Donald Trump Access Hollywood Tape*, accessed August 3, 2020, https://en.wikipedia.org/wiki/Donald_Trump_Access_Hollywood_tape.

15 Wolfgang Giegerich, *What Is Soul?* (New Orleans, LA: Spring Journal Inc., 2012), 204.

16 James Wolfensohn, *There Will be a Monumental Shift of Economic Power* (Video address to Stanford graduate students), Modified January 30, 2010, accessed, August 3, 2020, https://www.youtube.com/watch?v=6a0zhc1y_Ns

17 Encyclopædia Iranica, *Jamšid i. Myth of Jamšid*, accessed August 3, 2020, http://www.iranicaonline.org/articles/jamsid-i.

18 Encyclopædia Iranica, *Farr(AH) ii. Iconography of Farr(AH)/Xᵛarənah*, accessed August 3, 2020, http://www.iranicaonline.org/articles/farr-ii-iconography.

19 Giegerich, *What is Soul?* 293.

20 Wolfgang Giegerich, "The World Wide Web from the Point of View of the Soul's Logical Life," in *Technology and the Soul (Collected English Papers, Vol. II)* (New Orleans, LA: Spring Journal, Inc, 2007), 314.

21 Wolfgang Giegerich, *The Historical Emergence of the I* (London Ontario: Dusk Owl Books, 2020), 38.

22 Giegerich, *Historical Emergence*, 38.

23 Giegerich, *Historical Emergence*, 66.

24 Wolfgang Giegerich, "The End of Meaning and the Birth of Man: An essay about the State Reached in the History of Consciousness and an Analysis of C.G. Jung's Psychology Project," in *The Soul Always Thinks (Collected English Papers, Vol. IV)* (Woodstock, Conn.; Lancaster: Spring Journal, Inc., 2010), 225.

25 Henry Corbin, *Cyclical Time and Ismaili Gnosis* (London: Kegan Paul International, 1983), 18.

26 Corbin, *Cyclical Time*, 63.

27 Henry Corbin, *The Man of Light in Iranian Sufism* (New London: Omega Publications, 1971), 30.

28 Robert Zaehner, *The Dawn and Twilight of Zoroastrianism* (New York: Putnam's Sons, 1961), 56.

29 Zaehner, *Dawn and Twilight*, 302.

30 Wolfgang Giegerich, "The Ego-Psychological Fallacy" in *The Soul Always Thinks*, 352.

Chapter 16

The "Great Hunt"

Psychology and the Question of Truth

Marco Heleno Barreto

Introduction: Two Versions of "The Great Hunt"

"The human soul and its limits, the range of human inner experiences reached so far, the heights, depths, and distances of these experiences, the whole history of the soul *so far* and its yet unexhausted possibilities——that is the predestined ground for a born psychologist and lover of the 'great hunt'."[1] This passage from Nietzsche's *Beyond Good and Evil* could well have been quoted in *The Soul's Logical Life*, whose final chapter is dedicated to expose the notion of truth proper to psychology as the discipline of interiority by means of an interpretation of the myth of Actaion, the paradigmatic mythic hunter. Actaion's hunt is interpreted as the imaginal expression of psychology's search for (its own) truth. Psychology is thus symbolized as "the great hunt": the psychological I is the "hunter", and the encounter of truth——psychology's essential telos——is symbolized by Actaion's vision of naked Artemis.

Incidentally, a further semantic coincidence between Nietzsche's metaphorical presentation of psychology as the "Great Hunt" and the myth of Actaion interpreted in *The Soul's Logical Life* can be indicated: "*Supposing truth were a woman*——what then? Are there not grounds for the suspicion that all the philosophers, insofar as they were dogmatists, have been very inexpert about women? That the gruesome seriousness, the clumsy obtrusiveness with which they have usually approached truth so far have been awkward and very improper methods for winning a woman's heart?"[2] The associative bridge leading from the image-metaphor of "truth as a woman" to the naked goddess contemplated (*theorein*) by Actaion is all too obvious. Furthermore, and as is well known, Nietzsche's psychology receives the status of first philosophy—— or "the queen of sciences"[3]——in his thought, replacing metaphysics after the radical genealogical deconstruction to which metaphysical thinking is submitted by the most influential herald of the death of God. Psychology then would be the new method for winning that woman's heart, the new path to "the most fundamental problems."[4] At first glance, it seems thus that the notion of psychology presented in *Beyond Good and Evil* and in *The Soul's Logical Life*, based on a coincident image-metaphor, would be fairly the same. But evidently things are not so simple.

DOI: 10.4324/9781003381150-17

The *question of truth* is of paramount importance to the notion of psychology as the discipline of interiority. It is also what is at stake in Nietzsche's playful image of truth as a woman and psychology as the "Great Hunt." However, in *The Soul's Logical Life* Nietzsche is seen as "one of the greatest destroyers of the notion of truth", and by virtue of this standpoint of his he "failed to see and to say that precisely what he demanded hinges on our full commitment to truth", for "this is where the real danger and the true 'chaos' (the wild) are."[5] Therefore, despite all the semantic coincidences between Nietzsche's image of psychology as the "Great Hunt", with its dangers, Truth as a woman, and the structure of the myth of Actaion interpreted in *The Soul's Logical Life* as the image for human psychology, the standpoints concerning the question of truth in Nietzsche and in psychology as the discipline of interiority are not only different: they are presented as opposite, if not incompatible. Nonetheless, instead of simply taking this opposition and/or incompatibility for granted, without further reflection, it could be interesting to briefly explore Nietzsche's stance concerning truth, and to deepen our understanding of our notion of truth with Nietzsche's stance in mind, for this could shed light on and help us to better understand our psychology's innermost essence as the "discipline of truth." Differences, oppositions, and incompatibilities are precious to understanding one's own identity. And in the process of thinking contrasting standpoints, more than one common or tangential feature can surprise us.[6]

Now, Nietzsche is an extremely elusive thinker. It is difficult, if not impossible, to pin him to a particular position concerning a given topic. His style of thinking forces us inevitably to interpretations, perspectives, and thus the conflict of interpretations is remarkable in the case of Nietzsche scholars. This is valid even with regard to the question of truth. His standpoint changes according to the moment of evolution of his thought, and also to the particular strategy (or perspective) adopted at different places of a same moment. On the other hand, agreeing that "truth is inescapable",[7] even Nietzsche, known as one of the great destroyers of the notion of truth, cannot have been entirely successful in the attempt of such destruction. As a matter of fact, and as becomes clear in his playful and ironic image of truth as a woman, Nietzsche does not simply refuse truth: he gives it another sense, and arguably he substitutes *his* psychological approach to truth for the classical metaphysical form of addressing it. Something similar is also claimed by psychology as the discipline of interiority, inasmuch as it is defined as sublated metaphysics, providing "an asylum for a real presence of the notion of truth", in an age that "does not *want* truth", in which truth is "that which is abhorred most."[8] So, in order to differentiate both standpoints, according to the opposition pointed out in *The Soul's Logical Life*, we must ask: which notion of truth, indispensable to psychology as the discipline of interiority, is aimed at and criticized by Nietzsche's destructive intent? What are its essential aspects?

Here we have a fairly consistent position in Nietzsche's thought: he attacks truth as a "superior value", defined by opposition to error. This notion of truth supposes the *ontological* distinction essence-appearance, still accepted by Nietzsche at the time of *The Birth of Tragedy*, but subsequently abandoned in his mature thought. This distinction is correlative to another one, namely the distinction intelligible-sensible, also disparaged by Nietzsche, intrinsically related to the ontological distinction, according to the metaphysical postulate: the real is radically intelligible. To Nietzsche, all reality is appearance: "What is 'appearance' for me now? Certainly not the opposite of some essence: what could I say about any essence except to name the attributes of its appearance! Certainly not a dead mask that one could place on an unknown x or remove from it! Appearance is for me that which lives and is effective."[9] Appearances are thus the expression of life as will-to-power.

It follows from the Nietzschean absolutization of appearance that there are no grounds either for a strict opposition between truth and error, due to the latter's intrinsic connection to the specific ontological distinction between essence and appearance:

It is no more than a moral prejudice that truth is worth more than mere appearance; it is even the worst proved assumption there is in the world. (...) Indeed, what forces us at all to suppose that there is an essential opposition of 'true' and 'false'? Is it not sufficient to assume degrees of apparentness and, as it were, lighter and darker shadows and shades of appearance—— different 'values', to use the language of painters? Why couldn't the world *that concerns us*——be a fiction?[10]

The world as fiction is created by the will-to-power, it is its expression, and in such a fictive world the traditional question of truth simply makes no sense.

At first glance, it could seem that a somewhat analogous situation happens when we consider the standpoint of psychology as the discipline of interiority, because the notion of Truth disclosed through the interpretation of the myth of Actaion is not "the simple, undialectical opposite of mere appearances, lies or fictions", inasmuch as from the soul perspective "appearances, fictions, errors and lies can be one form in which truth manifests itself. It is absolute Truth (truth absolved from the difference between truth and fiction)."[11] However, despite its explicit departing from any ontological concerns, the psychological approach of interiority defines itself in *The Soul's Logical Life* with reference to the Kantian problematic of appearance versus thing-in-itself, a problematic which has ontological as well as epistemological aspects. The distinction between appearance versus thing-in-itself is kept, receiving a dialectical interpretation in psychology as the discipline of interiority. Therefore, the form of perspectivism associated with Nietzsche's *genealogical* deconstruction of the notion of truth (and of its classical ontological background) seems to be at odds with the psychological form of knowing presented in *The Soul's Logical Life*, since the latter is based on the *logical* distinction essence-appearance, intelligible-sensible. Nietzsche simply rejects such distinctions, and the word "absolute" qualifying "Truth", so recurrent in our psychological literature, would certainly awaken his most ironic criticism and the suspicion of a relapse into the despised dogmatic metaphysical form of thinking.

Most of all, the Hegelian notion of absolute negativity, essential to psychology's concept of absolute Truth, is completely absent from Nietzsche's frame of mind. The heirs of his *Denkform* in contemporary philosophy are the postmodern thinkers (of which Jacques Derrida is explicitly addressed in *The Soul's Logical Life*). They express the spirit of the age: "Postmodern philosophy also rejects metaphysics and the notions of truth, infinity, eternity, the absolute",[12] without accepting the logical level of absolute negativity reached by Hegel, and thus without being able to work with a notion of truth as logical negativity. It is likely that the dialectical method adopted in psychology as the discipline of interiority, only capable of disclosing the dimension of truth as absolute negativity, would be considered by Nietzsche as a form of that "clumsy obtrusiveness" with which "philosophers"——but not the Nietzschean type of "psychologist"—— approach truth. It would be seen as the epitome of the allegedly nihilistic perspective of "metaphysicians."

Therefore, the "prey" of the "Great Hunt" is conceived differently in Nietzsche and in psychology as the discipline of truth. There is not a consensual understanding of that "woman" in both stances. And this means that the very "hunt" is also differently conceived. The fundamental difference, as I suggested implicitly, might be in part due to the presuppositions backing up different views and methodologies. Nietzsche adopts a genealogical standpoint, whereas psychology as the discipline of interiority adopts a dialectical one. And dialectics is definitively absent from Nietzsche's approach to the question of truth. It belongs to the palette of rational tools used by the metaphysicians that Nietzsche ironically disparages in the quoted passage of *Beyond Good and Evil* as having been "very inexpert about women", meaning that they have approached truth with "very improper methods." Besides that, the logical distinction between appearance and thing-in-itself, correlative of the difference "fenced-in all-too-human realm" and "wilderness" in *The Soul's Logical Life*, is simply abandoned by Nietzsche. But this distinction is what allows the proposition of the fundamental notion of psychology as the discipline of interiority, namely the notion of the *psychological difference*.

True Knowing in Psychology and the Kantian Interdiction

The "gruesome *seriousness*" of the philosopher's approach to truth as seen by Nietzsche contrasts with his proposition of a *gay* science. On the other hand, if we invert the vantage point and take *seriously* Nietzsche's comment about the dangers of the "Great Hunt", if these dangers are logically *real*, and not simply a tongue-in-cheek *façon de parler*, then a simple light and joyful attitude would not be adequate for the hunter who exposes himself to the wilderness in which truth shall be encountered. This attitude is rather reminiscent of the character of the *Last Man*, who discovered happiness,[13] but does not seem to match the stance of the "lover of the 'great hunt'." Arguably, Nietzsche's *serious* commitment to his vision about the "Great Hunt" and its real dangers is proved by his tragic fate. Indeed, the "Great Hunt" (i.e., psychology) requires "our full commitment to truth." Thus, we *must* take seriously the question of truth. However, this seriousness, along with the dialectical method, seems to put us side by side with the metaphysical philosopher ironically criticized by Nietzsche.

And in fact, there are some very real underpinnings for this closeness. Not only does psychology as the discipline of interiority "provide an asylum for a real presence of the notion of truth":[14] this notion itself comes from the metaphysical form of thinking, and the whole "question of truth" belongs to metaphysics and is shared by our form of psychology. Now, what is fundamentally at stake in the question of truth is the claim for *true knowing*, which is the target of Nietzsche's destructive attack on the notion of truth. Besides that, true knowing is considered impossible or logically obsolete after Kant's "epistemological barrier" had prohibited any knowledge of noumenal "essences", restricting legitimate knowledge to phenomenal reality. Therefore, we must examine the relation of our psychology's notion of truth to the Kantian problematic of true knowing, leaving momentarily Nietzsche aside.

In *The Soul's Logical Life*, apparently, there is no problem with acknowledging the legitimacy of "true knowing" today. The whole question of truth revolves around the possibility of true knowing, which is unmistakably of a metaphysical nature. Evidently, one must admit that the anti- or post-metaphysical *Zeitgeist* in modernity abhors the notion of truth and true knowing. Nonetheless, the case for the *possibility* of beholding the absolute truth in our modern times is not definitively closed: "*How* this could in actuality be accomplished under the conditions of this 'metaphysically' anorectic age is an open question."[15] In *The Soul's Logical Life* we are admonished not to "simply accommodate the *Zeitgeist*",[16] with its process of abandonment of all meaning and truth. We should rather "consciously, soulfully accompany this process and rise to the level of the *Notion* of it", remembering that "the necessities of psychology/psychotherapy require a notion of Truth, of center, of meaning, of the subject (as the unity and difference of the person and the soul), of the necessity of our *inire* (initiation)———and thus a certain amount of courage."[17] In an age that despises truth, swimming against the tide and disclosing the truth of the untruth indeed requires courage.

If this is right, then psychological knowing should be conceived as one form of true knowing. And effectively, according to the interpretation offered in *The Soul's Logical Life*, in the myth of Actaion the soul "aims for knowledge, cognition, consciousness. The soul wants to *truly know* itself."[18] Psychology is the *medium* or *form* of such knowledge. Thus, psychological knowledge is a specific form of *true knowing*: soul truly knowing itself as Truth. The notion as absolute negativity is the *truth* that is reached in and as *true* knowing. Actaion is the image of the *soul as human psychology*, as the *empirical* desire to know the truth about itself and as the theory that it has been able to develop about itself so far in real life. (…) Inasmuch as soul is self-relation, it is in itself the unity of itself and of the (psychological) *theoria* about itself. The soul is not just the object of psychological investigation! It is not just its own one half. It is both at once: that which knows (or wants to know) and that which is to be known.[19]

When we consider that psychological knowledge is the dialectical unity of that which knows and that which is to be known, its nature as a form of true knowing must be even more explicitly admitted: "the soul encounters itself, as the sought for Other. *It as hunter* encounters and comprehends *itself as the naked truth* (Artemis in her virginity), as the unveiled image of Saïs, as absolute truth, as the Kantian 'thing-in-itself' (in contradistinction to 'appearance')."[20] But this true knowledge is absolutely forbidden within the Kantian level of reflection: "for Kant, the thing-in-itself cannot be known. He restricted the concept of knowing or cognition to the world *as appearance* only."[21] According to the *Critique of Pure Reason*, it is not possible to know the "soul that always thinks" (in Kant's language: the "I think" which is in every thought or concept) *as a thing-in-itself*. There is no *true knowing* of soul in itself by itself, as a noumenon. In any thinking activity whatsoever, we experience ourselves only as subjects "appearing" to ourselves (and empirical psychology stays at the level of this appearance or phenomenon).

To Kant, the "I" who thinks (the subject-matter of rational psychology, or "the soul" in psychology as the discipline of interiority) cannot be known *in itself*, only as an empirical object of inner intuition, as an appearance, a phenomenon, not as a noumenon. Psychology cannot be a *true knowledge* of soul by soul itself. But in *The Soul's Logical Life*, in the light of the interpretation of the myth of Actaion offered in Chapter 6, psychology is presented as not only soul's desire to *truly know* itself, but as the fulfillment of this desire: "The Notion is not only intention, desire, striving for cognition, it is also the *fulfillment* of this intention: *actual* cognition or the event of Truth."[22] This actual cognition is the event of "entering the wild", of knowing soul as the thing-in-itself. As such, it is true knowing.

Let us stress once more this extremely important point: soul as absolute truth has the logical status of the Kantian "thing-in-itself." It is the "wilderness" or "virginal nature", forbidden to knowledge through the Kantian "epistemological barrier." To move into this dimension means investigating (or exposing oneself to) the Kantian thing-in-itself,[23] which cannot be known according to the *Critique of Pure Reason*. Kant's level of reflection brings with it "the consequence that the concept of knowing no longer means *true knowing, or knowing the truth*."[24] Therefore, the Kantian concept of knowing cannot be psychology's notion of the Notion.[25] Conversely, psychology's notion of the Notion requires a concept of knowing that admits the possibility of true knowing. This is the fate that psychology as the discipline of *truth*, as presented in the last chapter of *The Soul's Logical Life*, shares with metaphysics: against the Kantian interdiction, both claim the legitimacy of true knowing with regards to the question of truth. "Psychology trespasses into the pristine wilderness the moment it accepts without reserve *the question of truth*", thus violating "the unwritten law of modernity that prohibits the question of truth under the guise of all sorts of methodological cautions and warnings against human *hybris*", and this means "nothing less than to trespass into 'infinity', into 'eternity', into the sphere of the absolute."[26] Again: this means very simply *true knowing*.

This is a very polemic point. But I cannot see how to avoid it without simply abandoning the bulk of what has been established in the last chapter of *The Soul's Logical Life*, this veritable *magna carta* for psychology as the discipline of interiority. If you consider true knowing impossible, then you forcefully admit that the question of truth is over, once and for all. True knowing means knowing the Truth as Actaion beholding the naked Artemis. Without true knowing, psychology as the discipline of interiority loses its scandalous identity as the "discipline of truth" and becomes nothing but a dialectical brand of modern psychology, which "is the study of ideas, feelings, experiences, and images, expressly apart from the question of whether they are true or not."[27] In this case, all the talk about "entering the wild" (as trespassing into the noumenal thing-in-itself), "disclosing the truth of the real" (as soul *truly knowing* itself), becomes nothing but sheer empty jargon.

A Problematic Shift: The Abandonment of True Knowing in Psychology

The question of truth, interpreted in the light of the dispute involving true knowing, is also what differentiates the rigorous notion of psychology aimed at in *The Soul's Logical Life* and Jung's "betrayal of his own truth", a betrayal perpetrated by the uncritical adoption of Kant's "epistemological barrier." As is well known, Jung was wholly committed to this post-metaphysical standpoint: "It is a thoroughly outmoded standpoint, and has been so ever since the time of Immanuel Kant, to think that it lies within the power of man to assert a metaphysical truth. (...) My apparent skepticism is only a recognition of the epistemological barrier."[28] Jung dismissed the question of truth, which to him "is unanswerable anyway and for epistemological reasons has long since become obsolete. Human knowledge has to be content with constructing models which are 'probable'——it would be thoughtless presumption to demand more."[29]

Now, an epistemological standpoint such as the one Jung adopts is presented in *The Soul's Logical Life* as the perfect example of a "fenced-in" form of consciousness, a consciousness that does not venture "into the wild", since "wilderness" is the forbidden Kantian "thing-in-itself." And in the article *Jung's Betrayal of his own Truth* (not accidentally first published in the same year as *The Soul's Logical Life*, 1998), this Kantian-like (anti-metaphysical) empiricism is revealed exactly as the source of Jung's betrayal of the truth that he offered us in his psychology. The effect of this Kantian bias is considered devastating to psychology.[30]

Therefore, apparently psychology as the discipline of truth, in contradistinction to Jung's and Hillman's standpoints in this regard, should conceive itself as the true knowing of soul by itself. And this is clearly claimed in *The Soul's Logical Life*. The interpretation of the myth of Actaion leaves no doubt about that. This claim is conceptually explicit and is explicitly spelled in written form in the passages that I have quoted here and in many others.

However, in *What Is Soul?* psychology is presented explicitly as having given up *any* claim to true knowing, this being one of its main differences from Hegelian philosophy: despite

> its fundamental structural closeness to the uroboric stance of Hegel's philosophy, psychology can also not be a continuation of the absolutely inwardized status that metaphysics had reached in the thinking of this philosopher. Hegel's thought was still a form of metaphysics. It came with the claim of being or achieving *true knowing*. (…) This is no longer possible for modern psychology. Psychology is no more than one of the possible methodological approaches to what happens and has given up any claim to being or striving for true knowing.[31]

Consequently, reading carefully both texts we realize that we are thrown into a difficult theoretical dilemma: in *The Soul's Logical Life* there are explicit statements signaling psychology's claim for true knowing, and this claim distinguishes the logical level to which the sought-for rigorous notion of psychology belongs; whereas in *What Is Soul?* this claim is denied no less explicitly. This blatant contradiction forces us to deepen our reflection and try to reach a better understanding of the problematic relation of psychology as the discipline of interiority with the question of truth.

On the one hand, one can interpret "true knowing" as constituted by ontological assertions, that is, as fundamentally belonging to ontology. "Ontology" here is defined in the particular sense of the study of *entities*, always understood as *existing positivities*.[32] Since "soul" is no such entity, psychology is not a particular form of ontology. In this sense, inasmuch as psychology does not talk about how things really are *ontologically*, by definition it would not claim ontological "true knowing." A psychological interpretation would have no ontological incidence.

On the other hand, this first solution of our problem is not completely satisfactory. True: psychology as the discipline of interiority deals with soul as absolute negativity, not with ontological positivities, even though *absolute* negativity is negativity "*absolved* from the opposition between positivity and negativity."[33] But absolute negativity is a *metaphysical* notion received from

Hegel's thought, and it is metaphysical because it is indissociable from the claim for true knowing——which is both *true* knowing and true *knowing*. Arguably, absolute negativity is (somewhat clumsily) represented in Jung's notion of the archetype in itself, pointing to its "fundamental and irrevocable unknowness."[34] If we stay at the level of "the positive (literal) concept of truth",[35] then the unknowability of the negativity represented (or interpreted) in the notion of archetypes in themselves is unsurmountable——here is the Kantian epistemological barrier. But if we advance to the "non-positive, negative notion of truth",[36] truth as absolute negativity, "*negatively* a form of being-in-the-world",[37] then we reach *soul* as *truly knowable*, and psychology as the discipline of interiority becomes a form of *true knowing*. This true knowing of soul is not reduced to a simple exchange of our metaphors, as it happens in Jung's naïvely critical stance.[38] True knowing, in contradistinction to the exchange of metaphors, is what renders meaningful the use of "truth" in the discourse of psychology as the discipline of interiority.

Now, if you dissociate psychology from true knowing, by giving up any claim for the latter, what is left of absolute negativity as the level in which the truth of the real is disclosed? It becomes nothing but a perspective, a methodological approach, without any real claim for truth *in the sense of the question of truth*. Therefore, without being a specific form of true knowing, psychology inevitably would have to drop out its essentially *real* and *serious* commitment to the question of truth. For in the moment that it is asserted that modern psychology has given up *any* claim to true knowing, all that previously (in *The Soul's Logical Life*) had been said about "soul truly knowing itself", "entering the wild", and so on, is emptied out of any reasonable meaning. That assertion decides the question of truth in favor of the Kantian stance, contrarily to the standpoint advocated in *The Soul's Logical Life*. "What Kant did was to state that the object, the transcendent, the thing-in-itself is absolutely inaccessible so that you have to once and for all confine yourself to the empirical world, to the finite, to what Kant termed the appearance."[39] For Kant, "we have to give up any hope of ever being able to achieve *true knowing*, part of which would of course also be (...) *true knowledge* of the soul."[40] In other words: giving up *any* claim to being or striving for true knowing amounts to giving up psychology as the discipline of interiority, as the discipline of truth, in the strongest sense presented in *The Soul's Logical Life*, and reinserting it in the Kantian level of reflection, responsible for the "unwritten law of modernity." But this is exactly what had been interpreted as the betrayal of psychology's own truth in Jung....

If we accept this abdication of true knowing on the part of psychology, talking about soul *truths* becomes just a rhetorical expedient, for no *true knowledge* of soul by itself is *really* intended. "Truth" now is presented as being no more than "a methodological guiding principle and aim", whose "validity remains enclosed within itself", and so psychology "is no more than one of the possible methodological approaches to what happens."[41] The Dionysian nature of truth as *logic* is lost, inasmuch as the Dionysian "is the unity of a way of seeing (style of consciousness, subjective, in our mind) *and the logical constitution intrinsic to the real world.*"[42] This Dionysian unity is what is refused in the Kantian notion of truth, in Kant's prohibition of true knowledge. This unity *is* true knowing, and it is argumentatively established in Hegel's thought. Abdication of true knowing means severing that unity, with two devastating interrelated consequences for psychology as the discipline of interiority: 1) "wilderness", which means the logical constitution intrinsic to the real world, cannot be entered anymore, because it cannot be *truly known*: without true knowledge, "wilderness" simply disappears; 2) psychology is reduced to one of its halves, a style of consciousness, *subjective, in our mind*, and it cannot "leave the fenced-in realm of the human-all-too-human",[43] because the only form of leaving this Kantian-built *epistemological* prohibition is in "venturing into the wild", which means claiming *true knowledge* for psychology. Hence, the sole difference between psychology as the discipline of interiority, on the one side, and analytical and imaginal psychology, on the other, would be methodological, not logical. *Logically*, with regards to the *notion* of psychology in its relation to the question of truth, all three would share the same level, the same Kantian premises which impose to modern psychology the giving up of any claim for being or striving for true knowing.

Back to Nietzsche

Our theoretical dilemma seems to be a dead-end situation. But the abdication of true knowledge could have another way of being thought without abandoning the Dionysian dimension of psychology: let us resume now the contrasting dialogue with Nietzsche.[44] Differently from the abstract Kantian notion of truth, in psychology as the discipline of interiority truth is "*negatively* a form of being-in-the-world, a state of existence",[45] so that "the psychological standpoint or perspective is itself that *lapis* that it tries to reach", and "not merely the perspective or method (tool) through which the psychological work is done."[46] The reference to "psychological standpoint or perspective" invites us to briefly examine the Nietzschean notion of *perspective*.

A perspective in Nietzsche's thought is not subjectivistic, or personalistic, but is associated to will-to-power, which arguably expresses what "life" means in Nietzsche. And life and its perspectives comprise "the human soul and its limits, the range of human inner experiences reached so far, the heights, depths, and distances of these experiences, the whole history of the soul *so far* and its yet unexhausted possibilities."[47] If true knowing is given up in psychology as the discipline of interiority, then "soul truth" can't help being envisaged as merely one perspective among others: "Psychology is no more than one of the possible methodological approaches to what happens."[48] "The psychological I is a methodological standpoint, a style of thinking and apperceiving, of interpreting and appreciating"[49]——again, this is compatible with a perspective, in Nietzsche's sense, since the Nietzschean perspective is also a form of being-in-the-world, a state of existence. "Psychology or the psychological I is its own purpose, it has its purpose within itself."[50] The psychological standpoint cannot be simply "switched on": it has to be produced each time anew[51]——just like a Nietzschean perspective, which is instituted by the creative will-to-power.

When one dismisses *any* claim for true knowing *in psychology*, adding that psychology's truth is valid only within its (psychology's) own boundaries (thus tightly closing the psychological bubble), then *logically* our interpretive psychological thinking is indistinguishable from mere *Schwärmerei*: even if only inadvertently, if we give up true knowing of soul by itself we confess that psychology-making through a dialectical methodology is just a new way of indulging in our particular dialectical kind of *Dreams of a Spirit-Seer*, a kind of dreams that can be *Illustrated by the Dreams of Metaphysics* (since soul statements have a speculative nature, and thus "must be read as 'speculative sentences' in Hegel's sense, the sentence subject and the predicate reflecting each other perfectly"[52]). But this apparently negative judgment, made from the critical Kantian stance, can take an altogether different aspect, if we leave Kant aside and adopt Nietzsche's standpoint about the world that concerns us being a *fiction* and all knowledge in this world being a *perspective*, an interpretation, and thus also a (creative) fiction. From this angle, psychology as the discipline of interiority could be interpreted as a kind of metaphysically inspired fiction (destitute of any pretention to true knowledge), based on a dialectical procedure which, though not admitted within Nietzsche's conception of psychology as the "Great Hunt", is nonetheless valid within its own boundaries, as any perspective is, once the opposition truth-error is abolished. The abdication of true knowing is all that is required to align psychology with the destruction (or rejection) of the notion of truth perpetrated by Nietzsche. We must not forget that the Nietzschean notion of perspective is the conceptual place in which this destruction is performed.

But from this conceptual standpoint, the question of truth, proclaimed in *The Soul's Logical Life* as being the specific and unnegotiable commitment of psychology as the discipline of interiority, simply makes no sense. In Nietzsche's perspectivism, the question of truth is abandoned, left aside. There is no sense in asking for the truth of soul's ideas and images (and perspectives!) from this perspectivistic skeptic standpoint: they are only that——ideas, thoughts, perspectives, imaginings, and no answer to the question of their truth is needed, for the question of truth is destroyed and replaced by perspectivism.

There is a further way to use Nietzsche's overall standpoint concerning perspectives, understood as the expressions of life as will-to-power, in order to interpret one essential aspect of the conception of psychological knowledge in *The Soul's Logical Life*, provided we abandon the notion of true knowing (or simply put into brackets the explicit allusions to it), following the stance presented in *What Is Soul?*. We have stressed that soul *as* truth is not the content of a proposition, but *negatively* a form of being-in-the-world, a state of existence. And truth is conceived as "the world of life as it really happens to be, *plus* the determined presence of man, his committed entrance into, and logical self-exposure to, life."[53] The *logical* existential dimension of Truth/soul as logical life, by means of which the split between theory and practice is abolished, is clearly included in the notion of absolute Truth (but, as becomes clear once more in the next quotation, expressly thought of as true knowing, which should be disregarded from a Nietzschean interpretive standpoint): "True knowing *immediately* and inevitably makes a difference. It is *immediately* compelling, puts under an obligation or fate. You have gained true knowledge only if it actually did make a difference and if it simply ignored, even abolished, the split between theory and practice. This is what is expressed by Actaion's becoming a stag. 'Becoming' a stag is what knowing Artemis ipso facto entails."[54] The issues at stake here "are not so much *theoretical* ones, but primarily concern the old question of ethics: *pōs biōteúein?* how to live?"[55] Psychology thus seen is not a body of doctrines, an ideology or a *Weltanschauung*, but a way of living, a state of existence indeed. All this is entirely in tune with the Nietzschean standpoint——except the explicit claim for "true knowledge."

The logically existential or Dionysian dimension of true knowledge in psychology as the discipline of interiority makes it transcend the limits of what an epistemological approach can say about it:

> Because the subject must become, *be*, Truth, the questions raised by theories of knowledge have foregone true knowledge and knowledge of the Truth to begin with. They all hope to get at truth without having to include the ideas of the subject's trespass and relentless self-exposure to the point of dismemberment as indispensable prerequisites of Truth. Science and learning are no ways to truth. Truth is not to be had except for the price of our *inire* (initiation) into it and our relentless assimilation to it.[56]

Again, a Nietzschean standpoint would drop out the reference to true knowledge and keep all the rest within the scope of the "Great Hunt." But even in this case the fundamental difference persists: whereas in psychology as the discipline of interiority all this process is *logical* (absolutely negative), in Nietzsche it is referred to the positivity of instincts, drives, and so on.

Nietzsche's appearance is neither a Kantian phenomenon, nor a positivistic fact: to Nietzsche, all that exists are interpretations. And interpretations are determined by perspectives. Truth is thus dissolved in the endless activity of interpreting. There is no reality to be interpreted or to be known, outside the very interpretation: the perspective creates reality.[57] Now, if once more we invert the vantage point and read Nietzsche through the lenses of psychology as the discipline of interiority, we could see in his notion of will-to-power a positivized form of attempting to grasp the logic of the real. We could submit that Nietzsche tries his best to formulate what we mean by soul as absolute negativity, but he fails because of his adhesion to the positivity of absolutized appearances. Thus his succumbing to madness could arguably be interpreted as his failure in reaching the level of soul, which led to his being concretely swallowed by a literally acted out Dionysian psychic dismemberment while performing the "Great Hunt"——a psychic catastrophe as the tragic price to be paid for not being able to perform the psychological difference and reach the level of absolute negativity.

There is another passage in *The Soul's Logical Life* that apparently seems to have a distinctive Nietzschean flavor: "the underlying psychological needs that were preserved and formulated in the metaphysical tradition, even if with inappropriate means, reach far back to before the age of metaphysics, before philosophy as such: to the age of the early hunters, the age of shamanism and ritualistic cultures——as reflected in the Actaion myth."[58] A Nietzschean genealogy of "true knowing" would say exactly this, but would interpret "psychological needs" in terms of instincts or drives, and not as logical negativity.

A further consequence of giving up the claim to being or striving for true knowing is that psychology would have to be thought of as nothing but a logical pastime, because it would play metaphysics in its methodological stance without claiming updated epistemological validity to this stance (now dissociated from its original intrinsic relation to true knowing). And astonishingly but coherently that is precisely the logical status attributed to psychology in *What Is Soul?*[59] Therefore, we are forced to suspect that something changed between 1998 (the year of publication of *The Soul's Logical Life*) and 2012 (when *What Is Soul?* was published). It seems that Jung's "deep-seated fear of appearing as a 'metaphysician'",[60] which led him to rule out the question of truth for the sake of Kant's "epistemological barrier", almost invisibly instilled itself into the veins of our psychology, leading to the giving up of psychological true knowing, the very heart of psychology as the discipline of interiority as boldly presented in *The Soul's Logical Life*.

By accepting the logical status of a pastime, psychology becomes an activity belonging to the form of living that Nietzsche described in the character of the Last Man. In fact, all the real dangers of life, in all of its events, are avoided by the Last Man: "One still worketh, for work is a pastime. But one is careful lest the pastime should hurt one."[61] A pastime provides that harmless and shallow form of happiness discovered by the Last Man. And Nietzsche's lover of the "Great Hunt" cannot be in the condition of the Last Man, for in this case there would be no *true* hunt, no *real* self-exposure to the wilderness of soul, but merely a simulation, a safely fenced-in human-all-too-human pastime. A Disneyland type of hunt.

We can now close the contrasting dialogue of psychology as the discipline of interiority with Nietzsche's thought, triggered by the common allusion to psychology by means of the image-metaphor of the hunt. We can say that in the two notions of psychology, the prime matter is the same; the procedures and their underlying presuppositions are different; the results may display superficial similarities but have deep structural differences (positivity in Nietzsche, absolute negativity in psychology as the discipline of interiority). The distance tends to be attenuated if one subscribes to the abdication of true knowledge in psychology as the discipline of interiority. But the disastrous[62] logical status of pastime attributed to psychology is a further feature of absolute incompatibility between the two forms of the "Great Hunt."

Conclusion

I will now summarize what I have presented here with some concluding remarks:

1   After Kant's intellectual achievement, one could not simply go back to previous positions that he had duly criticized. One should go *beyond* Kant, but taking his thought into consideration, pushing off from Kant. This was the accomplishment of German Idealism, and particularly of Hegel. In what concerns us here, the interdiction of knowability of the logical negativity definitional of the thing-in-itself was overcome, *not through a restitution of the positive/literal concept of truth, but through the step forward to the notion of truth as absolute negativity.* And *absolute* negativity is truth "*absolved* from the opposition between positivity and negativity."[63] This is the notion of truth proper to psychology as the discipline of interiority, a "non-positive, negative notion of truth."[64] *This* is the psychological real, the psychological thing-in-itself, soul as *logical* life, and as logical *life.*[65] And *this* is the "object" of the specific form of psychological *true knowing*: soul as absolute negativity *is* truly knowable. Without *this* claim, talking of psychology *as the discipline of truth* becomes nothing but a pompous and ridiculous way of referring to a discipline that has self-destructively abdicated absolutely of its notion as true knowledge of soul, becoming skeptic, and surreptitiously abandoning the idea of truth. "But, of course, the moment the idea of truth is dispelled from psychology, the word knowing loses its meaning."[66] Therefore, "we cannot afford the luxury of giving in to the fear of 'metaphysics', of truth, the absolute, and identity."[67]

2   The post-metaphysical framework applied to psychology as the discipline of interiority through the epistemological standpoint included in *What Is Soul?* is arguably a form of "accommodating the *Zeitgeist*", instead of seeing it through, instead of interiorizing it into itself and disclosing its Truth, instead of uncompromisingly standing by the bold statement: "The modern blindness to and dissociation from soul is the prevailing state of affairs, *but it is wrong.*"[68] The unquestioned adoption of this framework is perhaps a modern form of *participation mystique* that can lead to a cozy form of *sacrificium intellectus*. This framework is the position representative of the *Zeitgeist* in modernity: "our consciousness is under the spell of the *metaphysic of science and technology*";[69] "the positivistic logic underlying the modern sciences and technology (...) is the logic that was cemented by Kant's philosophy."[70] And regrettably, assuming this post-metaphysical standpoint leads to the inexorable betrayal of psychology's own truth and its imprisonment within a neuroticizing straitjacket.

3 When the psychological approach is given the logical status of a pastime, we can say that it is conceived as "a kind of peeping *into* the realm of 'pre-existence', but only *from* the safe side of ego country",[71] to which any pastime belongs. Consequently, *in truth* (or *logically*) one does not leave the fenced-in realm of domesticated world, the ego position. What is the consequence for psychology of this retreating into the logical status of a mere pastime?

Psychology then joins the mainstream of our civilization heading for Cyberspace and the world of multimedia. (...) If we are not willing to pay the full price that it demands from us by answering for the *truth* of our imaginings, thereby raising them to the level of knowledge and the Notion, reality will with might demand a much higher price from us. It will teach us (and is already teaching us) what the price is for eliminating the question of truth![72]

In brief: to attribute to psychology the logical status of a pastime means eliminating the question of truth and joining the mainstream of our civilization. If the question of truth has no place in modernity (if this is not an open question, contrarily to what is asserted in *The Soul's Logical Life*), then a soul perspective on the (modern) real is absolutely out of the question.

After all that has been exposed here, the theoretical dilemma previously mentioned persists. In face of it, we have two alternatives, as far as I can see: 1) ignore the statements about psychology having given up any claims to being or striving for true knowing, and of its having the logical status of a pastime, in order to stay uncompromisingly true to the interpretation of the myth of Actaion in *The Soul's Logical Life* as "the image of *soul as human psychology*";[73] or 2) accept those statements, but at the same time pretend that there is no contradiction between such statements with what is presented in *The Soul's Logical Life*, and in so doing performing the aforementioned *sacrificium intellectus*, but paying the price of a full neurotic betrayal of psychology's own truth. There could be still a third alternative, which I presented in *Psychology and Metaphysics*: give up the claim for psychology being true knowing but stressing that its logical status is not that of a pastime, providing epistemological justification for its dialectical methodological procedure. However, now I am not so sure that this third option is wholly satisfactory, as I am inclined to think that such justification necessarily involves the claim for true knowing. Without this claim, the notion of truth exposed in the last chapter of *The Soul's Logical Life* loses its meaning. And this notion is definitional for psychology as the discipline of interiority. Abandoning the former means giving up what ultimately distinguishes the latter. Therefore, I tend to stay with the first option, and definitely refuse the second one. Be that as it may, I leave to the reader the further meditation about these alternatives, welcoming criticisms as well as new perspectives other than the ones presented in my text.

Notes

1 Friedrich Nietzsche, *Beyond Good and Evil*, trans. Walter Kaufmann (New York: Vintage Books, 1966), 59 [aphorism 45].
2 Nietzsche, *Beyond Good and Evil*, 2, my italics [preface].
3 Nietzsche, *Beyond Good and Evil*, 32 [aphorism 23]. See also Robert B. Pippin, *Nietzsche, Psychology, and First Philosophy* (Chicago: Chicago University Press, 2010).
4 Nietzsche, *Beyond Good and Evil*, 32 [aphorism 23].
5 Wolfgang Giegerich, *The Soul's Logical Life* (Frankfurt am Main: Peter Lang, 2001), 222 (hereafter referred to as *SLL*).
6 I am aware that it is extremely risky——not to say temerarious——putting such contrasting standpoints in dialogue. But I believe that it is worth trying, and I hope that the reasons for this dangerous attempt will become clear in what follows.
7 *SLL*, 274; cf. Marco Heleno Barreto, *Psychology and Metaphysics. On the Logical Status of Psychology as the Discipline of Interiority* (London, Ontario: Dusk Owl Books, 2021), 105–107.
8 *SLL*, 224.
9 Friedrich Nietzsche, *The Gay Science*, trans. Walter Kaufmann (New York: Vintage Books, 1974), 116 [Book One, aphorism 54].
10 Nietzsche, *Beyond Good and Evil*, 46–47 [aphorism 34].
11 *SLL*, 231.
12 *SLL*, 232.
13 See Friedrich Nietzsche, *Thus Spoke Zarathustra*, trans. Thomas Common, in *The Philosophy of Nietzsche* (New York: Random House, 1927), 10–13 [Prologue, section 5].
14 *SLL*, 224. See also Wolfgang Giegerich, *What Is Soul?* (New Orleans: Spring Journal, 2012), 279–280; 307 (hereafter referred to as *WIS*).
15 *SLL*, 229. In *Psychology and Metaphysics* I leave the timidity of the quotation marks (the "deep-seated fear of appearing as a 'metaphysician'", *SLL*, 223) aside and suggest that this "metaphysical" anorexia is truly *metaphysical*, and that the "place" for the *real* encounter with the absolute truth in/of modernity is in the logic of nihilism, the absolute truth of the modern form of being-in-the-world.
16 *SLL*, 244.
17 *SLL*, 244.
18 *SLL*, 253, my italics.
19 *SLL*, 209–210. Note that there is a desire or will to know itself.
20 *SLL*, 207.
21 *SLL*, 216.
22 *SLL*, 207. "The Notion is the soul as (desire for) cognition, the soul in that 'archetypal' moment of its self-relation in which it, the soul, is cognizing, knowing, comprehending itself" (*SLL*, 204).
23 See *SLL*, 234.
24 *SLL*, 216–217 (my italics).
25 *SLL*, 217.
26 *SLL*, 213.
27 *SLL*, 229.
28 C.G. Jung, *Letters 2*, trans. R.F.C. Hull (London: Routledge and Kegan Paul, 1976), 368 [8 June 1957, to Bernhard Lang].
29 *CW* 10, § 853 [from Carl Gustav Jung, *The Collected Works of C. G. Jung*, vol. 10, trans. R.F.C. Hull (Princeton: Princeton University Press, 1970)].
30 Cf. Wolfgang Giegerich, *Collected English Papers, volume VI. C. G. Jung on Christianity and on Hegel* (New Orleans: Spring Journal, 2013), 300 (hereafter referred to as *CEP VI*).

31 *WIS*, 288. Nonetheless, just a few pages after this outright statement, one reads that the psychological I is a form of realization of "the internal not-I as the subject of *true knowing, the organ of truth* and of the syntactical or logical form" (*WIS*, 298, my italics; see also pp. 300ff). This shows that a tension——or conflict——concerning psychology and its relation to the question of truth persists internally in *What Is Soul?*, and not only between *What is Soul?* and *The Soul's Logical Life*. In *Psychology and Metaphysics* (chapters 1 and 2) I highlighted this conflict and interpreted it as the neuroticizing betrayal of our psychology's own truth, as presented in the interpretation of the myth of Actaion.

32 I will not discuss here other possibilities of understanding the subject-matter of ontology, which could show that an ontological presupposition is not necessarily incompatible with psychology as the discipline of interiority——as a matter of fact, it is required by statements such as "soul does not exist" and "soul is real." For more indications, see my *Psychology and Metaphysics*, 9 note 26; 48 note 101; 51 note 105.

33 *SLL*, 216.

34 *SLL*, 114. "Jung's distinction between archetypal image and archetype as such should be removed from the context of Kantian associations and, perhaps *against* Jung, be relocated into our new context of the distinction between the logical nature of the soul itself ('irrepresentability', *Unanschaulichkeit*, not having the character of an image) and the images which are its medium of expression" (ibid.).

35 *SLL*, 219.

36 *SLL*, 220.

37 *SLL*, 221.

38 See *SLL*, 159.

39 *CEP VI*, 296.

40 *CEP VI*, 296, my italics.

41 *WIS*, 288. Please note that all these statements have epistemological valence. They are akin to Kant's *epistemological* barrier.

42 *SLL*, 265, my italics.

43 *SLL*, 213.

44 Nietzsche's standpoint is at odds with Kant's. The absolutization of appearance and perspectivism abolishes the borderline concept of thing-in-itself and dissolves the Kantian much-valued notion of science into one interpretation among others (even natural laws of physics are no more than interpretive perspectives). Nietzsche's deconstruction of the subject also represents a blow in one of the fundamental pillars of Kant's philosophy: transcendental subjectivity. In this respect, there is also a fundamental incompatibility between Nietzsche's thought, faithfully subscribed by his post-modern heirs, and the notion of psychology presented in *The Soul's Logical Life*: "The manifold endeavors to overcome the philosophy of the subject seem, psychologically speaking, to serve the purpose of providing a philosophical justification for that development that I described above as 'man's having absconded from this world'. We need the subject and the philosophy of the subject——not to 'strengthen the ego', not to promote subjectivism and the split between subject and object [i.e., the 'unbridgeable difference'/mhb], but so that there may be an incumbent for that office whose job it is to be subjected to the Dionysian dissolution in order to bring about the event of Truth" (*SLL*, 257). Not only the deconstruction of the subject, but also the fear of metaphysics, of truth, the absolute and identity (see *SLL*, 245) are incompatible with the fundamental presuppositions of the notion of psychology advocated in *The Soul's Logical Life*. Without them, the "event of Truth" is either abolished or remains unintelligible.

45 *SLL*, 221.

46 *WIS*, 302.

47 Nietzsche, *Beyond Good and Evil*, 59 [aphorism 45].

48 *WIS*, 288.
49 *WIS*, 300.
50 *WIS*, 302.
51 See *WIS*, 301–302.
52 *SLL*, 234.
53 *SLL*, 224.
54 *SLL*, 253.
55 *SLL*, 244.
56 *SLL*, 256–257.
57 To interpret means bringing to light what is presupposed in a given phenomenon (in psychology as the discipline of interiority we call this the phenomenon's logic, or truth, its soul). This at first implicit and invisible (unconscious) presupposition is not *subjective*, not *arbitrary*, not "projected" into the phenomenon. It is *real*, meaning that it constitutes the reality of the phenomenon as its intrinsic and objective logic. At the same time, truth is *created* through the act of "entering the wild." Interpreting a given phenomenon means giving its notion (see *SLL*, 203), which is thus subjective-objective, "the dialectical unity of that which knows and that which is to be known."
58 *SLL*, 245.
59 See *WIS*, 307–308. In *The Soul's Logical Life* we find a reference to "hobby", *but not as the logical status of psychology*, and simply as a possible situation of the person who "does" psychology: "The 'wilderness', the 'naked Goddess', the 'unleashed dogs' require that there be no holding back. They require the realization that what goes into the primal forest is psychology as a totality, not merely the abstract *person* who *has* a psychology or who 'does' psychology (be it as a hobby or as a profession). Otherwise we would arrive at the idea of a 'checkmated' or 'domesticated wilderness'—— an idea which, if taken seriously, would self-destruct" (*SLL*, 213). The abdication of true knowing and the ensuing attribution of the logical status of a hobby or pastime *to psychology itself* does precisely this: it arrives at the idea of a checkmated or domesticated wilderness, thus self-destructing "psychology as a totality."
60 *SLL*, 223.
61 Nietzsche, *Thus Spoke Zarathustra*, 12.
62 Disastrous for our psychology itself, regardless of its confrontation with Nietzsche's thought.
63 *SLL*, 216.
64 *SLL*, 220.
65 "In psychology we are not concerned with life, but with soul, or, to put it another way, not with biological life, natural life, but with the soul's life, with Mercurial life. *Vita nostra non est vita vulgi.*" (*WIS*, 13 note 12).
66 *SLL*, 219 note 217.
67 *SLL*, 245.
68 *WIS*, 153, my italics.
69 *SLL*, 277, my italics.
70 *CEP VI*, 303.
71 *SLL*, 222.
72 *SLL*, 222.
73 *SLL*, 209.

Index

Pages followed by "n" refer to notes.

sharedness 178; fundamental impulse 178; logic of 189; and togetherness 187–189

Siegfried (in Jung's dream) 167–168

Simone, Nina 50

smeared-out self 152–154; acting-out and 160–162; and destructiveness 161; case example 161; communication technologies and 153–154; critical thought and 154; as cyborg 161; death of God and 154; deconstruction and 158; discourse and 152–163; drug use and 161; internet and 153–154; relation to oral tradition 153–154; relation to reflective thought 153; secondary orality and 153–154; social media and 153–154; impact on therapy 160–162; impact on the unconscious 162

soul 34–43, 45, 47, 70, 72–77, 79–80, 84, 92, 94, 177; abandoned music 201; absconded with music 201; absolute negativity of 8; adaptation to historical shifts 9; as archaic word 99; as basis of psychology 99; birth into the world 8; departed 200; desire for cognition 76; as dialectical unity of opposites 35; fundamental impulse of 178; as hungering for anxiety 42; as 'I' 35; identity and difference 80; interiorization of 77, 79; invisibility of 8; killing 80; as logical negativity 35–36, 40–41, 45–46, 76; logic vs. ego's logic 4, 9–10; as logically real 72; *logos* incarnated 186, 188; logos of 34; longing for initiation 7–8; made real 79; in music 196; nature of 3; negating itself 77; as negativity 74–75; as neurotic 35, 37, 39, 42–43, 46; notion of 99–100; and its *opus magnum* 181; as principles 72; in psychological difference 73; realization as thought 78; self-emptying 36; as self-negation 35–36; as self-sublation 37; as subject 24–26; as truth of the real 98, 104, 107

soul event 54, 56–57

soul-making 18–19, 22–25, 27–28, 30, 53, 148

soul of the real 123

"soul's logical life" 1–5, 7–10, 19, 70, 77, 84, 98, 147–148, 166, 168, 173, 178,

180, 186, 194, 204, 222, 224; as manifested in music 194

speculative: I-statement 114–115, 117–118, 121–122; subjectivity 114; turn 120

Spiegelman, M. 116–117, 120

spirit of Western culture 194

Spring Journal 97

Stengers, I. 30–31

"stepping backwards" in dialectics 5

'The Stone that is Not a Stone' 11, 36

Stravinsky, I. 201

student apathy 82

Sturluson, S. 64

subject as instrument of the soul 10

subjectivity vs. historical process 3

subjectivization 54–55

subject matter, giving over to 146

subject matter's I 114

sublation/sublated 27, 79, 179, 183, 188; blossom to fruit analogy 6; of the concept of money 180; of consciousness 6; of literal music 201; new form of knowing 79; of the soul 25; of status quo 8; substance to subject 113

suffering of the logos 130n53

symptoms: alterity of 42; as culturally determined 151–152, 161–162; conversion 151–152

syntactic level of consciousness 5

syntax 5, 41–42, 45; of music 193; shift in 193; syntactical 35, 45

Talmud 124, 129n41

tautological 73; presupposition of myth interpretation 73

technology, development of 193–195

temperament *see* Equal Temperament

temporality, significance of 148

Terence (Publius Terentius Afer) 117

Theoretical summit 27–26

Thich Nhat Hanh 7

thing-in-itself 213–214, 216–217, 219, 224, 227n44

thinking, psychological thinking 148

third of the two 114, 127n6

Thor's journey to Utgard 63–65

thought 66; as openness to truth 4; in psychology 3; vs. image 4

thought-based psychology 2

tonality, major-minor 194

For Product Safety Concerns and Information please contact our EU
representative GPSR@taylorandfrancis.com
Taylor & Francis Verlag GmbH, Kaufingerstraße 24, 80331 München, Germany

9 7 8 1 0 3 2 4 6 3 2 4 7